Sociology
for People

Sociology for People

Toward a Caring Profession

ALFRED McCLUNG LEE

Syracuse University Press

Copyright © 1988 by Syracuse University Press
Syracuse, New York 13244-5160

First published 1988

All Rights Reserved

First Edition

93 92 91 90 89 88   6 5 4 3 2 1

The paper used in this publication meets the minimum requirements of American National Standard for Information Sciences—Permanence of Paper for Printed Materials, ANSI Z39.48-1984. ∞™

Library of Congress Cataloging-in-Publication Data

Lee, Alfred McClung, 1906–
   Sociology for people : toward a caring profession / Alfred McClung Lee. — 1st ed.
   p. cm.
Bibliography: p.
Includes index.
ISBN 0-8156-2442-5 (alk. paper)
1. Sociology, I. Title.
HM51.L352 1988
301—dc19
                                     88-9672
                                     CIP

Manufactured in the United States of America

For my sons, Alfred McClung Lee III
and Briant Hamor Lee

ALFRED McCLUNG LEE is Professor Emeritus of Sociology at Brooklyn College and the Graduate Center, City University of New York, and is now Visiting Scholar in Sociology, Drew University, Madison, New Jersey. The author of many books, in 1975–76 he was president of the American Sociological Association.

Contents

Preface

In *Sociology for People,* an existential humanist tries to show what critical and emancipatory sociology can offer to individuals and to society. In characterizing myself as an "existential humanist," I want to insist upon simple and popular definitions of those terms. I am an admirer but not a follower of the existentialist Jean-Paul Sartre[1] and of the humanist Karl Marx,[2] to mention just two persons to whom those labels are commonly attached. But while existentialism and humanism of theirs and other sorts[3] stir up intellectual and social controversies and lead to innovations that are sometimes useful, I do not wish to be bound by anyone else's doctrine. It seems to me that such American writers as Thomas Jefferson,[4] Mark Twain,[5] William Graham Sumner,[6] and Franz Boas[7] have contributed other important dimensions to existential humanism.

My own intellectual focus is upon searching for reality in its historical and cross-cultural contexts and upon what appears most relevant and serviceable to our society. I consider this the most tenable orientation for a person dedicated to the scientific study of human relationships. In such a view, statements about first causes (or origins) and ultimate consequences, as well as of absolutes and infinites, are irrelevent except as human artifacts to be considered as such. Methods and tenets useful in other sciences are to be treated as possibly helpful suggestions, but techniques of social research and formulations of theory must deal with appropriate data and serve human understanding of the human lot. As the communications specialist Floyd W. Matson asserts, "our most pressing educational and cultural need is not for the indoctrination of men [and women] in the directives of science, but . . . for the enlistment of science in the cause of man [and woman]."[8]

The main preoccupation of the humanist sociologist, in the words of Herbert Blumer, should thus be "to lift the veils that cover group life. . . . The veils are not lifted by substituting, in whatever degree, preformed images for firsthand knowledge. The veils are lifted . . . by digging deep . . . through careful study,"[9] especially through participant observation. Our preoccupation is thus with sociology as a liberating and democratizing instrument.

But what about the bewildering complication, the "double bind," that the sociologist Robert P. Wolensky says confronts those trying to learn something about society? On the one hand, Wolensky sees "the communication of shapeless complexity . . . an infinitely complex and shapeless knowledge." On the other, he points to "the communication of closure . . . finality and comprehensiveness." He realizes that the "search for closure is a search for 'the answer,' or 'complete knowledge.'" He is concerned that "the idea of closure and perhaps even a closure mentality permeate sociology."[10] It is reflected in the growth of disparate schools and cults, each with its sacred personalities and texts.

Humanist sociologists reject cultish closure. They look for regularities they can discover in the societal chaos in all its relativism to time, environmental influences, and social processes. They usually find that interdisciplinary contacts, including ones with stimulating artists, are useful to build resistance against closure tendencies, against overlooking possible alternative views of reality.

Sociology for People owes much to a previous book of mine, *Toward Humanist Sociology,* [11] and to articles I wrote over the past decade. [12] In it, however, I have not only included new materials but have also rewritten any borrowings from previous efforts.

This book does not attempt to be a comprehensive treatment of such a complex subject as humanist sociology. The ideas discussed here are selected responses to salient personal and social problems that confront people as students and citizens, as social actionists, and as professional social scientists. These views were developed or brought together for lectures, discussions, and articles for both nonprofessional and professional audiences, and I have benefited much from the resulting give-and-take. Some of the ideas now reflect so many exchanges with so many people it would be impossible to indicate all of my indebtedness.

This book gained especially from the companionships I have enjoyed with members of the Society for the Psychological Study of Social Issues since the 1930s, the Society for the Study of Social Problems since 1950, the Society for Humanistic Anthropology since 1974, the Association for Humanist Sociology since 1975, and the Clinical Sociology Association (now the Sociological Practice Association) since 1978. The meetings and publications of these five innovative influences in the social sciences have encouraged constructive studies and reconsiderations of the human condition that stimulate corrective actions.

In addition to the acknowledgments in the references for each chapter, I wish to mention the following people who contributed intentionally or unintentionally to this effort: Among those now deceased, I remember especially Clyde Beals, Herbert Blumer, Ernest W. Burgess, Maurice Rea Davie, Charles P. C. Flynn, George Daniel Hamor, Howard and Lenore Turner Henderson, Helen Hall Jennings, John Kosa, Charles R. Lawrence, Jr., Robert S. and Helen M. Lynd, Abraham H. Maslow, Ethel Hamilton Murray, Robert E. Park, Hugh H. Smythe, and Willard Waller. Among those living: Sidney H. Aronson, Denis P. Barritt, Leo P. Chall, Elizabeth Clark, Ann E. Davis, Lynda Ann Ewen, Sylvia F. Fava, Franco Ferrarotti, Jan M. Fritz, John F. Glass, Irving Goldaber, Bruce T. Grindal, Beth B. Hess, Robert E. Kennedy, Jr., Louis Kriesberg, John R. Malone, Paul J. Nyden, Martin Oppenheimer, Victoria Rader, Thomas J. Rice, Pamela A. Roby, S. Stansfeld Sargent, George Simpson, J. Michael Sproule, Jerold M. Starr, Afif I. Tannous, Paul Von Blum, and Desmond Wilson.

Special thanks are due to another group of friends for their concern, encouragement, and aid. Terence M. Brunk, Stanley Hastings Chapman, Howard Elterman, Walda Katz Fishman, Richard F. Hixson, Edward Huberman, Glenn Jacobs, S. M. Miller, James M. O'Kane, Jonathan Reader, and Barbara Ann Scott all read typescripts of materials now included in this book and made helpful comments that were fresh and incisive. Susan F. Chase helped prepare the index. I trust that the final version reflects their friendly interest.

As always, my wife and fellow social scientist, Elizabeth Briant Lee, read critically each of this volume's many versions and has decidedly enriched each and every one of them. I also remember fondly how my work has gained from the influences of my other family members.

A. McC. L.

Drew University
Madison, New Jersey

Introduction

On Human Concerns

Writers of science fiction fantasies are prone to envision a future of absolute authoritarianism, but the day of the human ant hill is not an inevitable eventuality. More men and women than ever before are now spending at least part of their lives actively searching for better answers to old and new social problems. The manipulations of multinational corporate entrepreneurs, the depletion and pollution of our resources, the growing overpopulation in many areas, and the threats of nuclear horrors give this search increasing urgency. The extent of the quest is suggested by the growth of popular political organization and agitation and of critical — so-called "alternative" — communications media.

Human yearnings and temptations are at least latent in every polished social instrument, whether astronaut, military commander, cleric, corporation executive, academic administrator, political manager, or whomever. Human values find vivid expression in youths' revolts against war and depersonalization; in black resistance to white racism, hypocrisy, and exploitation; in female rebellion against traditional gender roles and male sexism; and in the work of vast numbers of dedicated scientists and artists, therapists, and administrators. They also appear in the growing dissatisfaction with organized religion, education, environmental pollution, militarization, colonialism and imperialism, and "made work" (contrived obsolescence, arranged mechanical failures, needless and endless duplications of effort). As the pollster Louis Harris reports, on the basis of annual surveys, only about one in five Americans now has a "great deal of confidence" in the press, business, organized religion, or Congress.[1]

Our unsolved problems are staggering, but social pressures are building to address them more effectively, to emancipate ourselves from debilitating and oppressive controls. These social pressures spring chiefly from growing dissatisfaction with the exploitative and depersonalizing tactics of those in control of power in the so-called social "system." People increasingly resent the myths and veils with which apologists obscure the nature of social arrangements. They are coming to understand, for example, as Karl Marx points out, how economists "express the relations of bourgeois production, the division of labour, credit, money, etc., as fixed, immutable, eternal categories," but that "what they do not explain is how these relations themselves are produced, that is, the historical movement which gave them birth."[2] We need to understand the shifting nature of such movements and how people can better cope with their consequences and potentialities for popular benefit.

As the sociologist Robert S. Lynd asserted in 1939, "A dangerously undemocratic vacuum exists in our culture between the individual citizen and political authority at the top, between the worker and the corporation that hires him, between the person and the city in which he lives."[3] Humanist sociologists try to reveal the nature of that vacuum even though, as Lynd adds, "Current social science plays down the omnipresent fact of class antagonisms and conflicts in the living all about us." Lynd worried about how "another and less democratic kind of control" has come and that "we may be asked to approve, after the fact, a Fascist-type seizure of power contrived in the name of 'anti-Fascism' and 'Americanism.'" A half-century later, Lynd's concerns still have validity.

Students of mine in a foreign university, deeply and sympathetically concerned about American affairs, in effect asked me: "Why do not your people and your educational institutions demonstrate in their behavior an actual attachment to democracy as a way of life and to the development of autonomous individuals such as you say a democracy requires for its full and effective operation? Why do we in universities outside of the United States get the impression that Americans are tremendously homogenized and fearful of nonconformism?"

Unabashedly and in spite of the many criticisms by social sophisticates in the United States and elsewhere who would undermine such a position, I have faith in the practical virtues of the democracy of Thomas Jefferson and John Dewey adapted constructively to contemporary conditions. In my estimation, democracy can be a tenable and highly useful way of life for the individual and for society. I trust that we can learn how to implement it more fully for more people in the United States and elsewhere in the world. Certainly some of the wisest and most admirable Americans do much to exemplify democracy as a way of life and to help us to realize its potentialities in social policies. In spite of the elitism and conformism of many American writers and professional people, I am convinced that American journalists and professors still include some of the most free and democratic intellectuals in the world.

Though I have great faith in democracy, I am vividly aware of its spotty application, its frequent denial in practice to women, nonwhites, and deviants, and its abuse in the hands of those we belittlingly call politicians. The authoritarianism that is too typical of many of our voluntary associations and schools, coupled with our anxious preservation of apparent stability through conformism and bureaucratization are further obstacles to democracy. As a public relations counselor asserted in a leading public relations journal: "We pride ourselves on individualism, yet each day dissent is looked upon increasingly as a form of perversity or, at best, mental aberration."[4] We seem to believe that individual autonomy is fine as long as it is respectable, nonthreatening, and directed toward the profit or enjoyment of the right people.

Democracy is a philosophy of social organization and participation that maximizes tolerance toward, and benefits from, internecine disagreements, competitions, and struggles, even conflicts. It is dedicated to equalizing opportunities without homogenizing aspirations. Democratic vitality comes from ferment, not from tranquility. Nevertheless, a great many of us mistrust the freedom that permits artists, scientists, philosophers, and agitators to break with old forms, to cast doubt on the familiar dependabilities of social life, and to offer new symbols, theses, observations, and organizational structures. Such innovators are rarely valued during their most creative periods, when their sense of autonomy is being given its greatest tests. After they have won their struggles or have died, after they have become self-plagiarists rather than newly creative, after their impact upon their specialty and upon society has been absorbed, or at least handled, they can become heroes rather than freaks or cranks. But even then they are rarely the individuals we Americans hold up as models for our children. Their lives are much too speculative or even hazardous.

Those compromisers who offer formulas for "pragmatic" change are the ones our society extols. Yet these people often serve chiefly to blunt the thrust of effective efforts toward needed social adaptations. From the standpoint of those with disproportionate vested interests in the status quo, democracy is largely negative. We Americans countrywide have yet to risk developing a citizenry sufficiently autonomous, aggressive, and creative to implement democracy comprehensively throughout our society. To the extent that we have had and still possess such citizens, they are "thousand upon thousand common men./ Cranks, martyrs, starry-eyed enthusiasts/ . . . And men with a cold passion for mere justice."[5] Before we preen ourselves with the accomplishments of these deviants, however, we should realize that a great number of them were developed elsewhere and fled to the United States to make their contributions.[6]

Only those who permit themselves to be merely conditioned instruments accept sexism, racism, heedless pollution and destruction of the environment, the population explosion, perpetual deprivation and starvation among millions throughout the world, and the possibility of the nuclear obliteration of humanity. Critically thinking human beings cannot accept such conditions.

When we look only at the appallingly wasteful and degrading sides of human life in the twentieth century, without considering the social history of previous centuries, humanity appears to have little future. We have only to ponder the lives of our diseased, vermin-infested, uneducated, and badly nourished ancestors, who were mostly exploited serfs and peasants, to take hope. Our history texts perpetuate a mythology that peoples our past with selected kings, nobles, and gentry, but it is principally the descendants of forgotten underlings who populate the earth. These descendants often still appear to be little more than faceless instruments, but they include millions who are aware of their human potential and are not about to surrender it.

This is not to say, as have so many analysts of social movements, that there is an automatic guarantee of progress in human affairs.[7] Evidence for that is lacking. The fortunes of social change turn both to favor and to oppose the welfare of the masses of the people, both toward and away from democracy and other equalizing schemes of social organization. Disillusionment with existing controls coupled with opportunities to struggle are currently giving activists hopes to achieve constructive social changes. More people are working to cope with such problems now than ever before.

This book attempts to stimulate interest in the following questions: How can we lift veils that hide or distort the character of social struggles? How can humane values be made to offset more effectively the dehumanizing instrumentalism so pervasive in our society? How can people resist such exploitative degradation? How can concerned social scientists help people to strive against such influences? How can they help equip individuals to participate more autonomously and also more cooperatively and thus more effectively in society? Can we develop further a sociology that will help us to see society more clearly and to serve as an instrument of social emancipation?

The book poses these other interrelated questions: With many social scientists and other professionals selling their services openly to the would-be controllers and manipulators of society, how can a larger share of such specialists be brought to aid rank-and-file people and thus to try to better the general human condition? How can we come to understand more adequately, with as little compromise and bias as possible, the oppressions, brutalities, and destructiveness as well as the creativities, kindnesses, and nobilities of individuals and their networks in society? How does such an effort at understanding differ from and yet complement an attempt to solve a specific social problem?

How can such understanding help us to cope more adequately with our social problems? Of what is our season of violence symptomatic? How autonomous can a person in mass society become and remain? How desirable is such autonomy and in terms of what values?

What are the personal and social roles of our ideologies and myths? Why is it so common now to claim their "death" or "end"? Why is it so difficult to perceive the birth or rebirth of significant ideologies and myths? Who are likely to be the midwives of social change? Women and men and those of different colors and contrasting ethnic traditions, education, occupations, religions, and wealth — how equal can they become in the late twentieth century? How can individuals and groups of each type be encouraged to make their own creative contribution to human welfare? Can we, with any confidence, see the possibility of achieving a more humane society beyond our contemporary confusion, tension, terror, and possible annihilation?

This book attempts to raise such questions and to provide some exploration and response to them. In doing so, it emphasizes our relations within changing social processes. As the sociologist Herbert

Blumer observes: "The life of any human society consists necessarily of an ongoing process of fitting together the activities of its members."[8] Society is constantly in process of change. Stabilizations and crystallizations of practices and of organizational arrangements, of interpersonal and intergroup relations, may give a temporary sense of security, but they can become logjams against which pressures for change accumulate.

Existential humanists can always find ways to involve themselves in existing adventures. They try to participate in group experiences that bring fulfilment to other people as well as to themselves. They attempt to help facilitate changes that will bring more humane interpersonal arrangements into being. They know how accurate Henry David Thoreau was when he asserted that people "have become the tools of their tools,"[9] and they also comprehend that men and women are not satisfied with being just tools.

The great challenge to sociologists and to social scientists more generally is not to ally themselves exclusively with social equilibrium or stability. This only serves the repressive status quo of the entrenched. Nor is the challenge to provide intellectual perspectives and instruments to self-serving entrepreneurs and administrators in the hope that they will somehow approximate the ideal of the philosopher-king. That is the elitist trap into which endless generations of intellectuals have all too often fallen.

The great challenge to social scientists is the development and wide dissemination of social wisdom and techniques of social action that will enable more and more people to participate in the control and guidance of their groups and their society. The German sociologist Georg Simmel concludes: "The deepest problems of modern life derive from the claim of the individual to preserve the autonomy and individuality of his existence in the face of overwhelming social forces, of historical heritage, of external culture, and of the technique of life."[10] Humanist social scientists regard this claim of the individual to be less a source of undesirable problems than one of challenging opportunities. They believe that the nourishment of individual wisdom and potential makes for a healthier society, and that it can lead to fruitful cooperation in efforts at democratic social emancipation.[11]

Sociology
for People

1

Sociology's Images

What should we expect of sociology? Rumors, common sense, and the mass media associate the discipline with all sorts of ideas and activities. They may identify it with social work or social reform. They may say that it has a strange and laughable jargon. They may describe it as involving sample surveys of public opinion. They may confine sociology to exploring the plight of the poor, the deprived, the deviant, and the criminal. They may limit it to studies of sexual and marital behavior. They may dwell on sociology's allegedly mysterious statistical manipulations, which somehow yield information useful in guiding politicians and business people in policymaking. And some gossips and journalists may even try to confuse sociology—more or less sarcastically—with socialism or communism. These are all quite contradictory images.

High schools rarely provide any introduction to or even definition of sociology. Thus confusion or ignorance of the subject persists at least into college years. In contrast with all this confusion, individuals who are well trained in sociology—especially those who are also literate and experienced in human affairs—are showing up in a wide range of responsible positions. On campuses you can see them not only in sociology departments but also ensconced in such positions as president, college dean, dean of students, and public relations director.

They are teaching and doing research in schools of communications, health, law, and business. Beyond academic walls, sociologists are more and more often found in the offices of newspapers, welfare agencies, trade unions, and a wide variety of "cause" organizations, or involved in such aspects of business as marketing, advertising, management, banking, planning, and new-product research. They are active in governmental and political party agencies on all levels from the White House to the city hall. Sociological training is thus becoming recognized in a de facto way as useful preparation for administrative, policy-research and policymaking positions.

Introductory Images

How can the confusing popular images of sociology be reconciled with the increasing social responsibilities of well-trained sociologists on the other? The variety of introductory courses now offered in our colleges helps to illustrate further both the range of the field's images and the uses to which the discipline may be placed. Let us look at five oversimple examples of what a first college course might be like. Then we will examine the possible practical applications of sociology in a career dedicated to the service of people and human welfare.

1. The teacher of the first course may be *philosophically* oriented. She or he may spend a lot of time on terms and conceptions said to deal with social life and with the nature of society. Somehow, nevertheless, those words and ideas may often remain rather blurry abstractions for the student. To illustrate, "social actors" are said to perform on diverse "levels of structural organization" that have "functional dimensions." The "collectivities" involved can be subjected to "structural-functional analysis." But do these terms convey senses of actual individual and group behavior, of people involved in the problems and joys of living? Do they help us to understand what happens in bars, on athletic teams, in factories, on dates, at home, in corporate board rooms? After intensive study and field work, they may aid the perceptions of the advanced student, and then they may just become verbal substitutes for actually going to look at human behavior and trying to understand it.[1]

The sociological historian Raymond A. Kent laments that "the vast majority of those sociologists who have written about the history of their discipline . . . have treated [it] almost exclusively in terms of the development of social or sociological thought." They often do not record that active social involvement in reform movements "was what united the pioneers of empirical sociology," because their research into controversial social problems often provoked criticisms that they were being unscientific, and "nonsociological." This criticism contributed to the separation of theory from investigation, Kent points out, and added to "the difficulties experienced by theorists — even by those who have been regarded as key figures in the litany of 'founding fathers'— in relating their ideas to an empirical data base." These difficulties, he says, "have been ignored or quietly overlooked" by too many disciplinary historians.[2]

2. The teacher may be oriented quite *technically* and try to give that slant to an introductory sociology course. She or he may feel that no one can even start to study sociology without first mastering research methods with which to observe, measure, and record the changing social scene, that only with such methods in hand can one start to understand the nature of human relationships.

These analytic methods yield what are called "hard data." These data are responses to questions or records of human acts that can be fed into computers and manipulated statistically. The results appear to be mathematical and thus objectively "scientific." They can indeed help to provide information about some limited and precise aspect of society. They may be quite necessary to the work of the advanced student, provided they do not become an end in themselves, a way of avoiding forays into a societal quagmire. For the introductory student, however, they may get in the way of broader and more useful perspectives.

3. In this scenario, a teacher in effect takes students on a selected reading tour of society's *chambers of horrors,* sometimes made more vivid by introducing them to such situations in the local area or by showing documentary films. This brings protectively reared middle-class teenagers face-to-face with serious social problems, often for the first time in their lives. These students thus become aware of decaying slums, deviant or criminal populations, deprived people, handicapped people, and others. They may also observe the ineffective attempts of politicians, business people, social workers, and government bureaucrats to mitigate or hide or ignore lower-class miseries.

Unfortunately, students typically come away from such a course with the impression that many of the problem groups are the causes of their own difficulties and not the victims of influences others should be expected to control or counteract. Students may be taught that the deprived and disturbed are to be pitied and helped, but not to expect that fundamental changes are possible. Students may not be shown what such groups have actually done for themselves when they have been moved to encouraging social environments. For example, racists once tried to bar European slum dwellers from our shores on genetic grounds, but the genes of those people must have had merits. The children and grandchildren of those slum dwellers include some of our country's current artistic, political, and business leaders!

4. A teacher may try to get students to approach the social situation from a quite different angle from the foregoing — to evoke discussion of their *basic concerns* about social life and living and of how they can find their way as adolescents through society's complexities into adult participation. Such teachers, as the sociologist Robert E. Kennedy, Jr., notes, "see people as shapers — and not victims — of society." Kennedy sees his role as helping "young adults to combine the sociological perspective with sound knowledge of the society in which they live, to judge their own life prospects and make their own life choices."[3]

This is an approach that takes these questions to be central: What is society doing to me and to other people? What purposes and whose purposes are thus served? How should I react to this knowledge? Is the misery which exists in my community and in the world necessary? How can I learn to lead a humane and constructive life in the society about which I am learning?

5. This last approach looks upon sociology as a *field of contention* among value-oriented influences and their practitioner-representatives. It takes the student a step beyond the fourth one. It explores the roles of competition, emulation, conflict, adjustment, and compromise in human affairs and in ongoing social processes. It points to the demand, implicit in the study of society, that one not be a disinterested observer, that one take sides. It shows how sociologists provide evidence for and against racial desegregation, education programs, health maintenance programs, housing projects, and criminal justice reforms. It demonstrates the influence of class, ethnic, and other value-forming factors upon the research and conclusions of social scientists.

When students are introduced to this social-conflict perspective upon sociology and social science without the underpinning of the fourth approach outlined above, they often do not know how to relate themselves to it. When this approach is presented in context, it leads students to agree with sociologist Victoria Rader when she says, "I believe that we human beings have the capacity to build social lives that truly delight us." She adds: "We are more likely to create such a world when . . . we develop our imaginations to envision a more satisfying social life; and when we experience an underlying alignment with all human beings."[4] Accurate social knowledge provides the basis on which humanists can help construct such patterns of life in a healthier environment.

When students understand that social science is a field of contention that can contribute to their lives and potentialities, they realize that they can take sides and thus become more mature participants. The "value-free" or "purely objective" stance is a pose. With social contenders stripped by humanist sociology of their usual disguises, students come to find that they can make wiser choices concerning which sides of various issues to join.

Sociology for People

The third approach (the chambers of horrors) may succeed in arousing students' curiosity, but the fourth (basic concerns) and fifth (field of contention) can appropriately be called "sociology for people" or "humanist sociology," even "liberation sociology." Students are not offered it often enough. They too frequently find only hit-and-miss parts of it in their private discussions outside of class.

The fourth and fifth approaches are sometimes called upsetting, radical, even outrageous and dangerous, but in fact they are deliberately down to earth. Still, many professors resist moving into these approaches. They fear their intimacies, their stimulation of greater empathy between them and their students. They may suspect that they have been serving as willing instruments for class-centered vested interests rather than as nurturers of autonomous future citizens, but they prefer to continue to give noble rationalizations for that role rather than hazardously to liberate themselves. It is easier and more profitable to produce controllable technicians and bureaucrats for those governing our lives than to stimulate creative social partisanship. As communications professor John Bremner points out: "Administrators and machines are taking over; the teachers are being squeezed out."[5]

In fact, university administrators do worry about instructors who insist upon discussing competition and conflict in society's power structures. Some deans, nervous about their budgets, do not like to think that their professors might be discussing with students the roles of the powerful occupants of boardrooms and executive offices in society's interlocking control structures. The deans know that such decision-makers constitute the boards of control of both public and private universities.

In these fourth and fifth approaches, the teacher may dramatize the contribution of sociology somewhat like this: Look, you have been born and assimilated into certain segments—a class and an ethnic group—of this society. As you were socialized, you learned rules of proper moral and social conduct. At some point, however, you became aware that not everyone in our society observes these rules.

There are the petty delinquencies of youth, to be sure, but more troubling are the frequent examples of corporate dishonesty—for example, the continued retailing of products like the Dalkon Shield that are known to be dangerous—and widespread political corruption, even at the highest levels. What are we to make of these discrepancies between what we were taught and what we so commonly observe?

Further, to what extent do these complex rule arrangements serve to immobilize us, as it were, so that we can be dominated and even exploited effectively by those who do not practice the same rules? Must there be what amounts to a slave morality and a master morality, as the philosopher Friedrich Nietzsche contended?

These contradictions bother students as they search for promising paths to maturity, to adult roles, to mature effectiveness. What can we do about these contradictions in our own lives? Should we say "So what?" or just "o.k." and try to live in terms of them? Or should we demystify such rules and try to help others demystify them? What would all such efforts accomplish for ourselves and for others? They are problems, as is suggested above, ordinarily addressed with some candor as well as passion only in student discussions and the adult strategy meetings of insiders, or with a trusted friend or counselor.[6] They raise questions about how contrived or mythical are the rules by which we are trying to live. They are central to the perspective imparted in a humanist sociology class.

How Can a Teacher Help?

A teacher may join with students to illustrate what it can mean to strip away some of the comforting myths that hide how social factors control and manipulate. When students hear talk about a "system of laws" based upon "equal justice for all," they can then begin seeking answers to such questions as why our prisons are filled so disproportionately with Blacks, Chicanos, and poor whites? Actual criminal behavior is rather evenly distributed among the members of all ethnic, "racial," and class groups in our society. Why then does this social justice system demonstrate so much greater understanding for the proportionately numerous white-collar criminals, most of whom continue to use our streets and other facilities? And when they hear talk about the promotion of freedom and democracy through American international negotiations and military interventions, students can ask why we almost exclusively implement those noble sentiments with military bases and weapons and aid deals around the world that serve chiefly to benefit foreign elites and protect exploitations by multinational corporations? Why do we spend so little effort trying to develop genuine democracy and human welfare in the countries under the shadow of American-centered corporate imperialism?

With such illustrations, a teacher can reveal to his or her myth-conditioned students something of the hypocrisies and conspiracies — the dark underside — of our society. This is not to say that democracy and human welfare cannot be defined to have highly estimable goals toward which many try to struggle. It is to say that such terms have often been used in delusory propaganda to forward quite undemocratic and inhumane objectives. Such is often the case today, and it needs to be offset by attention to alternative versions of reality.[7]

Students can thus start to understand how sports and sensational trivia in the news not only intrigue and amuse but also divert our attention from political malfeasances and business exploitations. They can observe how anti-strike propaganda — advocacy of faith in employers — can make it easy for employers and their cooperating labor leaders to exploit workers. They can learn something about how other schemes in the name of social welfare, democracy, and Americanism can direct education into narrow, industry-serving channels, can counteract efforts to make medical services more widely available, and can protect the adulterers of food and the destroyers of environmental assets. They can also discover something about the vast manipulations in the name of our ideals that lead to wars, the overthrow of governments unfriendly to corporate interests, depressions, inflations, stagflations, and the exploitation of people in less developed parts of the world.

At times the mass media do tell us about such scandals as those of Teapot Dome in the 1920s and President Nixon's Watergate in the

1970s, but those events are presented as rare aberrations. They are treated as the iniquities of bad individuals and not, as they more accurately should be, as standard operating procedures in struggles to obtain and maintain power and advantage in our plutocratic society and in the world. They are significant symptoms, not unique events. Similarly, the lessons of our costly imperialistic defeat in Viet Nam are being swept under carpets as rapidly as possible both by politicians and by media people; its history is being rewritten to make it appear a noble venture, albeit possibly a mistaken one.

Once well launched, as the philosopher Barrows Dunham observes, "social myths, precisely because they are socially entertained, require great changes for their abandonment." As long as they serve dominant interests, their accuracy and their relations to general human welfare are irrelevant. As Dunham notes, "someone can always be found who will propagate the myths for pay."[8]

What Is the "Social System"?

To point out these things is not to insist that there is an integrated and overarching social conspiracy, a carefully constructed, worldwide, American-centered plutocratic imperialism. On the contrary, our world is dominated locally, nationally, and internationally by a military-industrial complex of growing proportions and power, but that complex consists of more or less independent and competing units. Those conglomerate corporate units are linked together occasionally by financial ties but more significantly by common class and economic interests among their executives and owners. The top operators have learned how to behave as long as there is not an overwhelming international catastrophe. They do not need to censor the mass media. The latter, whose top officials are part of the same group, know the limits within which they can profitably operate.

As the economists Richard J. Barnet and Ronald E. Müller conclude, "the global corporations are constantly accelerating their control over the world productive system and are helping to bring about a profound change in the way wealth is produced, distributed, and defended." Their strategies make them "an antagonist of local interests everywhere." They add: "Driven by the ideology of infinite growth, a religion rooted in the existential terrors of oligopolistic competition, global corporations act as if they must grow or die, and in the process they have made thrift into a liability and waste into a virtue."[9]

In their competitive manipulating, these contending corporate interests penetrate much of societal life with their views and values. They are reflected in the school classroom, the pulpit, and the mass media, in trade union halls and the civil and criminal courts, in the internationalized markets, and in the special-interest lobbies and political slush funds that control governmental operations.[10]

Sociology can help citizens understand the mythological and jerry-built nature of this "social system" upon which they depend but which means so many different things to so many different people. Sociology can help people to confront their social predicaments shorn of obscurities, and then to realize they can organize to cope more directly and effectively with their problems.

Unfortunately, many times when we have learned something about sociology, we may be trapped in one of the first three types of limited sociology mentioned earlier — the abstract, technical, "chamber-of-horrors" approaches. Theories, methods of research, and exposés may provide some useful ideas about the nature of society to those who are motivated to go out and see and hear and even smell and feel what is going on in a variety of social situations. By themselves, however, those focuses can become mere diversions from more thorough explorations of the nature of the human scene and its complex scenarios. If we do not acquire understanding through first-hand investigation, we have to satisfy ourselves with second-hand analyses without any criteria with which to judge their accuracy.

Purposes Served by Sociologists

How easy it is to agree on an idealistic statement of the purposes properly to be served by sociologists: Sociologists as scientists discover, verify, and conceptualize what actually exists in society. In the process, they try to analyze and report their findings and seek critical appraisals by other sociologists. Few would disagree that findings so produced might, in their aggregate, serve many purposes, including popular human needs, concerns, and desires.

This is all very well as an abstract and idealistic model for the scientific advancement of knowledge. It neglects, however, a crucial factor in social scientific as well as other scientific research. It neglects the personality of the scientist, including his or her gender, social status, ethnic background, educational and other experiences, motivation, and current terms of employment. As the physicist Victor F. Weisskopf reminds us, "the activity of science is necessarily embedded in a much wider realm of human experience" than is specified traditionally for a discipline itself. He then contends, "Science itself must have a nonscientific base," but he does not seem to realize how the "emotional and social embedding of science" is not only, as he says, "the precondition of the quest for scientific truth," but it is also a powerful influence upon what may be taken to be "scientific truth."[11] This latter is much more the case with sociology than with physics. In the real world faced by sociologists, facts and values merge.

The idealistic statement of purposes for sociology seems straightforward and uncomplicated enough in an elementary textbook. It very quickly becomes muddied and complex when sociologists are observed actually at work as practitioners in academic, business, or governmental circles. The idealistic statement serves to justify a confusing variety of careerist practices that stretch the terms of the definition in many directions. The practices challenge notions of the possibility of purely objective research uncluttered by ideological biases. Practices can and often do turn the conception into a shambles.

The "Knowledge Industry"

The Columbia University philosophical sociologist Robert Nisbet upset many social scientists who had been doing profitable special-interest research with his 1975 article, "Knowledge Dethroned." In it he claims that the scientist-scholar "was a hero in the public eye only a decade ago," but that more recently such a person "seems only a combination ne'er-do-well and enemy of both nature and human community." He blames this on "the behavior of men of knowledge during the last quarter-century and in the whole structure of what came to be called, so pretentiously, the knowledge industry." He notes that as part of this an "alien spirit of pride, even arrogance, seized the learned disciplines." This led social scientists in particular to "assume," as he puts it, "the role of priests in the new church of knowledge."[12] This pretense had long ago been made explicit by the positivist Auguste

Comte (1789–1857) and his followers with their religion of humanity, but a similar notion sometimes appears implicit in the teachings of more recent social scientists.

Nisbet says, "Grantsmanship, at first a wry joke among academicians, is by now a publicly recognized source of banality, trivialization and pretentiousness." But as he continues, he reveals that his bias is against governmental social planning research. He belittles programs "aimed at the quick ending of urban blight, the termination of ethnic tensions, the eradication of poverty, the reduction of crime." Nisbet claims that the liberal sociologist's "litany begins, 'Crime is caused by poverty; poverty is caused by racism,' and proceeds predictably from there."[13]

Nisbet asserts that such efforts "will always rank among the most prodigal and worse, inept in American history." He adds, "As a sociologist myself, I find all this tragic and humiliating," especially because he saw it bringing a "vast deflation of prestige and a concomitant loss of public confidence"—in such conservatives as himself.[14]

What such writers try to avoid is a realization that philosophy, the humanities, the social sciences—indeed, all of the intellectual activities of humankind—develop in settings of social processes. The competitions and conflicts of such processes in ancient Greece helped produce both the elitist Plato and the humanist Protagoras. All intellectual disciplines reflect contentions among those more or less openly representing special interests as well as those voicing diverse conceptions of the public or general interest. That creative theorists overshadow establishment and special-interest writers in intellectual influence is a painful reality to established conservatives.

What About Values?

A very large percentage of sociologists contend that they do not knowingly propagandize, that is, create or help perpetuate manipulative myths or ideologies that serve special interests. They claim that their strivings for academic preferment and for stipends and grants have nothing to do with the orientation to special interests to be found in their teachings or writings.

If this claim had enough substance, there would be no need for the Society for the Study of Social Problems and especially the Association for Humanist Sociology and humanist organizations in other social science professions. This is not to contend that these bodies consist only of people who have managed somehow to dissociate themselves entirely from any such influences. Quite the contrary. But their members seem to realize that social scientists must be conscious of the pressures under which they function, and they must choose whom they will represent.

The Society for the Study of Social Problems came into existence in 1950–51 to help rescue sociology from the dehumanizing influences of abstract theorizing and of fancifully complex research methods. The Association for Humanistic Psychology, the largest of the avowedly humanist bodies, dates from a conference in 1964 held at Old Saybrook, Connecticut. The psychologist Rollo May recalls: "That conference developed out of a groundswell of protest against the theory of man of behaviorism on the one side and orthodox psychoanalysis on the other."[15] The Society on Anthropology and Humanism (now the Association for Humanistic Anthropology) appeared in 1974, and the Association for Humanist Sociology began taking form in 1975 and held its first convention in 1976.

These bodies thrive because many social scientists feel the need to reinforce each other in their efforts to serve people. As nearly as they can, many try to strip the incrustations of class, ethnic, and gender biases from texts, monographs, journal articles, expert testimony, and other professional work. They want their profession to find its justification in caring for the needs of people rather than in erecting rationalizations for the status quo.

Skepticism versus Cynicism

Those who belong to the associations mentioned try to dedicate themselves to the doubting, questioning, or incredulous state of mind, the skepticism so long typical of creative scientists in all fields and among them the democratic humanists in the social sciences. They disclaim any similarity between such cleansing and demystifying skepticism in the service of humanity and what is usually called cynicism. The latter is an intellectual stance so typically that of pillars of the status quo in our society. Oscar Wilde characterized the cynic as a person "who knows the price of everything and the value of nothing."[16]

Cynicism is a posture common among those who fear to be identified with the creative loneliness of those who do independent work heedless of currently accepted and legitimated views. The followers of the predominant fads in sociology—quantification or structural-functionalist abstraction—sneer at the presumptuousness, even at what they may assert to be the subversiveness, of independent investigation, thinking, and writing. Little wonder that our professional journals often appear so dull and repetitious. Plagiaristic embroidery pays off! Little wonder that many introductory texts bore students—as evidenced by declining sociology enrollments in a great many colleges and universities.

As the sociologist Jerome Davis wrote in an introductory sociology text in the 1920s,

> Sociology should be a coordinator which helps [us] . . . to brush aside the mental cobwebs of particularistic explanations and to see society as a whole. How many Americans now see clearly, for instance, that we have a dualism between our ideals and practices? How many sense the aesthetic starvation in our life, the obedience to blind regimentation, the slavery to the folkways which bind us whether we will or not?[17]

Cynicism bows to such notions as that little can be done to improve human society in a significant way and thus give more people opportunities for self-improvement. It goes along with contentions that genetic factors—as promoted by sociobiologists—make it impossible to improve the human lot through environmental changes. It accepts that elites are powerful because they are the fit while the oppressed and poor are what they are because they are the biologically unfit,[18] despite the fact that a wealth of comparative data indicates the adaptability of human beings to many circumstances and opportunities.

Cynicism of a more or less overt sort is a pervasive characteristic of the operating theories and practices not only of business and political entrepreneurs but also of their middle-class followers in managerial, professional, and technical positions. Those middle-class functionaries elaborate that posture into palatable myths for mass consumption and thus for mass manipulation. Typically they build cynicism into social myths by focusing attention on society's victims—women, nonwhites, the unemployed and underemployed and unemployable, the psychologically disturbed, and those they label delinquent and criminal. They ask what such people have themselves done to be as they are. Isn't it because they are absorbed into a "culture of poverty" that they do not want to break out of? They avoid the basic question: What have other people and the general social situation done to those people to make them as they are?

This spirit of a cleansing and creative skepticism offers an alternative version of reality. This critical concern for humane values and for the future of humanity has thus brought into existence the humanist scientific bodies mentioned. They are not to be thought of as creating new directions in human aspirations, but they are surely demanding changes in their disciplines. They are efforts to reinforce and to update existing humane concerns. As the anthropological society's statement of purpose so well formulates it: "While varied in form and expression and not adhering to any one academic discipline, humanism has historically sought to reaffirm the intrinsic value of the human being by creating other possibilities for human thought and action, and by keeping alive humanity's habit of continually reshaping its own image, hence its own reality."[19]

2

_____

Humanist Emphases
in Sociology

How does a liberating, "humanist" sociology differ from other types? The term "humanist" is so diversely and controversially employed that its meanings and the contexts of those meanings require specification and consideration.

A dictionary definition of "humanism" states it to be "any system or mode of thought or action in which human interests, values, and dignity are taken to be of primary importance, as in moral judgments."[1] This definition is vague and general enough to leave it open to identification or at least rationalization with many religious viewpoints as well as with many secular philosophies, programs for social action, and scientific efforts.

The same dictionary offers as a briefer alternative definition of humanism "devotion to or study of the humanities" and describes the humanities as "literature, philosophy, art, etc., as distinguished from the sciences." A science is "systematized knowledge of any kind" and "any skill that reflects a precise application of facts or principles."[2]

Popular dictionaries appropriately enough report common usage, however contradictory it might be. These summations point to an untenably precise distinction between the humanities and the sciences. They also suggest how the fields do overlap and how both "humanism" and "science" may accurately be linked with sociology.

Prominent among the concerns of students both of the humanities and of the sciences are the ideas with which people live. These ideas provide senses of environment and community, of worth and dignity, of identity and purpose, of accomplishment and frustration, and of fear and dread. Suggested innovations or reinterpretations of such ideas may change people's conceptions of what their own interests and concerns might well be.

How the Humanities and the Sciences Differ

The chief differences between the humanities and the sciences arise from the greater inclusiveness and permissiveness of the former. Innovative works valued in the humanities can be based on speculation or traditional mythology or careful observation. They can take a graphic, poetic, ritualistic, or prosaic form. The sciences typically limit their sources of information to what can dependably be observed and their media of expression to the prosaically precise. At the same time, as the sociologist Willard Waller observes, "All science depends upon perceptions reconstructed and fitted together in imagination, upon an artistic re-creation of events. This holds *a fortiori* for sociology, for sociology must also include imaginative insight."[3]

The German theorist Max Weber had a similar view when he contrasted the interests of "subject matter specialists" with those of "interpretative specialists." He said: "The fact-greedy gullet of the former can be filled only with legal documents, statistical worksheets and questionnaires, but he is insensitive to the refinement of a new idea. The gourmandise of the latter dulls his taste for facts by ever new intellectual subtleties." In consequence, a social scientist's "genuine artistry . . . manifests itself through its ability to produce new knowledge by interpreting already *known* facts according to known viewpoints."[4] Weber did not appreciate the utility of firsthand observation.

Many scientists try to demonstrate the human benefits of their searches and products even when their work appears remote from general human concerns. The social sciences, however, clearly can serve both humanist and scientific values. The humanist social scientist is self-committed to do so.

Humanist sociology in particular is related to and integrated with the findings and expressions of similarly oriented humanists in other scientific, literary, philosophical, and artistic disciplines. Findings and opinions among humanists can contrast quite sharply, and that makes them all the more stimulating and creative. Humanist sociologists' searches for more dependable social knowledge, for ways of communicating it, and thus for contributions to making people's lives more practicable and fulfilling are also central concerns of the other liberal arts and sciences, each discipline from a somewhat different approach.

Efforts to establish a formal sociological discipline since the nineteenth century have aroused amused rejection among "hard" scientists. More than a few physicists and biologists brush aside sociological "claims" to scientific precision and insight. The American Association for the Advancement of Science admits social scientists to membership and even to fellowship, but its weekly periodical, *Science,* only rarely contains social scientific articles.[5]

Those involved in the traditional humanities also resent sociologists' efforts. They perceive the "newcomers" as diverters of their constituencies and invaders of their perquisites. They criticize sociologists' "artificialities," "presumptions," and lack of historical orientation and literary expression.

Especially with regard to the relations of traditional humanists with sociologists, the sociologist Edward Shils notes: "Mutual distrust, derogation, and avoidance have been the common traits of the relationship. Defensive ignorance has played a larger part in engendering this relationship than awareness of each other's procedures and objects."[6] Relations with physical and biological scientists have been similar. This sharing of mutual aversion has not characterized our greater social scientists.

What about Religious Humanists?

Mystical humanists and other religious specialists, defensive of their beliefs, object to the respect of humanist social scientists for scientific criteria, procedures, and theorizing. They urge social scientists to mix their professional work with religion, to follow more speculative and poetic lines of thought for purposes of policy determination as well as for self-gratification and entertainment. For example, the sociologist Peter L. Berger claims, "A rediscovery of the supernatural will be, above all, a regaining of openness in our perception of reality."

He contends that "it will be an overcoming of triviality. In openness to the signals of transcendence the true proportions of our experience are rediscovered."[7] The criminologist Richard Quinney attempts to identify sociology with "a theory of nature, . . . the supernatural mystery of the natural world." He says that "all is related to God." As a part of this, he claims that there has been a "collapse of the metaphysical dualism (the material and natural world versus the nonmaterial and spiritual world)."[8]

These statements remind one of the contentions of medieval scholars, so well exemplified by St. Thomas Aquinas's "baptism of Aristotle," his rationalization of secular and religious philosophies. Great social benefits demonstrably come to both church and state from their separation, and similarly great ones derive from distinguishing scientific procedures and findings from religious theories.

Interdisciplinary Conflicts Persist

Why do all these interdisciplinary conflicts — this mutual aversion — continue? Perceptive and insightful social scientists have long demonstrated the utility of their procedures in the service of human needs, values, and aspirations. They have looked long and intimately at wide ranges of human behavior and social myths and theorizings. They have carefully checked their findings with those of others. They have recognized the historical and environmental settings and relationships of their data and understandings. They have developed a clinical sense and ability to diagnose social situations, to prescribe adaptive efforts, and to interpret such wisdom for popular understanding and benefit. Their formulations are not perfect, but they are constantly trying to improve them. Above all, they have cast doubt upon unproven and unfairly exploitative or oppressive allegations and practices.

The degree of success of humanist social scientists in achieving verifiable reformulations of social knowledge is a real social problem for them. This is especially so when they indicate with evidence the probable benefits of emancipatory or liberation movements. As George Savile pointed out in 1750 on the basis of his extensive experience in public affairs: "A man that should call everything by its right name would hardly pass the street without being knocked down as a common enemy."[9] The more productive humanist social scientists are such whistle-blowers on those who exploit humankind, and whistle-blowers are too often "knocked down as a common enemy." Nevertheless such scientists continue their dedicated work. They do much to combat racism, classism, sexism, and imperialism and to point to needed re-constructions of society.

How Some Strive to be "Respectable"

These implications of humanist emphases repel sociologists who insist upon being given "respectable" characterizations as "scientific" and "professional." They, and especially their employers, as sociologist Edna Bonacich observes, now choose "to curtail the independence of the social sciences and make them subservient to sustaining the current social order."[10] In consequence, many sociological monographs and journal articles are dehumanized. They lack recognition of pressures necessitating adaptation to changed conditions. They are too often peripheral or irrelevant to human needs. They fail to look behind the manipulating social myths promulgated by institutional spokespeople and reinforced by the mass media.

Why is so much sociological fact-gathering and theorizing so remote from actual human struggles? Why are so many "scientific" sociological research methods so artificializing, so trivializing, so oversimplifying and over-complicating, so distorting of human affairs?

An exchange between Bonacich and applied sociologist Cynthia B. Flynn illustrates the nature of the problem. Flynn asserts: "Like fine artists, we are taught to be wary of being coopted by 'the system' which pays for our work." She asks: "If you can sell an hour for three times as much outside of academia and reinvest it in your academic research, does not the whole academic community profit?"[11] Bonacich replies that "serving as paid consultants to the business community (or, for that matter, to the government or bureaucratic labor organizations) will quell any critical role that sociology might play in helping to improve the quality of life for all members of this society." It makes for "an emphasis on technical training at the expense of critical thought." She does not oppose applying sociology, but she "would hope that sociologists would move out of the university with more than that almighty buck in mind."[12]

The necessarily controversial nature of important social data and theory repels those concerned with the institutional status of social scientists. Such persons are also anxious to confront the related contention that social science "is all 'subjective' anyway." As the social scientist Nancie L. Gonzalez replied in a *Science* editorial: "It is not subjective, . . . but it is apparently very difficult, even for the scientifically sophisticated, to keep in mind that there is an external social and cultural world independent of the perceiving subject, a belief which, as Einstein said, is the basis of all natural science."[13]

Institutionalization in our current society demands of social scientists what passes for indubitable proof of entitlement to public images of "scientist" and "professional." This places premiums on being allegedly "value free" and "consistent," contentions that humanist social scientists reject. The sociologist Alvin W. Gouldner saw "all the powers of sociology . . . entered into a tacit alliance to bind us to the dogma that 'Thou shalt not commit a value judgment,' especially as sociologists." He regarded the acceptance of this "myth" as a "sign of professional senility."[14] The sociologist Joseph Gusfield points to the "need to stay close to the historical and empirical situations in which perspectives emerge." He calls consistency "the hobgoblin of the theoretical mind"[15] that can override or erode considerations of social relevance and accuracy of data and theory.

Noncontroversial public images or reputations for producing apparently "hard" data and conclusions favorable to those in power pay off readily in academic appointments, in consultantships, in grants of aid, in research contracts, and in opportunities for media attention. In response, humanists raise the question: Doesn't this result in the reduction of social science more or less to colorless routines and to pro-establishment propagandizing? If one does not object to being a follower, why not take oneself, garbed in scientific raiment and status, wholly and honestly into the more profitable outside world?

About the "hard" data criterion, Gonzalez asserts: "Even the educated and highly credentialed may be so ignorant of what social science is all about that they see science only in the dating or identification of artifacts, or in the demonstration of statistical correlations, such as those between divorce and educational level or between crime and urban congestion." She adds: "What is desperately needed is a better understanding of how rigorous, impartial investigation of social and cultural facts, including acts, objects, ideas, and sentiments, leads to increased knowledge of the patterns and processes which affect how we and others think and behave."[16]

President Derek Bok of Harvard illustrated in 1985 the establishment preference for "hard" data and especially for statistical manipulations by accepting an outside committee's recommendation to deny tenure to sociologist Paul Starr. The department faculty had voted seven to three to offer Starr a continuing contract. Starr's 1983 book, *The Social Transformation of American Medicine,* had gotten him a Pulitzer Prize. A reviewer in *Science* praised it as "the most ambitious and important analysis of American medicine to appear in over a decade."[17] His detractors claimed that he was a "journalist" or a "social historian." Sociology chair Aage Sorensen wanted researchers and teachers with a quantitative approach who would help Harvard sociology obtain "a more dominant influence in the profession."[18] Research and students of statistics rather than of social history would presumably be more important and more marketable.

In 1980, expert on welfare-state sociology Theda R. Skocpol had also been denied tenure by the all-male sociology faculty at Harvard at least in part because of her humanist orientation. Probably because of the affirmative action grievance that she filed, Skocpol accepted in 1985 an invitation by Bok to return to Harvard as a tenured professor. [19]

Curiously enough, in another connection at about the same time, Bok took a very different position. He asserted: "Humanistic learning has suffered enough from ill-considered efforts to ape the scientists by concentrating on what is quantifiable, verifiable, and value free." He contended: "With all its powers, the computer cannot contribute much to the learning of open-ended subjects like moral philosophy, religion, historical interpretation, literary criticism, or social theory — fields of knowledge that cannot be reduced to formal rules and procedures."[20] And yet he let Starr depart to Princeton and Skocpol be absent for a number of of years!

In considering these related controversies, it is over-simple to assert that there are only two stances that can be taken toward those prestige-giving labels, "professional" and "scientist." It is the rare person who is either all subservient or completely independent and autonomous. All but the obsessive are given to some degree of practical compromise and even occasional sycophancy as well as of idealistic aspiration.

Those who pander to establishment values and personalities love to see the innovative and daring works of their more autonomous competitors attacked as being radical, irresponsible, misinformed, method-

ologically naïve, journalistic, or simply unscientific.[21] Yet these off-beat social scientists can sometimes become influential, recognized, memorable. It is well to consider the statement of the psychologist Percy Black: "Among the great dilemmas of our age is the recognition that although we can't get along without science we don't know quite how to live with it."[22]

Ideal Definitions versus Group Mores

The clash between ideal definitions of a scientific sociological role and definitions to be found in the mores of the more pandering groups is striking and significant. It disturbs humanist sociologists, challenges them, and helps them to become and remain more autonomous. The contrast annoys many of the entrepreneurially minded—when they become at all aware of it—and makes them try to ignore or rationalize the existence and implications of such differences.

Plato, in his efforts to speak for intellectuals, wanted *episteme* or "science" to become recognized as an authentic and valuable item of merchandise to be accumulated, processed, and purveyed by himself and his fellows. This is one of the reasons why this elitist critic of humanist, relativist, and democratic Sophists, such as Protagoras, has been so highly valued by subsequent generations of elitist intellectuals. Only in recent times has the relativism of knowledge and its changing nature gained greater recognition and application under the leadership of cultural anthropologists, comparative historians, and such innovators in the physical sciences as Charles Darwin and Albert Einstein. Outstanding contributions to more accurate social knowledge typically come from the labors and dissents of nonconforming humanists, not from members of Platonic cults.

The development of the modern sciences of physics, chemistry and biology, the vast elaborations of mathematical conceptions and procedures, and their great politico-economic acceptance have provided stereotyped images of "scientist" for the less secure social scientists to try to emulate. The "hard" sciences suggested rhetoric and methods with which to give weight to social scientists' efforts. Sociologists borrowed this magic from the "hard" scientists by appropriating their terms and methods and attempting to adapt their theories. Despite resulting distortions of social data, these efforts have appeared to work because the products have often been of service as pro-establishment propaganda, justifications or reinforcements for the status quo.

Borrowings from the "Hard" Sciences

Examples of these borrowed scientific efforts are numerous enough. They continue to the present time, but here are a few older, influential examples:

Herbert Spencer in the nineteenth century made substantial contributions to reactionary propaganda through his application of Darwinian evolutionism to human affairs, his racism and classism, and his insistence that society has the characteristics of an organism.[23] It was he who introduced the concept of the survival of the fittest that was later taken up by Darwin.[24] Spencerian views are still exemplified in sociological literature.

When the paleontologist Lester F. Ward invaded sociology in the 1880s, he brought with him such biologistic terms as "sympodial development," "social karyokinesis," "social synergy," and "social telesis."[25] His optimism about the human lot was contagious, but he lacked contact with social realities. His artificializing influence still has adherents.

Franklin Henry Giddings seized upon Spencerian doctrines and statistics to provide his work with "scientific" respectability. In spite of this, "he was inclined to base his judgments . . . on immediate impressionistic reflections,"[26] often on apparently opportunistic considerations. Thus, from the late 1890s, he welcomed the imperialism of the Spanish-American War[27] and the militarism of World War I.[28] Following the latter war, Giddings' devotion to the status quo led him to crusade against any tendencies he suspected of being socialist. His influence through his texts[29] and some fifty Columbia University Ph.D.s fledged during his tenure there has been significant in American sociology.

Others such as the German Max Weber and the Harvard professor Talcott Parsons sought legitimacy for their "scientific" theorizings in the traditional baggage of European and especially German speculative philosophy. They did some delving into published sociological, ethnological, and historical materials, but they did not reveal the deepening intimacy of perception that William Graham Sumner brought to his cross-cultural analyses in his *Folkways*[30] from his extensive and intensive field experiences in Connecticut and elsewhere. Sumner was not, like his successor and distorter, A. G. Keller, a social Darwinian or Spencerian.[31]

The rise of contract research during the Depression of the 1930s and especially during World War II had as leaders such operators as Paul F. Lazarsfeld of Columbia University and Samuel A. Stouffer of Harvard. They helped to make special-interest arrangements predominant in the sponsorship of the research of both faculty members and students in many key graduate sociology departments. The formation of the Society for the Study of Social Problems in 1950–51 and then of the Association for Humanist Sociology in 1975–76, mentioned in the previous chapter, became reactions against this dehumanizing movement. Those bodies seek to provide mutual support for those concerned with the autonomy and ethical commitment of sociological scientists.[32]

Outstanding Sociological Contributions

Our greatest contributions to the knowledge of human affairs are usually based squarely upon intimate participant observation of clinically significant situations. They typically gain orientation from historical and comparative cross-cultural materials. Those responsible for such creative efforts avoid the artificialities and pretentious scientisms mentioned. Unfortunately, our "professional" histories of sociology deal chiefly with accounts of theorizings, with theoretical and methodological controversies, rather than with the many available studies that humanistically probe observational data.[33]

The genealogy of humanist empirical sociology is more accurately traced to social reformers and explorers and to novelists and investigative journalists dealing with nineteenth-century urban horrors than to the vaunted philosophical "sociologists" of that and earlier periods. To illustrate, the influential and scientific Karl Marx (1818–83) is often spoken of as a rather abstract theorist, but he was a perceptive observer and investigative journalist as well as a scholar.

A few examples of the many outstanding humanist sociological contributions are the following:

In the early 1840s Friedrich Engels, as an immigrant in England, sought "more than mere *abstract* knowledge" about the underprivileged there. As he told the underprivileged later, in his *Condition of the Working Class in England in 1844,* he "wanted to see you in your own homes, to observe you in your every-day life, to chat with you on your condition and grievances, to witness your struggles against the social and political power of your oppressors."[34]

Even though Charles Booth was the owner of a successful shipping line out of Liverpool, he "developed the habit of exploring the East End of London, mingling with the people and becoming familiar with their lifestyles."[35] In consequence, he decided to undertake with associates a comprehensive survey of the *Life and Labour of the People of London,* eventually published in seventeen volumes.[36] It was "a gigantic undertaking, unparalleled in its time and unsurpassed by modern empirical sociologists. Yet his work has generally been dismissed as mere fact gathering and unrelated to sociology proper. Such views are mistaken." Booth's analysis contains "the pervasive conception of class as a 'style of life' involving a multiplicity of criteria and as a force in the community having considerable impact on various types of social institutions." Booth's work contains "no shortage of sociological insight and much of what he said was suggestive of what would now be regarded as in the best tradition of sociological research."[37]

A similarly significant investigation in the United States, Paul U. Kellogg and his associates' *The Pittsburgh Survey*[38] "revealed to that community and to the nation at large the dangers to workers and citizens inherent in a community of rapid and uncontrolled industrial expansion."[39] Its penetrating generalizations about city life are similarly neglected by sociologists, to their loss. Fortunately, the popular acceptance achieved by Robert S. and Helen M. Lynd's *Middletown* and then by their *Middletown in Transition*[40] helped to convince sociologists that such observational reports and analyses can provide more dependable knowledge than philosophical disputes and mechanized surveys.

The influential University of Chicago sociologist Robert E. Park[41] based his work on firsthand observation and inspired his students to do likewise. Engels, Booth, Kellogg, and the Lynds all shared that enthusiasm for participant observation. It helped to free them all from bourgeois preconceptions so that they could traverse social gaps among class and ethnic groups.

Reactions to a recent symposium, *The Apple Sliced: Sociological Studies of New York City,*[42] illustrate well the conflict between abstractionists and efforts to portray and understand social realities. Lyn H. Lofland, for example, asserts, "Like many of the studies produced by the students of Park and his colleagues, the reports published here tend to be more descriptive than analytic." The nineteen articles are admitted to be "fascinating, intriguing, suggestive. But their links to generalizations about the structures and processes of urban life are, at best, tenuous." She admits to a "vitality in evidence here, and healthy doses of sociological snoopiness about everyday life."[43] But she apparently does not realize that too many theorists lack any such touch with "everyday life," that this book communicates a great deal more about "structures and processes" than do abstractions.

Other notable exemplars of humanist sociology in this country and elsewhere are numerous. In addition to *Folkways,* Sumner offered a long series of significant macro-sociological essays, notable for his opposition to plutocracy and plutocratic imperialism.[44] As we have suggested, Park personally and through his stimulating writings on urban life, interethnic relations, and mass communications inspired many younger sociologists. Charles Horton Cooley[45] published such intimate studies of interpersonal relations as *Human Nature and the Social Order* and *Social Organization.* W. I. Thomas and Florian Znaniecki delved deeply into the experiences of migrants and their resettlement in *The Polish Peasant in Europe and America.*[46] W. E. B. DuBois,[47] as a sociologist, social actionist, and writer, brought to black concerns a rich depth of perception.

Memorable more recent humanists in sociology include Oliver C. Cox, C. Wright Mills, Willard Waller, and Erving Goffman. Cox[48] continued the examination and analysis of black roles in American life with fresh insights. Mills[49] fearlessly attacked myths about social control and manipulation. Waller[50] did notable work on marital relations, teaching, and the military. Goffman[51] contributed novel additions to our knowledge of interpersonal interaction. The annual C. Wright Mills Awards of the Society for the Study of Social Problems provide significant additions to this list of illustrations.

Help from Other Humanists

In giving these examples of humanist contributions to our knowledge of society, it is not to be assumed that humanist sociologists do not recognize contributions from those not labeled sociologist. We can still learn a lot about the human condition from such ancients as the Arab Abd-ar-Rahman ibn Khaldûn, the Italian Niccolò Machiavelli, the English Francis Bacon, and the Spanish Baltasar Gracián y Morales. Ibn Khaldûn's[52] social-clinical experiences in North African governmental circles gave sociological depth to his historical and ethnological analyses. Machiavelli's *The Prince*[53] and Gracián's *The Art of Worldly Wisdom*[54] are keen social satires, based upon their extensive and intensive observations of the run of people and also of manipulators of social power. Bacon's *Novum Organum*[55] offers thoughts on propaganda analysis and scientific procedures that are timeless.

How often have I wished that my students might spend more time pondering the social wisdom of the many writers available to us who are not called sociologists. Think of what one can learn from the plays of Henrik Ibsen, George Bernard Shaw, or Sean O'Casey; from the novels of Honoré de Balzac, Feodor Dostoevski, Charles Dickens, Mark Twain, Sinclair Lewis and John Steinbeck; and from the shrewd writings of Thomas Jefferson, Lincoln Steffens, Vernon Louis Parrington, and Upton Sinclair, to name only a few of the more prominent.

The Usefulness of a Bacon Analysis

To illustrate the current utility of such outside writers to humanist sociologists, think of the four types of idols that Bacon says beset human minds. He calls these the Idols of the Tribe, of the Cave, of the Market-Place, and of the Theatre or of Systems. They represent influences of which humanists try to be aware and with which they attempt to cope.

The Idols of the Tribe are distortions of thought due to class, ethnic, and nationalistic biases. Gender needs to be added to Bacon's list.

The Idols of the Cave refer, as Bacon puts it, to the fact that every one "has a cave or den of his own, which refracts and discolours the light of nature, owing either to his own proper and peculiar nature, or to his education and conversation with others, or to the reading of books, and the authority of those he esteems and admires, or to the differences of impressions, accordingly as they take place in a mind preoccupied and predisposed or in a mind indifferent and settled, or the like." As he says, people thus often "look for sciences in their own lesser worlds and not in the greater or common world."[56]

With regard to the Idols of the Market-Place, Bacon is concerned with the influence of "commerce and concert" among people and especially with how the related conniving warps words and concepts and thus patterns of thought. Words as used in the markets "plainly force and overrule the understanding," he contends, "and throw all into confusion, and lead men away into numberless empty controversies and idle fantasies."[57]

Then, finally, there are the Idols of the Theatre or, as he adds, of Systems. These "have immigrated into men's minds from the various dogmas of philosophies and also from the wrong laws of demonstration." In consequence, he perceives that "all received systems are but so many stage-plays." He contends this because he concludes that "human understanding is of its own nature prone to suppose the existence of more order and regularity in the world than it finds."[58] Lofland's review of *The Apple Sliced*, mentioned above, is an illustration of this idolization of the theatricality of "received systems" that haunts so much sociology.

Bacon surely holds with the humanist scientists when he claims: "Now the true and lawful goal of the sciences is none other than this: that human life be endowed with new discoveries and powers." At the same time, he realizes the fear "the great majority" have of innovation, how they are mostly coopted by being "merely hireling and professorial." Humanity benefits because "it occasionally happens that some workman of acuter wit and covetous of honour applied himself to a new invention, which he mostly does at the expense of his fortunes."[59] As the lives of Karl Marx, Thorstein Veblen, and W. I. Thomas as well as of Bacon himself illustrate, this point about the costs of innovation to the innovator can be especially acute in the social sciences. Marx fought against suppression and lived in exile. Veblen and Thomas were dismissed from academic positions. Bacon's critics were happy when his involvement in corruption got him banished from the English court.

In referring to these influences, I am not trying to be "holier than thou" in behalf of humanist sociologists. We try to be aware of such influences, and we try to deal with them as best we can. To the extent that we succeed, we are able to pursue more effectively the humanist concerns, needs, goals to which we are dedicated in our efforts to create an emancipatory sociology.

Any implication in the foregoing that humanist sociologists necessarily come to similar conclusions or have precisely the same conceptions of humanist concerns, needs, goals is surely to be disavowed. Much can be learned from the disagreements as well as from the agreements to be found in humanist social science literature.

The Influences of "Concert"

In closing, let us look a little further at the concern Bacon called the influence of "concert," in other words of "networking." That influence plus related increased legitimation and recognition are the chief values social scientists seek in such bodies as professional associations.

Just what is a profession? It is a group of people initiated into a given common body of knowledge and practice, with each person certified to be so qualified, and formed into one or more associations presumably for self-disciplining and networking purposes. The associations "lay down rules of entry, training, and behaviour in relation to the public (*professional ethics*), see to it that the standard of knowledge and skill of the practitioners is not lowered, defend the level of their professional remuneration, try to prevent competing groups from encroaching upon the boundaries of their professional activities, and watch over the preservation of their professional status."[60] In other words, professionals utilize their association as a cultish conspiracy that may or may not serve public interests but that surely needs critical probing and prodding. Members should be aware of the costs in scientific integrity that the Idol of the Market-Place can exact.

Let us look briefly at some of these associational activities. To what extent do they raise problems that humanist sociologists should confront?

The rules of entry and training are especially significant. With the conversion of so many Ph.D. sociology departments into contract research establishments serving the military-industrial complex or other biasing interests, how many fledgling Ph.D.s are now able to obtain their degrees without being exploited and sometimes intellectually damaged? How many doctoral dissertations are now really pieces of independent research? As C. Wright Mills has written: "The idea of a university as a circle of professorial peers, each with apprentices and each practicing a craft, tends to be replaced by the idea of a university as a set of research bureaucracies, each containing an elaborate division of labor, and hence of intellectual technicians."[61] Thus do administrators, research promoters, and subservient technicians take their places alongside or completely replace "more old-fashioned scholars and researchers."

The topic of professional ethics is important. In 1950–51, I chaired an American Sociological Society (ASS) committee on problems of the individual researcher in which professional ethics was discussed.[62] The next year, that committee was renamed one on standards and ethics in research practice, and I continued to be its chair.[63] Since then, I served four terms on the ASS/American Sociological Association Council, one as a write-in president of the Association, and a year as a member of the committee on freedom of research and teaching. I mention that record of experiences with the ASS/ASA only to furnish my background for the following generalizations about that sociological association's efforts concerning ethics. They are propaganda ventures. They protect the tenured against the untenured. They do little to give security to the controversial innovator. They try to convince potential providers of research grants and customers for contract research of the legitimacy of what they are buying. I place the ASA code of ethics in a class with those of the medical, advertising, public relations, and legal professions. They are all façades that may or may not have any resemblance to actual practices.[64]

Another consideration is the level of professional remuneration: Can you imagine the ASA cooperating with the teachers' unions or concerning itself with minimum wages for graduate assistants? So-called "professional remuneration" is on a much "higher" level, the level of merchandising professional wares in competition with the wares of other professions.

Finally, encroachments from other professions and preservation of professional status are to be examined. ASA tactics in this regard are curious. The American Psychological Association and the American Anthropological Association are both federations. They try not to permit disciplinary innovations to become splinter bodies that escape from their organizational networks. The dedication of ASA stalwarts to a salable commodity consisting of abstract theory and methodological exercises plus their anxiety to control the principal sociological body have, in contrast with APA and AAA procedures, permitted a whole raft of groups to form their own separate and competing organizations: the criminologists, the family specialists, the rural sociologists, the social problems people, and others. This is a price that ASA insiders pay for "purity," but selfishly and in the short run it is apparently a rewarding investment. They do control the professional logotype, as it were, and get whatever perquisites the "principal professional association in the field" can glean from that claim.[65]

A Song of Joy

Parts of this chapter may look to some like a sad dirge, the sour grapes of an outsider, but it is really nothing of the kind. It should rather be interpreted as a song of joy that there are so many who know where sociological wisdom can be found and who are willing to dedicate themselves to that search.

As the sociologists Walda Katz Fishman and Robert Newby have it, humanists feel an "imperative, in both theoretical understanding and political practice, . . . to participate in the creation of a more humane society in which the human rights and needs of all people are recognized and met." This means that our social "system must be basically altered if the poorest and most unequal are to realize the benefits of their labor and of life in the most 'advanced' society in the world."[66] The needed social movements, as the sociologist Jerold M. Starr avers, "must adopt a position of humanist reason, reason based on the principle that individual freedom and rational social planning must be rooted in democratically organized social relationships and concerned with ultimate ends or values." This calls for "a dialectical synthesis of rationality and moral community, individual creative freedom and collective solidarity, head and heart."[67]

These are difficult challenges, but they are ones many social scientists and others are now trying to do what they can to meet. That there are so many making such efforts turns one from discouragement with the darkening national and international scene to the encouraging possibilities for change that do exist. Sociology can help with human liberation.

3

To Magnify the Individual

Concerned students like to talk about what society is like and how they may be able to relate themselves to it. If they are taking a course in sociology, they may ask each other: "Can we really use the stuff we're getting? Does it work when you try it out in life?" Years later, in homes, clubs, and bars, they may still be struggling with similar problems.

Such discussions can become quite personal, even intimate. Autobiographical bits and items concerning close friends and relatives serve as illustrations. The most intimate revelations are often disguised as experiences of some unnamed person. The subjects range from encounters with members of the other sex to how to reform the university, stop militarism, get a job, or build a fortune or a political constituency. The more concerned often wonder about how our jerry-built world, with all its iniquities, inequalities, and brutalities, can be made into a society that is likely to persist and be more worth living in. Many focus on short-term improvements—hopefully with constructive longer-term implications—to which they can contribute during their lives.

When teachers of sociology, as presumed experts, participate in such discussion sessions, they suddenly may find themselves thrown on a dissecting table. They may have to cope with imperious demands for self-revelation. The nature of social controls, exploitations, and mass communications makes for exciting reading and discussion, students admit, but they want to get down to "where we live and where we are likely to live." How do professors convince themselves that the viewpoint they present is that suitable to a professional? The viewpoint may or may not be a pose — on that the students are not at all sure, and they want to know. The attitude is so different from any they have known before that they just have to demand fuller and more adequate explanation. Is such an orientation of use only to a professional sociologist and perhaps just as a hobby or a luxury to anyone else? How is it that the affirmed positions of sociologists differ so much, as the first chapter indicates?

All these questions are significant, but let us turn first to the last one. There are sociologists concerned about helping people to live more effectively and satisfyingly as fuller participants in society, and then there are others who lean more to the manipulative or just to the dilettantish. Some are games-playing statisticians and other precise methodologists who can show how to learn very little about society, but how to determine that little bit in a most correct fashion. There are also social theorists who offer a scintillating supermarket full of alternative explanations, subtle distinctions, exact terminologies, and conflicting theoretical models of people and of society. They can discourse grandly about almost anything, well out of touch with actual starvation, disease, war, exploitation, and hopelessness. And then, not to make the list too long, there are the existential humanists to whom sociology and related disciplines (including history, philosophy, and literature) must yield knowledge for life and living or not be worth the struggle. What they ask you to consider may at times not be pleasant, romantic, flattering, or elegant. It may mean delving into outrageous ways of life and repulsive events. But what they offer often strikes students as being relevant to their futures, as contributing, in effect, a kind of initiation into "real life." It is an initiation that contrasts sharply many times with an introduction to the instrumentalism of such trade disciplines as business administration and engineering.

Looking at "Slices of Life"

When students discover that a given professor actually has roles in exciting events "out in the world," they become all the more insistent upon a revelation of the nature of those involvements. If they feel that the professor is likeable, they may try to learn from her or him the risks, consequences, and tensions, the human drama of such experiences. Such a relationship can lead to such questions as these:

What is to be learned from taking part in a work party to detoxify walls covered with scaling lead paint or powdering asbestos fibers poisoning school pupils or slum dwellers? To whom is such work controversial? Why?

What insights can be gained from visiting meetings of Alcoholics Anonymous, Addicts Anonymous, or Gamblers Anonymous?

What can be learned about such organizations as the Black Muslims, the Black Panthers, the Jewish Defense League, and the Ku Klux Klan? What are the stated and the real, the voiced and the unacknowledged, the consciously believed and the unaware points of view of the members of the Daughters and Sons of the American Revolution, the Chamber of Commerce, the Junior League, and trade and professional associations? How do their members work to get what they want? Are those organizations sometimes used for purposes their members do not comprehend and perhaps would not sanction? If so, how?

What happens when a white neighborhood is desegregated? What sort of people help? How? What kinds of actionists work against desegregation? How?

What is the nature of the various anti-war or pro-peace efforts? What are the differences among the objectives and tactics of conscientious objectors to any war, objectors to a specific war, advocates of peace through preparedness, advocates of peace through war, and agitators of internal social revolution? What evidence can be marshalled to support the wisdom and agitations of each group?

Can scientific studies be made that contribute usefully to the efforts of socially constructive actionists? How can we evaluate the alleged constructiveness of an actionist?

Is concern with individual social problems worth the bother? Doesn't such concern merely lead to efforts wasted upon attempting to prop up an outworn social system? Doesn't the whole "system" need an overhauling or replacement?

Students soon learn that the existential humanist classroom is not bounded by four walls and that its subject matter includes experiences more vivid than lectures, text assignments, discussions, term papers, and even spontaneous informal discussion sessions. They begin to realize how much easier it is to listen, read, or talk wishfully, and thus selectively and defensively, than it is to participate in social events that confront them with mind-changing observations. Protective and distorting thought-curtains often prevent us from assimilating mind-modifying facts and ideas as we hear or read them, but a close-up view of an actual event can tear great holes in such comforting veils. Active participation in an event can be most stimulating mental therapy. Fieldwork in social action may suddenly and sharply bring students to the conclusion that a great deal in society is not what they had assumed it to be.[1] This constrains them to read anew, to rediscuss, and to rethink their social perspectives. Thus does their fundamental education for mature social participation get under way.

The mention of teachers with something more than teaching experience does not imply that courses should be of a trade school character. Working with a social worker or farmer or trade-union organizer might forever enrich the life of a future industrial manager or banker. Becoming involved in a biologist's laboratory or newspaper editorial work might help a sociologist or anyone else to mature more than would several extra courses in any given subject.

Can "Sociology" Be an Escape Device?

Many students do not identify with a professor who has actionist exploits. Many future sociology professors would not appreciate the hearty worldliness of an existential humanist. They would be more comfortable with a more theoretical teacher. The Harvard professor of government Carl J. Friedrich, in accounting for the elitism and cultism common among intellectuals in our society, notes that "the intellectual is apt to be maladjusted in childhood and youth. Frequently he is ridiculed and even persecuted by his more normal schoolmates. His superior mind becomes the avenue of escape from his hostile environment."[2]

Since sacred academic precincts can be invaded successfully via elegant theory and glossy methodology, the language and tools of select cults, those intellectuals in effect ask: Why reopen the sores of childhood and youth? Why not make a career of escapism? As one professor in a prestigious graduate school once frankly told me: "I was an avid stamp collector as a youth. I have enjoyed thoroughly my graduate work and my research since then because they are my psychological equivalents of stamp collecting." Whether philately's loss was sociology's gain in this case depends upon what one expects a sociologist to accomplish. For the humanistically inclined, this professor's teachings and example have dramatic negative value. Fortunately other professors demonstrate that sociology has made them more effective social observers, diagnosticians, theorists, and citizens.

Enticements of the Laboratory

Many a striving sociologist looks enviously at the laboratory of an archeologist, physical anthropologist, experimental psychologist, or entomologist. They note the scientific aura such an orderly workroom gives to a discipline, the apparent authority it imparts to its inmates. But let us look candidly at an experimental psychologist's problems and labors and then at a sociologist's.

Even the most specialized experimentalist among psychologists sooner or later finds it necessary to lean heavily on the studies of social and clinical psychologists, sociologists, and ethnologists in order to learn the individual and social contexts within which subjects live and within which to experiment. For all the precision of testing instruments, measurements, and statistical manipulations, they cannot but realize how much significant information has had to come from outside the laboratory. Much of that data is no less useful because it may have to be in the form of unmeasurable observations.

When psychologists go beyond experimentation with individuals and attempt to deal with arranged group situations, the artificialities of the laboratory become all the more limiting and all the more dependent upon outside observation. They realize that each of their subjects is a person torn out of many group contexts and that each experimental group is fitted by its members into many remembered contexts. Both sociologists and psychologists engage in this type of experimental social-psychological work focused upon a small group or upon several groups in a controlled environment.

What these illustrations highlight is that scientists must take their subject matter — not their tools — as their principal preoccupation. Archeologists have as their goal the reconstruction of part or all of an ancient way of life, not the mere piecing together of single pots. The physical anthropologists try to shed light on the evolving anatomy and functioning of human beings as they have lived through the ages, not merely the reconstruction of single skulls or skeletons. The entomologists do not stop with an orderly display of variations in the form or color of beetles; they attempt to relate their findings to those of others in the search for how beetles and other insects live, modify, and reproduce under changing conditions. Thus scientists must not be enticed into oversimplifying or otherwise distorting their data through the overuse or inappropriate use of gadgetry such as a computer or of stage sets such as a laboratory. Such artifacts can too easily become ends in themselves, ends that obscure scientists' basic jobs.

Uses of the Sociological Laboratory

The above is not meant to suggest that sociologists should always be strangers to laboratories. In studies of appropriate problems, they may well find a computation laboratory to be most helpful in processing complicated data that can be reduced to comparable units. They may save many hours of library research through employing a mechanized data-retrieval system, such as has been developed by Sociological Abstracts, Inc.[3] They may be able to interview informants more efficiently and accurately in a neutral laboratory environment, equipped perhaps with a recording instrument, than they could in the street or in the subjects' homes. They may achieve special insights by arranging confrontations between groups of competitors or antagonists in a laboratory situation. They may gain useful knowledge by the extended study of play groups or work groups placed in controlled environments. In each case, however, sociologists need to be vividly aware that what they are doing in a workroom is artificially abstracted from society. It has to be brought into relationship with what takes place spontaneously in society. It should also be added that a great deal of highly important sociological analysis and synthesis has been done upon the basis of observations made only in the midst of life.

How Intimate Should Sociological Learning Become?

Many students agree that a personal report from an observing participant in social action can give them much more than they are able to learn from a formal text, even from a text by the same participant observer. A person — a human "document" — portrays more through words and actions than can be gained from printed pages or even from documentary cinemas. This advantage of the use of persons as classroom study materials can be possible especially through encouraging the students themselves to report their own meaningful outside experiences. They return to class from having labored in volunteer carpentry efforts, been observers at a debutante ball or a fox hunt, had firsthand experiences in a factory assembly line, worked in a prison, mental hospital, or tuberculosis ward, accompanied social case workers on their rounds, or attended a Rotary or a trade-union meeting. When students are so enlightened with what they have taken part in outside of their customary class and ethnic — even age and gender — groups, they become vivid documents both for themselves and for their fellows. They help translate sociological observations and theories as set forth in words and pictures into intimate aspects of living.

Such live expeditions permit students to perceive different personalities interacting among themselves and with various situations, data, and ideas. A long step beyond this in educational effectiveness is field or project work of a more sustained sort under trained and permissive guidance — that is, under leadership that encourages and stimulates individual work and creativity and does not dominate or exploit.

Field work can raise some difficult problems associated with the possible unwanted invasion of privacy. Investigations can be overt or covert. In either case, students need to be alerted to how their prying might offend those observed. If the inquiry is a covert one, the anonymity of subjects should be carefully protected against possible embarrassment. In overt studies, diplomatically carried on, students can learn the extent to which people and organizations may welcome or resent opportunities to have their problems and accomplishments better known and understood. The subsequent analytical report should be as unqualifiably accurate as possible, but it need not identify individual subjects.

Empathy and the Power to Choose

Students are fortunate when they can empathize with at least a few of their teachers and fellow students. Empathy is vicariously to experience feelings and thoughts of another. It does not imply identification and certainly not idealization. Clear-eyed empathy may stimulate or facilitate learning, but idealization may only block it. One's critical ability must be preserved.

In addition to personal ambitions, such empathy plus personal experimentation with what is being studied provide great stimulants to personal growth. Empathizing with a "working model" of what may be ahead in life, whether in or outside of school, makes the route appear more traversable. Personal experimentation with ideas in practical situations gives a realistic sense of taking steps along a route "into life," into autonomy.

As the sociologist Robert E. Kennedy, Jr., notes, "Some people claim they have little or no choice, that society and social pressures entirely determine their lives." To this, he replies: "But they don't have to." He contends "that while 'society' or some mix of 'social forces' may constrain your options, they do not entirely determine your life. . . . Opportunities can be exploited or squandered; difficulties can be overcome or compounded."[4]

As C. Wright Mills, another sociologist, has put it, a sociologically trained imagination can help people understand better their own experiences and gauge their own probable fate by placing themselves in historical context and by perceiving how their own chances in life compare with others in similar circumstances. "In many ways," he says, "it is a terrible lesson; in many ways a magnificent one." He points out that "the limits of 'human nature' are frighteningly broad."[5]

A lot depends upon how one interprets Mills's advice. If one takes sociological findings about historical context and life chances as opportunities or difficult challenges, the choice of alternatives can become a productive and creative way of life. Otherwise, the "terrible lesson" can help one sink into routines and discouragements others apparently exemplify, advocate, or accept as unobtrusively "normal."

Sociological Writing as Autobiography

The autobiographical element or quality in novels and sociological writings helps readers empathize with authors with whom they can make some identity. It is inescapable in sociological reports and texts even though very few of them contain frank personal history. Evidences of an author's life history and ideological orientation appear even in the most formal dissertations.

One would think that a historical treatment of sociological research and theory would need to bring the personal lives and social settings of the protagonists into the changing picture. How else can one understand the positions they take in such struggles as those centering on evolutionism, values versus value freedom, quantification, and functionalism? In many ways, Roscoe C. Hinkle's *Founding Theory of American Sociology: 1881–1915* is an accurate portrayal of what leading figures wrote in such conflicts, but it is strangely lacking of a portrayal of the human contexts out of which the writings emerged. For example, Hinkle notes that W. G. Sumner and E. A. Ross "offered broad indictments of most or all of the main features of Social Darwinism." On the contrary, F. H. Giddings and Sumner's student and successor, A. G. Keller, "are prevailingly social Darwinists." In consequence, because Keller attributed the senior authorship of the four-volume *Science of Society* to Sumner[6] long after the latter's death, what Hinkle recognized as "the substantial divergence in their positions"[7] is obscured. This made Sumner look like a social Darwinian and his substantial social insights and criticisms thus easier to discard. Unfortunately, Hinkle did not dig into the highly relevant personal background factors that made Sumner and Ross so different from Giddings and Keller.

More autobiographies have begun to appear in the discipline in recent years. Such writing is still thought by some to be narcissistic or egotistical, but it takes some such quality to lead one to become a professor, author, actor, or other type of public figure. Since biographies depend heavily upon a sociologist's writings, they tend to be only a step away from the autobiographical. The resulting accounts are typically selective and biased, but they help to humanize the discipline.

An intriguing and instructive autobiographical statement by a sociologist is Charles Horton Cooley's[8] candid *Life and the Student,* which his biographer observes "might just as well have been *My Life as a Student,* for it was, in a sense, his autobiography."[9] Other useful autobiographical accounts include E. A. Ross's[10] *Seventy Years of It,* Pitirim A. Sorokin's[11] *A Long Journey,* Robert M. MacIver's[12] *As a Tale That Is Told,* William Foote Whyte's[13] appendix to his *Street Corner Society,* John Kosa's[14] collection of autobiographical essays in his symposium, *The Home of the Learned Man,* and Charles H. Page's[15] *Fifty Years in the Sociological Enterprise: A Lucky Journey.* Such biographical treatments as

Harris E. Starr's[16] *William Graham Sumner* and Robert E. L. Faris's[17] *Chicago Sociology* are, as is suggested above, only a step away from being autobiographical. All such documents help to place social findings a little more precisely in their social and psychological contexts.

What Sociologists Can Give to People

In the discussion here of ways in which sociology can magnify the individual, there is no point in pursuing further the esoteric and technical aspects of the field. Here our concerns are with sociology as an awakener and stimulant and as intellectual equipment with which an individual can more effectively deal with problems of life and living. As the sociologist Joseph Gusfield states it, "humanistic social science, like imaginative literature, creates an experience for the reader." He adds that it "is not the same as imaginative literature. Its unique virtue lies both in its encounter with a world of real people and events and in its systematic presentation of the framework through which the authors experience and analyze that world." He does not see it as cinéma vérité but as engagement for the reader "with experience and reflection, finding its effect in the combination of both."[18]

What can humanist sociologists thus offer to people? Sociologists can give people an ever-refreshing sensitivity to all kinds of other people, groups, and social problems. As consciousness-raisers, they may help to make people feel that action and change are possible and even desirable, preferable to anxious and habitual attachment to a stability that cannot and does not exist. They can destroy enfeebling respect for and fear of charismatic persons and statuses and then help to replace them with more accurate and useful assessments. They are able to reveal human dimensions and limitations of the social "system" and of its alleged legitimacy and orthodoxy, which when accepted uncritically are so destructive of individual autonomy and effectiveness.

Sociologists can show people how control procedures of family, school, and other social agencies which tend to push most of us — not just minority-group members — toward accepting roles as trucklers, as willing and dependent instruments of others. They can substitute an accurate conception of what is happening and can happen to us for an unthinking and sentimental notion of social controls. They may demonstrate how the control of power in our society depends more upon loyalty than upon competence, and that therein lies the controllers' greatest vulnerability. They can spell out the insecurity and frailty of any one who controls some social power, whether in finance, politics, religion, entertainment, or knowledge.

Sociologists point to the omnipresent morass of manipulators behind any individual who appears to be a dominant figure in our complex and multivalent society. They detail how habituation and power-fatigue eventually benumb those in influential statuses as well as their followers. All power—whatever its seeming form—derives from the conscious or unconscious consent of the controlled. That consent, regardless of how it is given, can be withdrawn in any of a myriad of ways.

Sociologists and other social scientists serve to inform people about how mass-communications agencies attempt to influence them. They suggest ways to analyze, compare, and otherwise deal with such manipulative procedures. They can also clarify the nature of pressuring groups and institutions so that people can relate such interests more accurately and beneficially to their own concerns. In other words, these scientists provide "consumers" with ways to analyze propaganda, agitation, and social organization.

Sociologists suggest the relative merits of becoming even a modest power crystallizer rather than a servant or courtier of a power wielder or power group. To help keep such agitation from becoming too obsessive, too much of an end in itself, sociologists can help people keep accurate perspectives on persons and events and themselves.

Sociologists and other social scientists tell people how to penetrate a mass-communications network, even for purposes contrary to those held by a given medium's nominal controllers. They furnish data on how to interact with and also how to use voluntary organizations in order to launch acceptable social projects. "Acceptable projects" may be projects that might not otherwise be launched but that actually can serve popular interests and can gain popular support.

Why do many sociologists treat such problems—if they do—under heavy veneers of obscure terminology and unconvincing or irrelevant fact? The reason is, briefly, that this is risky stuff. This is not a high school course in "civics" or "American society" or their college equivalents. This kind of sociology means stripping the disguises from social controls and manipulations and trying to understand how they work.

The sociology advocated here demands that the primordial promise of democracy in education actually be implemented. Its promise thus for society can also gain greater acceptance. It means that people must be given a chance to become responsible citizens by again being given an opportunity to feel the sense of independence and responsibility some find in frontier or rural conditions, after emigration, in unsettled times, and in agitations for novel efforts or social causes. This kind of realistically humanist sociology can help people to make our society into what it can well become if it is to survive—an egalitarian and participant one. Some sociologists try to achieve these effects both in their classrooms and in their books, articles, and outside activities. In our society, this constitutes a calculated professional risk as well as a valuable basic ethical commitment.

Sensitivity and Action

How can sociologists refresh people's sensitivity? How can they raise social consciousness and thus stimulate participation in constructive social actions? How can they help provide realistic models of actionists and of action strategies? These are sociological queries, but answers to them require more than what is reported in sociological texts. As the sociologist Charles H. Page points out, sociologists gain much from borrowings from other disciplines. As he words it, "The fact that major contributions to our subject are made by 'outsiders' rarely gets attention in sociology's major journals—a reflection perhaps of the provincialism associated with academic success, long marked, for example, in history and psychology."[19] These queries also call for immersion in what is being called "clinical" sociology, a point to be illustrated below.

The problem of sensitivity recalls a passage in a book by the sociologist Jerome Davis. He mentions "speaking about the dangers of a possible and 'theoretical' future World War II" before a student group in the 1930s. In response: "Two American college boys retorted: 'We can't do anything about the problem of war. What do we know about foreign affairs? Leave such matters to the War Department and the State Department.' Time passed. One of these boys is dead and the other spent four years in the army fighting on a foreign battle-front." A young female college student in the same audience insisted: "We have no influence. We can't change foreign affairs. Why bother?" To this, Davis adds that since then, her husband "had died fighting and she is struggling alone to support two children."[20]

These young people were acting "normally." Their perspectives were typically short-term, narrow, and self-centered, and they gained long-term suffering for themselves and associates.

Increased social sensitivity can become a significant byproduct of broader and more varied social experiences. It can grow quickly through participating or at least observing in ethnic, racial, or class groups other than one's own. Such groups can force us to think in terms of a subculture or culture different from our own in order to understand them, in order to deal with them. It is like learning to perceive people through another person's quite different glasses. If the contrasts are great enough, it can give us a sense of culture shock, a disturbing but unfolding and enlightening experience.

The anthropologist Philip K. Bock reminds us how possible it is "to go around the world without ever once directly experiencing anything different from one's normal routine, no matter how many quaint scenes are captured on color slides." Or if one "views anything foreign as inferior and/or disgusting," the result is much the same. Such ethnocentrism shields one from upsetting realizations. On the contrary, "direct exposure to an alien society usually produces a disturbing feeling of disorientation and helplessness that is called 'culture shock.'" At first, it usually involves "inability to make any sense out of the behavior of others or to predict what they will say or do." It then becomes an opportunity "to *understand* an alien way of life, by choice or out of necessity." It is "the best way to learn about alien modes of life or to gain perspective on one's own culture."[21]

Investigative reporters, socially conscious novelists, film makers, cartoonists, and other artists, and literate humanist social scientists can sometimes give a similar sense of shock. As the art historian Paul Von Blum points out: "War, slavery, class exploitation, racism, sexism, imperialist adventures in foreign affairs, internal assaults on civil liberties—all these and more have caused artists to respond with passion and indignation."[22] Many who are cartoonists, socially conscious painters, or humanist social scientists have had training in "realistic reporting"; it sharpened their eyes to real life. As Von Blum adds, "The engaged posture of socially conscious art . . . stimulates ethical controversy and resolution, which in itself is an admirable effect in a world that is often pervasively indifferent."[23]

Once we comprehend more accurately what intergroup cultural differences can mean by having gone through one or more intergroup cultural barriers, through having suffered the travail of culture shock and thus of becoming somewhat marginal, we can gain a much deeper appreciation of humankind. It adds depth and scope to sociological wisdom. It even makes clearer to us the extent to which, as we grew up in our society, we were assimilated into more than one subculture with contrasting values. This is something many people only subconsciously recognize and do not understand. Such astute politicians as the late John F. Kennedy and the 1984 and 1988 presidential candidate Jesse Jackson repeatedly refreshed their cultural perspectives and their sensitivity by participating in frank discussions with diverse groups.

Marginality's Benefits and Handicaps

The marginal person or cultural hybrid is an individual who has become more or less assimilated into more than one distinct ethnic or class culture. Marginals include immigrants, Blacks, and others forced to live and work in more than one culture, parvenus and others who have changed class level, migrants from country to city, ex-members of American ghettos, and those who have had other types of mind-stretching experiences.

Sociological literature frequently treats marginality only as a maladjustment, an individual handicap or a social problem. The focus often falls on the difficulties of marginals to find and hold jobs, to accept the norms of their new community, and on their violations of custom and law. Marginality can contribute to psychopathic and criminal behavior, but it can also help provide the stimulus for greater creativity in the fine arts, scientific and scholarly research, education, and other social activities.[24]

Intergroup contact produces not only marginality but also the divisive influence of prejudice. The social psychologist Gordon W. Allport formulated in 1954 a much-used hypothesis on how prejudice may be diminished. He summarized a wealth of evidence by saying that it "may be reduced by equal status contact between majority and minority groups in the pursuit of common goals." He stressed the usefulness of "institutional supports (i.e., by law, custom or local atmosphere), and . . . the perception of common interests and common humanity between members of the two groups" in achieving such a reduction.[25] This hypothesis has the same thrust as the statement signed by Allport, Kenneth B. Clark, and thirty other social scientists that was acknowledged by the U. S. Supreme Court in 1954 as having been influential in their decision in the landmark school desegregation case, *Oliver Brown et al., v. Board of Education of Topeka, Kansas, et al.*[26]

Norman D. Humphrey and I had found substantial evidence to support such a hypothesis when we made a firsthand study of the 1943 Detroit race riot. As we reported: "People who had become neighbors in mixed Negro and white neighborhoods did not riot against each other. The students of Wayne University—white and black—went to their classes in peace throughout Bloody Monday. And there were no disorders between white and black workers in the war plants."[27] A symposium on "Intergroup Contact," edited by the psychologists Walter G. Stephan and John C. Brigham, gives a wealth of more recent evidence in support of the Allport hypothesis. Its authors also illustrate many of its ramifications.[28]

Marginality thus has its unfortunate and even disastrous aspects, but it is also an effective manner of shaking individuals and groups out of complacency, of stimulating autonomy, social awareness, and creativity, in other words of magnifying the individual.

To Stimulate Individual Participation

Efforts at social action can serve both society and also the interests of individuals who become its participants. Clinical sociologists provide realistic models of activists and of social strategies that help to give individuals and groups a realistic sense of what they may actually accomplish with their available assets.

As illustrations, let us look at the work of the Italian sociologist-actionist Danilo Dolci, the negotiators Holly G. Porter and Irving Goldaber, and the applied clinical sociologist Thomas J. Rice. The effectiveness of these activists suggests only a few of the many possible ways in which the individual—magnified by social sensitivity and wisdom—can engage in constructive social action.

A Nonviolent Confrontationist

Now that both Mahatma Gandhi and Martin Luther King, Jr., have become victims of violence, Dolci is today one of the outstanding living exemplars of nonviolent methods for the achievement of social change. A north Italian, Dolci as a young man turned away from being trained as an architect to begin what he calls his real education — working at Nomadelfia in Italy. That Christian community "gathered together in a vast family boys and girls left homeless by the war" of 1939–45. There he says he had his "first opportunity to acquire some knowledge through direct experience. Hoeing weeds, building latrines in the camps, living with orphans, former petty thieves, many of them sick," he learned "what it means to grow together; after several months of common endeavor, even abysmally stupid faces became more human, and sometimes beautiful." Dolci observes that he "became deeply aware that even as each man must take stock of himself and learn to live according to his convictions, so the life of the group, community life, is an indispensable instrument for stock-taking and for individual and collective maturation."

Dolci did not feel that he was doing enough to forward his concerns at Nomadelfia. It came to be too much just "a warm nest that tended to breed complacency," so far as he was concerned. In 1952, therefore, he set out for "the most wretched piece of country I had ever seen," Trappeto, a fishing village in western Sicily.[29] Together with a deep humility, a rich background in the humanities and in social studies, and a drive to learn ever more, Dolci brought to this area's problems a wealth of practical know-how.[30] As Aldous Huxley has said: Dolci "knows what specialists in other fields are talking about, respects their methods and is willing and eager to take advice from them."[31] Always working with only a small staff in a limited area, Dolci succeeded in creating an experimental situation in which techniques for social change are developed and demonstrated. He is a practical social innovator who seeks to show how even the most deprived and exploited can improve their lot.

Dolci wanted to help western Sicilians to lift themselves out of poverty through adequate irrigation, better health facilities, better opportunities for their young, and better living conditions. First, however, he had to perceive the area and its problems as intimately and as accurately as he could. This took painstaking observation, study, discussion, and analysis. He also had to gain the confidence of the highly suspicious and secretive people he sought to help. This required involvement — for him, even marriage to a local widow. And then he had to stimulate volunteer organizations to plan, to pressure the government for aid, and to implement whatever programs that might result.

To do this social action job, Dolci faced Mafiosi, ecclesiastical indifference and even opposition, and political-business venality on many levels, as well as the deep-seated fear of experimentation or even of change among those who had been so exploited for centuries. He sought joint or communal decision making. He wanted to encourage the people's potential leaders to come forth and to function. He wanted to raise social consciousness, not to "sell" people answers to their problems. Dolci hoped: "The struggle must be nonviolent—taking the form of active or passive strikes; refusal to cooperate on what is deemed to be harmful; protests and public demonstrations in all the many forms that may be suggested by the circumstances, one's own conscience, and the particular need."[32]

Dolci believes in human potentialities, in discovering as precisely as he can those with whom he can work and the nature of their problems, and in encouraging people to organize, to inform themselves, and to take responsibility for social action. As he summarizes his viewpoint:

> People learn rapidly when they find it is to their advantage. . . . Already a good part of this area has had clear proof that when a large enough group works together with determination and a spirit of nonviolence, some very important things happen, such as getting a dam under way. And one democratic development follows another. For example, for the first time in their lives the sharecroppers and landowners, both of whom stand to benefit from the dam, are getting together to make certain that they will get their fair share of water; not, as in the past, the share that the Mafia would or would not let them have.[33]

As a researcher and resource person for the oppressed, and as a teacher and facilitator, Dolci offers no miracles:

> Such struggle carries penalties with it, and the people must know it. Those who want things to remain as they are, to preserve the present "order," will try to put out of the running anyone who promotes change. . . . It is naïve to be surprised or shocked by it. Instead, responsible men must diligently look for those methods and strategies which can be used by the weak to bring about the triumph of reason, i.e., effective alternatives to violence.[34]

Dolci thus counteracts traditional exploitation, brutality, and callousness, with cleverness, with facts, with a variety of methods and guises for social pressure locally, regionally, and nationally, even internationally, and with dogged persistence and abiding faith in common people. He constantly helps western Sicilians to find appropriate nonviolent social-action levers and the strategic times and places for using such levers to force change. These methods have included, in addition to fact-finding, fasting, organization of cooperatives and unions, lobbying, a "strike in reverse" (building a needed road in defiance of the authorities), the occupation of a public plaza, demonstrations, long marches, stimulating support groups throughout Italy and in many other countries, and constant publicity through conferences, speeches, clandestine and regular radio programs, books, and items in magazines and newspapers. Dolci says that "the struggle must be carried on, peaceably but energetically, until common sense and the sense of responsibility have won the day."[35]

Dolci's sense of winning the day is of a long-term sort. He knows that current gains may or may not add up to a long-term victory. The only sense in which he or any other clear-eyed clinical sociologist can see "victory" for a humane effort is through maintaining persistent movement toward needed adjustments. As Dolci phrases it, "There are difficult moments, and one feels overwhelmed. But it's senseless to speak of optimism or pessimism. The only important thing is to know that if one works well in a potato field, the potatoes will grow. If one works well among men, they will grow. That's reality. The rest is smoke. It's important to understand that words don't move mountains. Work, exacting work, moves mountains."[36] It is thus that western Sicilians have been getting some roads, sanitary facilities, democratic cooperatives of agriculturalists, vintners, and artisans, democratic trade unions, the Iato dam, voices in self-government, and much more — a realistic sense of growth and accomplishment.

Dolci's academically trained sociological associates, sent to him by various European and American universities, have systematically studied many aspects of western Sicily — Mafia murders, underemployment, living standards, educational procedures and needs, and agricultural arrangements. These studies have been helpful, but the accumulating knowledge of social strategies and their consequences — in other words, of clinical sociology — is the greatest local and exportable contribution of all these efforts. Dolci's talks on his clinical findings have inspired university students in many parts of the world. Those who have worked with him at his Center for Study and Action in Partinico are forever impressed by the accomplishments and ideas of the "practical visionary" who inspires and guides it.

This example is not meant to suggest that young men and women who study sociology necessarily have to try to approximate Dolci's spectacular performance. There are many ways in which sociology can magnify the social effectiveness of students, and through them, that of others. That Dolci accomplishes so much among *gli ultimi* (the last) suggests how much more others can do with less heroic measures among people whose problems are not so entrenched and so desperate. As a prototype, he has encouraged many to learn and to face their local social realities, to find levers with which to facilitate change, and thus to contribute to human welfare.

Clinical Sociologists in American Conflicts

On the American scene, many city, state, and national authorities have usually responded to incidents of disorder with immediate physical repression. Then they may follow that by having recourse to the old political device of appointing a prestigious study commission. This is popularly referred to as "the appointing-a-committee gimmick."

At best, the suppression of violence might buy some time in which constructive changes might be planned and implemented. Unfortunately, study commissions often fill that time with great promises but provide little more than a forum for public debate. They stimulate and publicize investigations that may only give rise to temporary interest and concern; their reports are too quickly filed and forgotten.[37] Such stalling may solve no problems other than the personal ones of the politician who creates the commission and thus contributes to his or her own political survival. From schooling in political folklore and from long experience, the politician is well aware that time's passing can often blunt issues and see them lost in some new crisis or turn of events.[38]

Any effective dynamic for change comes from outside establishment circles, chiefly from the deprived people themselves. Sociologists can serve in these struggles as resource persons and as facilitators. They can furnish data to social therapists working democratically for social change. Above all, they can help members of competing or conflicting groups to perceive each other as persons. They can do this in such a way as to make the problems of competitors or antagonists, and their social context, vividly clear. Such clarification helps to relate real people and real organizations to thinking and planning for change rather than—as is too often the case—to stereotypes or caricatures.

Since the 1950s, American social scientists have helped to clarify and facilitate the resolution of tension in three significant ways. All are described as efforts to convert the impact of intergroup violence into gains toward a more egalitarian society. They center on (1) the improvement of data and pressure strategies for the deprived, (2) the opening of two-way paths to intergroup empathy through carefully organized confrontations, and (3) the development of negotiation media and procedures. The first is the thrust of such organizations as MARC, the Metropolitan Applied Research Center in New York City. It was founded and headed by the psychologist Kenneth B. Clark whose research played a significant role in the 1954 U.S. Supreme Court desegregation decision. The other two will be illustrated here with the work of Porter and Goldaber and of Thomas J. Rice.

Many names are given to procedures that stimulate two-way paths toward empathy among members of disparate groups who then can reap benefits from such increased understanding. The "quiet" or "unstructured" meeting of the Religious Society of Friends (Quakers) is often cited as a tested and durable folk model for such activity.[39] Professional terms for "tension reduction" efforts include "intergroup problem solving,"[40] "group conversation method,"[41] and "laboratory confrontation."[42]

The Laboratory Confrontation Method

Holly G. Porter and Irving Goldaber organized the nonprofit Community Confrontation and Communication Associates (CCCA) of Grand Rapids, Michigan, in order to forward the use of the "laboratory confrontation" method. Porter is the serene and comely mother of four, the wife of a successful manufacturer. Goldaber, a sociology professor at the time at Brooklyn College of the City University of New York, skilfully combines classroom theory with street lore he learned growing up in Brooklyn's crowded Brownsville section and as long-time executive of New York City's Commission on Human Relations. Porter and Goldaber share the belief that antagonistic factions really prefer talk to violence and that conditions, attitudes, and behavior can be changed through dialogue and resulting action.

As Porter describes it, their technique of conflict transformation was "originally designed to create a productive working relationship between a given community's black ghetto residents and police personnel — long-time adversaries but increasingly victims of similar social neglect." In that, and then in other types of community adversary relationships, "laboratory confrontation" became a means of nondirective group therapy and community decision making that "did the impossible: It dealt in the formerly dealt out. It designated as special resource in the community those individuals thought to be most deeply alienated from the general welfare and most destructive. And it gave responsibility for roles in future community direction to individuals who formerly had had little or no say and no basic information about why things were as they were."[43]

How does the laboratory confrontation program of CCCA work? In each case, a facilitator team spends considerable time on advance planning and arranging with appropriate local sponsors and with leaders of adversary groups. These CCCA facilitators try to assure themselves that participants will be leaders representative of, and chosen by, the significant adversary groups in the tension situation, "groups who find it difficult to work with one another although they are in some way mutually dependent upon each other." This planning and organizing stage is crucial to the effectiveness of the whole program. The group-selected leaders — for each confrontation project usually a total of six to ten from each of the adversaries — must be ready to resort to an egalitarian confrontation.

Then comes the most dramatic phase, "a closed-door, issue-oriented, eyeball-to-eyeball group dialogue . . . conducted in a neutral setting over a three- to five-day period." For this actual laboratory confrontation, there has been advance agreement on the following simple ground rules:

> Anything is on the agenda, nothing is taboo.
> Everyone participates and one-at-a-time.
> Facilitators will not be involved in content-input.
> Facilitators' process direction will be followed at all times.
> There shall be no weapons in the laboratory.

Only those who witness or participate at length in such a confrontation can appreciate the skills and knowledge of human relations such ground rules require of facilitators. This is equally the case of all other phases of this nondirective social therapy.

At the outset of each confrontation, homogeneous groups of participants are asked to segregate themselves and to write an agenda for discussion in the form of their own specific grievances. In consequence, "the hostilities of members are expressed. Specific complaints are identified, explanations are offered, communication skills are developed, trust is built up, and, as feelings are altered, forces are joined to formulate common objectives and to prepare a scheme for implementation."[44]

Laboratory confrontation is something different from the much-discussed "sensitivity training" and "T-grouping."[45] The latter attempt to modify individual personality in more basic and rather comprehensive ways. On the contrary, laboratory confrontation focuses practically upon "issues and problems affecting the relationships between groups of people." It seeks to modify such behavior "in mutually desirable ways." It provides "reinforcement for continuing that modification and benefiting from it by means of community-organized follow-through."[46]

Porter and Goldaber thus arrange "a setting of minimal threat in which the participants move from positions of polarized antagonism to collaboration through a process which encourages 'gut level' ventilation of hostilities."[47] They admit that they have only "imprecise methods of identifying 'destroyers'" (disrupters, irreconcilable persons) who might be included in a confrontation and that the "tolerance level of the process is unknown." After many confrontations in many cities, however, they report that "somebody from the group always saves it from destruction."[48]

Tensions in Asbury Park

Porter and Goldaber do not pretend that one laboratory confrontation of twelve to twenty people during three to five days will permanently alter the course of an organization's or of a community's intergroup relations. Working from October 1970 through the summer of 1971 to cool the very tense interracial situation in the mile-square seaside resort of Asbury Park, New Jersey, they arranged repeated confrontations that eventually involved a large number of "individuals known to be 'opinion leaders' in the various factions represented in the city . . . people known to be critical of the 'status quo' and of the activities of other groups."[49]

Asbury Park had had disastrous rioting in July 1970 in which 180 persons were injured, 167 were arrested, and four million dollars were lost in property destruction. The once-thriving vacation spot was in trouble. No one wanted to be city manager. The Chamber of Commerce had collapsed. Businessmen commuted to homes outside Asbury Park. Whites were dismayed by rising taxes, muggings, and robberies. Blacks could find few year-round jobs and had to contend with high slum rents and omnipresent drug dealers and junkies. "Twenty-nine percent of the city lived on welfare. Racial antipathies were fast acquiring the face of hatred, particularly between the blacks and the hard-pressed, clannish Italians, the largest white ethnic bloc."[50] Rumors had it that on July 4, 1971, there would be another riot, one even more devastating than before.

The 1971 riot did not take place. As repeated laboratory confrontations involved more and more leaders of all types, ripples of consequences spread through the city. The Chamber of Commerce arose from the dead and developed a program to help the whole city, blacks as well as whites. The City Council yielded to joint black-white pressures and obtained state support for additional laboratory confrontations. In the ten additional sessions, policemen confronted black and white teen-agers, senior citizens, businesspeople, and street-wise ghetto dwellers who labeled themselves Brothers of the Mud Hole. Summer jobs were found for needy teen-agers. "Local planning stimulated a Model Cities grant, including funds for a swimming pool in the black area and a youth-development program."[51] Many other details might be given, but most convincing to the community was the favorable comparison of 1971 with 1969 figures for crime rates, for business levels of downtown merchants and beachfront concessionaires, and for applications for employment as police officers from both blacks and whites.[52] Full credit for all such developments can scarcely be given to the laboratory confrontation series, but it is accepted in the community as having had a key role in redirecting community energies.

Clinical Sociology Consultation

During the years that Thomas J. Rice was a university sociology professor, he had increasing involvement in a range of nonprofit organizations. Then he decided to join the firm of Interaction Associates as a full-time consultant clinical sociologist. The firm, with offices in Boston, Washington, Detroit, and San Francisco, specializes in organizational consulting. It offers "collaborative problem-solving, conflict resolution, and consensus-building for large scale systems change." It serves a variety of commercial, governmental, and nonprofit clients, but it has a policy of rejecting those "who are engaged in socially destructive activity." Rice's own clients are mostly nonprofit organizations: "an international famine relief organization, a project for health care delivery to the homeless, a city food bank, a state hospital, and a liberal arts college." The firm's private-sector customers "include the automotive industry, computer manufacturers, financial services, telecommunications, insurance and pet food manufacturers." Rice devotes himself to educating "task forces, facilitating retreats, coaching individuals, and planning change processes." As with Porter and Goldaber, a focus of the firm's methods is "on running effective meetings, a deceptively simple proposition."

Rice values his educational background in participant observation, sociodrama, conflict and other social theory, psychology, and economics. He regards "interdisciplinary boundaries" as a "luxury we cannot afford to indulge" in clinical practice. "The reality of consulting," he says, "is that you draw on whatever knowledge you have to solve the problem at hand."

Rice lists skills — other than "a lot of chutzpa" — that are required for such work as follows: "(1) Listening; (2) Watching for symbols, rituals, and cultural indicators; (3) Assessing the formal and informal organization from reports, policy manuals, accounts, and bulletins; (4) Defining and redefining the situations from varying perspectives; (5) Reframing issues (problem statements) in such a way that clients can see them more clearly; (6) Using data to test assumptions (hypotheses); (7) Positing relationships between parts of the system that are difficult to imagine; (8) Coaching and training for interpersonal effectiveness; and (9) Resolving interpersonal and intergroup conflict."

In reviewing his career shift, Rice adds, "I felt the need to apply sociology directly to the task of social change, and I'm doing that. It's not easy; it's not glamorous. But I feel very effective."[53]

Who Co-opts Whom?

Some critics belittle such methods as those used by Dolci, Porter and Goldaber, and Rice. They say they are ways of co-opting dependents, that they make the oppressed or exploited come to believe that the present system works, that it buys them off with brainwashing or tokens.

Such critics are people who look upon current society as a fixed configuration that only a sweeping revolution might make more satisfactory. They do not perceive how that apparently stable structure can and does change. They do not understand how much more extensive and constructive are the gains that can be achieved by carefully planned nonviolent aggression rather than by violence.[54]

The powerful enter into such confrontations when they learn that the less powerful are far from powerless. The "underdogs" participate in such adaptive procedures as a possibly useful recourse. They find it becomes more realistic and constructive as their sensitivity increases. Both sides know that they can reserve other strategies to use in case there is a breakdown of the traditional procedures.

More Than Just "Interesting"

These examples and the other discussions in this chapter suggest something of the range of social actions for which individuals can be responsible. They illustrate how knowledge of social dynamics and methods utilizing social leverages can facilitate social change nonviolently. Quite appropriately, they stress the significance of efforts to help people to grow. They suggest ways in which sociology can help magnify the effectiveness of the individual through nondirective social therapy. Far less spectacular ways, but nonetheless workable ones, are available to all in everyday life — at school, at work, in voluntary organizations, at home. It is hoped that the discussion helps underline

Karl Marx's statement that people "make their own history, but they do not make it just as they please; they do not make it under circumstances chosen by themselves, but under circumstances directly encountered, given and transmitted from the past. The tradition of all the dead generations weighs like a nightmare on the brain of the living."[55] It also provides starting points for the creative to help launch new patterns of individual expression and of community life. As the 1953–61 Secretary General of the United Nations Dag H. Hammarskjold stated: "We are not permitted to choose the frame of our destiny. But what we put in it is ours."[56]

Sociology is thus much more than just another "interesting" subject in the curricula of liberal arts and sciences. With it, the ancient David could have achieved far more than he did with his fabled slingshot — and without a violent weapon! It is a powerful and nonviolent weapon with which the Davids of the twentieth century can successfully deal with the influence of many of our society's Goliaths.

4

Ideologies
in Social Struggles

Ideologies are always with us. They rise, change, sometimes merge, and sometimes disappear. Popular ideologies are the simplified bodies of doctrine by and with which people live, aspire, dream, succeed, and fail. Institutional functionaries, pressure-group spokespeople, and agitators constantly attempt to restate or reorient accepted ideologies for their purposes. A common stance among business and political leaders is to claim that they do not have an ideology; instead, they are down to earth and practical. They assert that only academics, reformers, and radicals have ideologies. In making such claims, they are merely revealing their own ideological biases. In our day, publicists are forever subjecting ideologies to propagandas and to other manipulations aimed at modifying, activating, or replacing them.

At the outset, it must be admitted that a fashionable sociologist has already announced "the end of ideology" as a consequence of the "tragic self-immolation of a revolutionary generation that had proclaimed the finer ideals of man; destructive war of a breadth and scale hitherto unknown; the bureaucratized murder of millions in concentration camps and death chambers." He also contends that "all this has meant an end to chiliastic hopes, to millenarianism, to apocalyptic thinking—and to ideology." He thus asserts that "ideology, which once was a road to action, has come to a dead end." Beyond what he calls "ideology," he appears to see and to hope for the growth of "intellectual maturity," for the "end of rhetoric, and rhetoricians, or 'revolution,'" but somehow not "the end of utopia as well. If anything, one can begin the discussion of utopia," he insists, "only by being aware of the trap of ideology."[1]

These sweeping dogmatisms were published at the beginning of the 1960s — before the renewal of black uprisings, of student revolts against militarism and educational irrelevance, of women's liberation efforts, and of restless agitations against the pollution of our environment, urban decay, suburban isolation, and so many other problems. In order to understand the alleged "trap of ideology" to which the above quotation refers, however, one has to comprehend the trap of definition in which its writer and so many other social-scientific students of social and scientific ideologies appear to be caught.

The terms *ideology, intellectual,* and *propaganda* all have at least one significant characteristic in common. When they are employed in the generic senses suggested by their etymologies, they tend to bring into relationship phenomena with value adhesions that contrast sharply and that by such juxtaposition, point to undesired comparisons. These phenomena include ideas, activities, and persons that are esteemed and also ones that are hated or feared. They help to emphasize similarities between "their" and "our" ideologies, intellectuals, and propagandas. As a consequence, scholars, as more or less subconscious apologists for themselves and their kind, as well as other more obvious public apologists, often try to control such comparisons by giving these terms arbitrarily limited, value-laden meanings.

Ideology: For many social thinkers an ideology is not merely "a pattern for beliefs and concepts (both formal and normative) which purport to explain complex social phenomena with a view to directing and simplifying socio-political choices facing individuals and groups."[2] For them an ideology is instead a kind of infective growth, or even a poison, responsible for the distortion of facts and beliefs in ways they take to be either objectionable or even repugnant. "Ideology is the conversion of ideas into social levers. . . . What gives ideology its force is its passion." Thus ideology creates, it is said, a "false consciousness," while philosophy can reveal a "true consciousness."[3] In other words, quite oversimply, "my philosophy" is rational and true, and "their ideology" is passionate and false.

Intellectual: Similarly, academic apologists are annoyed by opposition from the nonacademic, those who think and speak without suitable accreditation. They develop, therefore, elegant ways to differentiate between intellectuals and intellectualism on the one hand, and types to be called anti-intellectuals, cynics, or irresponsible agitators and their ideologies or propagandas on the other.

Generically, the newspaper writer, the industrial technician, and the political strategist can each be as intellectual as the liberal-arts university professor. In the struggle for the minds of people, however, the professor is often more than tempted to glorify himself and to denigrate intellectuals lacking formal institutional certification and status. When similar denigration of the academic is attempted by those pushing nonacademic intellectualism, it becomes an academic sin. *Anti-intellectualism*[4] is a term more than a little reminiscent of the more ancient one, *heresy.*[5]

Propaganda: In the same vein, propaganda is defined generically as a way of conveying ideas rapidly to many people. Through combinations of symbols — words, personalities, music, drama, pageantry, and others — the propagandist attempts to use communications media to make impressions upon specific or general publics. The impressions may be wholly or partly true, confusing, or false. When similar information is transmitted in our society in a detailed and more accurate manner rather than in the stimulating shorthand of the propagandist, few bother to listen. In moments given to decision, vividness and emotion quite often override common-sense demands for accuracy and for an opportunity to question and discuss.[6] Consequently, literature abounds purporting to distinguish between *our* communications or *our* educational materials and *their* propaganda.

To understand ideologies, intellectuals, and propagandas as social phenomena, we need to avoid confusing objective considerations with values. Objective conceptions of these three terms include their nature, development, and social roles. The values arise out of personal, status-group, and national involvements and uses. We need to try to perceive as clearly as we can and to compare many sorts of these social products, with many value orientations, and to try to discover as accurately as possible their cultural and social-interactional ingredients and functions.

To Understand Conflicting Viewpoints

Aware of the "multiplicity of conflicting viewpoints," the sociologist Karl Mannheim put forward his *dynamic relationism* as "the only possible way out." Each ideology, "though claiming absolute validity, has been shown to be related to a particular position and to be adequate only in that one." Thus, in order for an "investigator to be in a position to arrive at a solution adequate to our present life-situation," the investigator has to have "assimilated all the crucial motivations and viewpoints, whose internal contradictions account for our present social-political tension." Mannheim called for a "total view" and said that this "implies both the assimilation and transcendence of the limitations of particular points of view." This would have as "its goal . . . the broadest possible extension of our horizon of vision."[7]

In contrast with this vague Mannheim goal, we need to realize, as the sociologists P. L. Berger and Thomas Luckman point out, "Definitions of reality have self-fulfilling potency. Theories can be *realized* in history, even theories that were highly abstruse when they were first conceived by their inventors."[8] When they gain acceptance and even utility, it is not because a theory has shaped an event or development but rather because events became hospitable to interpretations of events or aspirations in terms of a given theory.

One can share Mannheim's concern for "the profound disquietude of modern man" in the face of "the multiplicity of conflicting viewpoints" without oversimply interpreting this, as he does, as a crisis to be resolved. He attributes this crisis to the "disruption of the intellectual monopoly of the church." He defines the "greatest exertion of mankind" in current society as "the attempt to counteract the tendency of an individualistic undirected society, which is verging toward anarchy, with a more organic type of social order." This calls, he claims, for the acceptance of dynamic relationism as "the only possible way out."[9]

The multiplicity exists, as it has for a long time. Like all stimulating situations, it is disquieting, disturbing, even upsetting. It is only claimed to be at a critical point by advocates of one or another integrating ideology who stand to gain from its acceptance. Such advocates are not only academic rationalizers but especially religious and political propagandists. We are probably no more at a decisive historical moment or turning point in the matter of multiplicity than we have been for centuries.

Ideological multiplicity appears to hold more promise than danger, except for those trying to find the alleged but delusory peace and quiet of a homogeneous society, one more monovalent culturally. Many influences other than the decline of imperial Rome and of ecclesiastical power helped to bring forth modern multiplicity. Mannheim might have cited longtime Jewish, Muslim, heretical Christian, primitive

magic, commercial, military, and other diversifying influences opera-
tive in Europe as sequels to Rome's multiplicity.[10]

Talk of a single possible way out, like Mannheim's quest for a tran-
scendent sense of reality, raises such questions as these: A way out
for whom? For society? For intellectuals only? Why only one way out?
Society's multivalence provides and is likely to continue to furnish many
perceptions of reality, thus many bases for ideological formulations
and interpretations. Certainly each group seems to move in a separate and distinct world of ideas, but one neglects the social realities
of cultural conditioning when one says, as does Mannheim, "that these
different systems of thought, which are often in conflict with one another, may in the last analysis be reduced to different modes of experiencing the 'same' reality."[11]

Objective societal symbols, artifacts, and basic environment are
presumably present for all to experience, but they differ in their avail-
ability and accessibility. They are perceived and conceived differently
by members of different social status groups in each society of which
we know. Are there not strengths as well as handicaps in ideological
multiplicity when it is faced with frankness and tolerance?

Finally, Mannheim's apparent anxiety in the 1920s to replace un-
planned individualism with "a more organic type of social order"
stresses a type of solution for living in a giant society well-illustrated
by modern states in a variety of forms. It is a type of solution that
has scarcely proven itself in this war-torn century as a way to avoid
anarchy more than temporarily. Our vast, centralized, integrated states,
with their persistent conformist pressures to homogenize individuals
and their values, may merely be more efficient ways to prepare for
eventual chaos.

Let us look at an approach or orientation that is more receptive
to the implications of cultural multivalence and more appreciative of
change and diversity in social life through time and space. Mannheim's position is explored because it resembles that of too many social theorists.

Ingredients of Ideologies

The principal ingredients out of which ideologies are constructed
are notable for their lack of novelty. They typically include symbols

for generalities drawn from a societal culture that were long embedded in moralistic preachments. The conceptions (of "reality," of deprivation, need, challenge, and tactics) and referents associated with such symbols, as well as general theories binding them together, derive from the subcultures of the groups to whose concerns the ideologies are chiefly related. Messianism, regal divine right, egalitarian aspirations, puritanical devotion to entrepreneurism, and class conflict are folk theories that long antedated Christianity, absolute monarchy, democracy, the so-called protestant ethic, and Marxism.

The contributions of the formulator of a given version of an ideology lie chiefly in pattern, relative emphases, topical applications, and rhetorical artistry. The formulator may be an individual writer, a drafting committee, or the impersonal and continuing discussion processes of a group or society that gradually crystallizes a folk aspiration with some clarity and influence. When an ideology is to be mass-communicated in whole or in part, it is often applied to a specific competitive or conflict situation. The same ingredients become those of the related propaganda. In a sense, propaganda is ideology on the march. Much of the continuing impact of a legitimated ideology is through its permeation of a society's formal and informal educational processes.

Bridges of symbols: Ideologies consist of symbols with which propagandists build bridges from their clients to diverse publics. The symbols represent traditional and habitual values that are placed in relation to a given leader's or organization's aspirations. Ideologies contain claims to support and thus legitimation from some source of authority—theological, popular, military, economic, historical, scientific—or from a combination of several. "The strength of such legitimations is that they are perceived as independent of the social and political climate in which they are produced. But they can be better understood as reflections of it."[12]

An ideology is often used for purposes other than those for which it was presumably developed and given popular acceptance. For example, "Christianity . . . was harnessed by powerful interests for political purposes with little relationship to its religious contents. . . . There may be large elements in an ideology that bear no particular relationship to the legitimated interests, but that are vigorously affirmed by the 'carrier' group simply because it has committed itself to the ideology."[13] Thus Freudianism has been used to combat Marxism. Darwinian theory has been seized upon to give intellectual support to unbridled free-enterprise capitalism.

Current examples of ideological misapplications and distortions are furnished by British Prime Minister Margaret Thatcher and President Ronald Reagan. Thatcher is reported as insisting that crime increases are "not connected to record unemployment, poverty, homelessness or the institutional and individual racism of a decaying and deindustrializing society." On the contrary, she attributes them to "the decline in family authority, the rise in moral permissiveness and the presence of a disaffected black minority which is 'swamping' the lawabiding indigenous population." In other words, "In Thatcher's Britain, as in Reagan's America, accounting for the social crisis by blaming the victim is again the order of the day."[14]

Moral literalists and social scientists disrupt such appropriative and distorting efforts. Unfortunately their audiences are more limited, and they are decried as "radical" nuisances by the prestigious manipulators of ideological materials.

To Typify Ideologies

Rather than by their subject matter alone, it would appear more practical to typify ideologies in terms of their stage of development and vogue (folk, somewhat formulated, crystallized, decadent, modifying), in terms of the groups to which they are related (interest, ethnic, class or stratum, societal), and in terms of their current social role (revolutionary, reformist, legitimated). Interrelations among these three sets of typings could give us sixty possible combinations in a three-dimensional diagram. There are, for example, emerging folk-societal ideologies that are reformist, such as some of those developed by black action groups for the modification of United States society. The ideologies most commonly discussed are those that can be characterized as societal, crystallized or modifying, and revolutionary, reformist, or legitimated. Some of the ideologies most influential in the subtle coloration of the thoughts and writings of intellectuals in largely unrecognized fashions are those of class, ethnicity,[15] occupation, gender, and age. These are often of a folk nature or are only partly (often inaccurately) acknowledged. These ideologies are rationalized and are frequently made to work within the overall legitimated ideological patterning.

In offering such a typology as a way of characterizing ranges of ideological phenomena, it is insisted that actual examples of ideologies are usually typologically "impure." Other dimensions of ideology are also subsumed under the types given — for example, relative absolutism, inclusiveness, or exclusiveness and relative charisma, authority, or pathos. What is principally implied in this suggested typing is that the characteristics of ideologies are relative to their social purposes and roles and to their degree of establishment or nonconformity.

As their social purposes and roles change, ideologies constantly modify, but less in symbolic representation than in associated concepts and referents, in interpretation. As the sociologists Severyn T. Bruyn and Paula Rayman conclude: Such interpretations enabled "the centralized institutions of the state to perpetuate violence in the 'legitimized' battlefields of World War I, the extermination camps of World War II, and the tiger cages of the Indochina War. On a more daily basis, states legitimize the continuation of racism, sexism, and growing worldwide hunger."[16]

What is also implied by this suggested typing is that rather than announcing or even seeking an end to ideology or to the influence of ideologies, it would be more useful to study their amazing persistence and adaptability, their many guises, and the deep roots of the most useful and the most disastrous ones in family life and in multivalent individual personalities. These roots include the prototypical and successor roles and groups in socialization patterns.[17] As such studies proceed further, social scientists will be able to offer more data about the utility or lack of utility of ideologies to specific types of groups' social actions and to societal welfare broadly considered.

Emotionalism, adroitness, trickery, irrationality, and the use of force recur as one studies ideologies and phenomena related to them. Ideologies are part and parcel of social competitions and conflicts. They demand much more than scholarly wishful thinking or social-scientific technique to brush them aside or to deny them.

For all the alleged increase of popular sophistication in political and economic matters through expanded educational facilities, the number of docile voters, soldiers, and customers continues to be abundant and not very questioning. After all, many of the educational facilities are accurately described as impoundment operations devoted to brainwashing and homogenizing. "The ideology operates not only as a unifying force and a guideline to action in ambiguous situations, but also as a *language,* a set of semantic guides, that makes possible rapid and efficient communications of the wishes of central authorities."[18] As Martin Luther King, Jr., put it, "How often are our lives characterized by a high blood pressure of creeds and an anemia of deeds!"[19]

Ideologies in Interethnic Relations

John Stuart Mill claimed in 1861 that democracy is "next to impossible in a country made up of different nationalities."[20] This view has helped rationalize restrictions on civil liberties and the forceful suppression of ethnic rights movements. After studying interethnic conflicts in many parts of the world, the political scientist Donald L. Horowitz recognized "recurrent tendencies to ethnic cleavage and identifiable patterns of conflict, but the outcomes of conflict are various rather than uniform." His findings did not point to "the futility of democracy or the inevitability of uncontrolled conflict."[21]

Southern white folklore to the contrary notwithstanding, African blacks never did accept slavery or remain in it willingly. Revolts began in the slave-accumulation compounds of West Africa and continued across the Atlantic.[22] Nonwhite-white struggles have since gone through at least ten significant phases: (1) the 200 slave conspiracies and revolts prior to 1861,[23] (2) black cooperation with Union armies during the Civil War, the "greatest and most successful slave revolt — a sort of general strike against slavery,"[24] (3) white repressive violence featuring the Ku Klux Klan during the so-called Reconstruction at a cost of at least 5,000 black lives,[25] (4) following Reconstruction, white lynchings of 5,000 and killings of uncounted others in terrorist raids on black ghettos,[26] (5) from the 1890s, the development of a clearer two-sidedness in interracial clashes,[27] (6) white rioting against the industrially mobile blacks, especially during the World War I to II period,[28] (7) nationalism achieving some crystallization in the black Garvey movement of the 1920s and later among Amerindians, black Muslims, and Hispanics,[29] (8) in the 1950s and later, continuing widespread disorders of blacks and Hispanics against oppression and exploitation,[30] (9) the emergence of nonviolent confrontations led especially by Martin Luther King, Jr. (1929–68), and his followers,[31] and (10) the rise of black political power in the cities and nationally under such leaders as Andrew Young and Jesse Jackson.[32]

American whites have yet to give nonwhites adequate aid in their struggles toward equal status and thus toward a more healthful society. Such aid would be a reparation for more than three and one-half centuries of degrading domination and exploitation.

The anti-minority positions of the more radical and more conservative white churches are often to be observed in inter-ethnic conflicts. Martin Luther King, Jr., recalls that churches "often served to crystallize, conserve, and even bless the patterns of majority opinion" in this area. He mentions their "erstwhile sanction . . . of slavery, racial segregation, war, and economic exploitation."[33]

The emergence of what is often called "our secular religion" bridges gaps among some ethnic and racial ideologies. It tends to minimize conflicts among the more established or "respectable" segments of the population, to make a degree of "democracy" possible. As King points out: "Success, recognition, and conformity are the bywords of the modern world where everyone seems to crave the anesthetizing security of being identified with the majority."[34] Here is thus another social ambiguity: We need a degree of adherence to an overall "secular religion," but it must be subject constantly to review and criticism in terms of social needs and ideals. As King appropriately adds: "The hope of a secure and livable world lies with disciplined nonconformists, who are dedicated to justice, peace, and brotherhood."[35]

Ideologies in Wars

People with a variety of motives accept ideologies as reasons or excuses for participation in wars as well as in other social conflicts. Propagandistic interpretations help to obscure unfortunate possible consequences or give a sense of irresistible urgency. As the late clergyman Harry Emerson Fosdick said, "Christianity joined with the state, became sponsor for war, blesser of war, cause of war, and fighter for war." Too often, it tried "to carry the cross of Jesus in one hand and a dripping sword in the other."[36]

The record of European participation in wars suggests that the United States has carried on its Old World heritage in this respect with little alteration. From the twelfth through the nineteenth centuries England and France were at war with one another or with some other country from thirty-six to sixty-five of the years in each century.[37] Citing similar figures for those and other European countries ranging from ancient Greece to modern Russia and for the United States, the sociologist Pitirim A. Sorokin noted in 1947 that peaceful periods have been unevenly distributed, have lacked periodicity, and those "as long as a quarter of a century have been exceedingly rare in the history of these countries." Only Holland had a full century of freedom from international military conflict.

Sorokin stresses (1) "that frequency of war is considerably higher than most of us usually think," (2) "that the most primitive peoples — that is, the least literate — are the most peaceful; that with an increase of 'liberalism,' 'humanism,' 'modernism,' and 'relativism' wars have not decreased," (3) "that democracies and republics are not more peaceful than autocracies and monarchies," (4) that more literacy, educational opportunities, scientific knowledge, and mechanical inventions have not diminished the time devoted to war, and (5) that there "is no perpetual historical trend toward either a decrease or an increase of war. . . . The theories claiming a progressive pacification of the race constitute merely wishful thinking." The twentieth century's bloodiness he contends "is sufficient in itself to refute such utopian theories."[38]

Sorokin's sweeping conclusions are perhaps less surprising today than before the dawn of atomic warfare. In World War II, under various ideological banners, some 16,933,000 soldiers were killed or died of wounds, and 34,325,000 civilians were slaughtered, a total of 51,258,000. The "winning" Allies lost six-sevenths of that total; the "losing" Axis powers lost only one-seventh! When coincident warborne epidemics are also included, the grand total killed was perhaps 60,000,000 in the five-year period, one and one-half times that of World War I.[39] Our technological efficiency is now such that the same number of people or more could be exterminated in the first few days of a third world war.

Do such unbelievable destructions of human lives accomplish the goals promised in any extant ideology? It is possible that the mobilization and militarization of life among the Allies did at least as much to nurture as to destroy authoritarianisms. Military action did not save the lives of six million Jews, Poles, and others in and on the way to Nazi extermination camps.[40] Effective coping with what became Nazism would have had to start at least as early as the Versailles peace conference, preferably earlier through steps that would have prevented World War I.[41] As the sociologist Willard Waller cogently pointed out on the eve of United States participation in World War II, "Any valid theory of war . . . must consider the fact that it grows out of the totality of our civilization. . . . War settles nothing because defeated nations will not accept defeat. War is an arbiter whose decisions the contestants refuse to accept as final, for there is always the chance that another trial will turn out differently."[42]

Ideological rationalizations for a Hitler's existence became complex. In the highly interrelated world of today, the blame — whatever "blame" might be determined to be — for a Hitler is shared so widely by those in power as to be well nigh universal. The trials of Nazi war criminals dealt only with a few obvious instruments. What about the Americans and non-German Europeans who backed Hitler and Hitler's supporters with funds, materials, and silence? Americans too often prefer nationalistic (so-called "consensus") historians who carefully select events supportive of pleasant nationalistic myths rather than those who, like Charles A. Beard[43] and Harry Elmer Barnes,[44] insist that unpleasant facts about the American past and present be remembered, pondered, and hopefully used. The latter seek to reverse, at least for a few decision makers, Hegel's futilitarian dictum that "peoples and governments never have learned anything from history, or acted on principles deduced from it."[45]

How can we explain the depressing frequency of wars, rebellions, riots, and murders throughout the world? No instinct of pugnacity needs to be assumed to account for them. "Peoples have always gone to war with various degrees of relish or repugnance; but such sentiments have been in their traditions and not in any inherited instinct, one way or another,"[46] a great many comparative students of society have concluded.

In spite of the efforts of such instinctivists as Robert Ardrey[47] and Konrad Lorenz,[48] the anthropologist Ralph E. Holloway, Jr. insists that the problem of war "is a political one, not a biological or psychological one."[49] Anthropologist Margaret Mead argues "that man lacks instinctual controls, and not, as Lorenz and Ardrey do, that warfare is an extension of built-in aggression towards rivals for mates, territory or food."[50] Recourse to interpersonal or intergroup violence varies so greatly in terms of ethnic (including so-called racial) and class differences that it can be traced to social learning (culture) and to happenstance rather than to biologically inherited "instinct."

Is American Ideology Especially Violent?

How violent are Americans? Domestic and international violence since the 1960s raised this question with increasing insistence. Television screenings of citizens being attacked by police dogs, of armed conflict on American streets and college campuses, and of the battlefield horrors of Vietnam made violence vivid daily. It made it immediate and even intimate. The National Commission on the Causes and Prevention of Violence reported 239 violent domestic outbursts in 1964–68 that were sufficiently extensive to be termed "riots" by the police. Of the estimated 200,000 participants, 191 were killed and about 8,000 were injured. Property damages were said to have totaled hundreds of millions of dollars.[51]

During the same period the United States forces dropped 2,948,057 tons of bombs on North and South Vietnam, almost one and one-half times the grand total dropped by Americans during World War II on all European, Asian, and Pacific targets. Some of the bombs contained napalm. They were supplemented by defoliants with aftereffects on humans and their environment that were not then wholly recognized. The amount of damage inflicted upon this small country caught between two superpowers can scarcely be estimated even yet. American battle deaths in this war totaled just a few thousand less than those of World War I.[52] It was the fourth most bloody war in United States history, an undeclared war!

Little wonder that 1964–68 included 370 civil rights demonstrations and 80 counterdemonstrations with at least one million participants, hundreds of student protests involving the occupation of school facilities, rioting, property damage, injuries, and deaths, and some 700,000 participants in antiwar and antidraft confrontations on campuses and in towns and cities.[53]

But the principal ways in which Americans get slaughtered are not in riots and battles. During 1964–68 about twice as many citizens were murdered in the United States (some 55,000) as were killed on the Vietnam battlefields. Accidental deaths at the same time totaled about 550,000: 250,000 in street traffic, 125,000 in homes, and 175,000 in other types of accidents. Just how many deaths reported as accidental were suicides and homicides is anyone's guess. In addition, about 106,000 deaths were officially recorded as suicidal. Compared with 1980–84, accident deaths have declined, but murder and suicide have risen.[54] These violent losses of life in *either* of these five-year periods comprise more than the number of Americans killed in *all* of our wars.

Wars and Social Inequality

Those two five-year periods furnish all-too-typical samples of American violence. A large share of the organized violence in and between countries is associated with efforts to facilitate or to prevent social changes, especially those that might develop more or less social equality. Only through the use of physical coercion can any dominant group continue for long to maintain a given condition of intergroup inequality.

A relationship of intergroup inequality usually begins with the use of force and is given its justification by mythmaking later. Masters flatter themselves or accept the flattery of their lackeys about the reasons for their superiority and their consequent high social status. The dominated do not fail to find ways to resist the propagandas that assert and attempt to legitimize their inferiority and their consequent low status. The dominated develop their own counterlegitimacy with which to confer on themselves some degree of dignity and often also some share of social benefits. Intimate views of those living in any deprived area, whether in Calcutta, Tokyo, London, Belfast, Rome, or New York City, provide vivid authentication of this and give pause to any curious-minded person who enjoys power, privilege, and high status in that city.

Our ideological justifications for inequality have become increasingly sophisticated and labored. The more widely held ones are no longer officially based on such disproven crudities as alleged racial superiority and inferiority or the special genetic virtues said to be "bred into" a social-status-group-defined human stock.[55] They are now more commonly couched publicly in terms of IQs, academic grades and degrees, and other types of achieved certification, including the control of powerful social structures, such as those that do the certifying.[56] But the dominated still remain just as "unreasonable" as always about accepting their "inferiority" as a justification for their low status and for their economic and political deprivation. That the criteria are "scientific" or "realistic" or "necessary" for the maintenance of "the system" based upon so-called "incentives" somehow fails to impress those excluded nationally or internationally from a more proportionate share in what society controls and produces.

Think about what happens to rationalizations for inequality nationally or internationally when we grasp adequately the implications of the statement by the psychologist Kenneth B. Clark: "Children who are treated as if they are uneducable invariably become uneducable."[57] That statement has a bearing not only on our expanding prison population but also on the growth of international terrorism and of riots, revolts, and wars. Belief in any child can accomplish educational wonders. On that lesson may hinge significant aspects of society's future, especially whether or not we shall continue to use violence to maintain an unequal society.

The Growing Military-Industrial Complex

What is now sometimes called the MIC has been growing in the United States all through this century. The journalist Seymour Waldman concluded in 1932 from attending the hearings of the joint Cabinet-Congressional War Policies Commission: "The hearings revealed the gigantic machine, whose intricate parts touch the entire nation, which is being constructed by the War Department and industrial magnates for use in the event of war. . . . They revealed the dangers inherent in a militarization of industry, an industrialization of the military forces, or a combination of the two."[58] The *Washington* (D.C.) *News* on March 14, 1932 told how "it was the hope of the men who conceived the plan" for the War Policies Commission "that war might occur much less frequently if it were known in advance by munition makers and their bankers and all the thousands of business men who might be affected that war would mean acute financial suffering for them, instead of profiteering." The newspaper called the recommendation of the Commission "inadequate, unsatisfactory."

Subsequent wars and the injection of nuclear bombs and other high tech products into the situation stimulate this overwhelming MIC influence all the more. What can be done about it? The historian Paul A. C. Koistinen offers this proposal: "First the idea that the nation can and should play world policeman must be abandoned, and military solutions to what are essentially social, political, ideological, and economic issues must be foregone. This . . . means a foreign policy of sane and reasonable priorities for the world's major power." Koistinen is hopeful, but he realizes the "inextricable global ties" of the U.S. economy, and he therefore wonders if such a rational procedure might be accomplished "without a fundamental reordering of our entire social system."[59]

Representative Les Aspin points out that the MIC consists of a lot of "factotums, who might otherwise be brawling with one another," and who "rarely link arms in pursuit of the ends of the MIC, but the decisions they take in the pursuit of their perceived self-interest have the same result." These "decisions are taken not only by the services and their contractors, but also by labor unions, local politicians, and a press inflicted with community boosterism." And he adds: "Even the Soviet equivalent of our MIC promotes our Military-Industrial Complex."[60]

The Need for Nonviolent Aggression

The fireworks and the dramatic shifts of apparent control in violent confrontations stimulate or inhibit social change, but nonviolent developments can be far more effective and less costly to the masses. The greatest American revolutions have been nonviolent ones that followed the violence of 1776–83 and 1861–64, and they are still coming.

We need to know more about how desirable nonviolent changes can take place, to what extent they can be selected and stimulated. How might a nonviolent popular complex (NPC) work to offset the damaging influences of the MIC? How would it utilize negotiation, aggressive confrontations, popular resistance, courage in intergroup and interpersonal relations to bring about desirable outcomes?[61]

Middle-class functionaries traditionally try to brush aside threats to the status quo or to compromise them "at all costs"—to the oppressed, not to those in power. They accompany such efforts with appropriate rationalizations and appeals to idealistic moral vagaries. This has the effect of storing up resentment by the deprived and the exploited. When the middle class was relatively small in our society, it could anxiously and profitably devote itself to serving as a kind of social balance-wheel, to trying to resolve the aggressive and sometimes violent thrusts of upper- and lower-class activists. As both the middle-class and the unemployed and underemployed underclass expand, the old-fashioned middle-class ideology becomes more obviously a tool of dominant entrepreneurs. More sophisticated professionals, managers, and technicians come to realize that they must attempt moving beyond superficial compromises or rationalizations for ignoring underclass problems. Some see the need for taking a longer-term view, for taking hard looks at the probable implications of on-moving social processes.[62]

Theories of social change and revolution too often depend upon old ideologies rather than upon intimate observation and analysis of evolving social conditions. Herbert Marcuse's contention that the

United States is and will remain a prerevolutionary society, "capable of containing qualitative change for the foreseeable future," is possibly accurate in a military sense. He asserts that, if revolution (as he defines it) should come, it would be because "forces and tendencies exist which may break this containment and explode the society."[63] This is based upon a narrow view of historical processes, a misconception of the nature of social revolution. Our contemporary social revolution, of which our season of violence is an unnecessary symptom, is a phase of the continuing American revolution that reactionary forces are attempting unsuccessfully to terminate. Egalitarianism, literacy, and politico-economic activism become more and more integrated into our popular culture, and they can go much further. A more effective nonviolent popular complex (NPC) could stimulate those tendencies and help build a more viable society without the highly speculative and probably authoritarian alternative of a violent uprising to resolve our problems.[64]

Violence is used to achieve goals for which no other *known* and *accepted* technique appears to the participants to be as available and as useful. Popular backlashes against using Americans in foreign military adventures have led the United States government to seek recourses "to give the appearance of peace while continuing its war."[65] These alternatives include automation and Vietnamization and the employment of client armies, such as the "contras" trying to overthrow the Nicaraguan government, soldiers trained, equipped, guided, and paid by the United States. General Ellis W. Williamson thus summarizes the services of automation: "We are making unusual efforts to avoid having the American young man [in Vietnam] stand toe-to-toe, eyeball-to-eyeball, or even rifle-to-rifle against the enemy."[66] Col. Robert D. Heinl indicated in 1971 in the *Armed Forces Journal* the need for such automation when he asserted that "our Army that now remains in Vietnam is in a state approaching collapse, with individual units avoiding or having refused combat, murdering their officers and noncommissioned officers, drug-ridden, and dispirited where not near-mutinous."[67]

Since mechanization maintains and even expands the market for military gear and supplies, it helps "wed industry to the military more firmly than ever before" while assuring "the aggressor that he need never see the eyes of his victim."[68]

As riots, revolts, and wars become more frightful and more destructive, experimentation with alternatives to violence has gained increasing urgency and support. Martin Luther King, Jr., told a congregation: "Violence brings only temporary victories; violence, by creating many more social problems than it solves, never brings permanent peace." Nonviolence, he insisted, "combines toughmindedness and tenderheartedness and avoids the complacency and donothingness of the softminded and the violence and bitterness of the hardhearted."[69]

More and more, chiefly the emotionally disturbed, inexperienced, and incompetent among those in positions of leadership try to precipitate armed conflict. Such persons too often achieve great power in social movements and states. When they confront the more competent, the latter get seduced into treacherous spirals of retaliation or of "preventive" violence — fighting to "make the world safe for democracy." Chaotic and overtense social conditions, often carelessly or cynically maintained and stimulated by interests powerful in their own or other states, provide opportunities for the Stalins, Hitlers, Mussolinis, Francos, Japanese war lords, and Third World dictators, not to mention our own members of the list.

The social historian Quincy Wright recalls "that, when faced by conditions resembling those of today, most civilizations have begun a fatal decline ending in death to be followed, after a period of dark ages, by a new civilization." But our so-called civilization is different from those of the past in that it "is worldwide, and therefore, without the roots of new civilizations on its periphery, the situation may be more ominous."[70] In spite of this, the United States spends hundreds of billions of tax dollars, as the Center for Defense Information indicates, "to support the largest peacetime military buildup in American history while social programs are cut, the debt becomes unmanageable and the probability of nuclear war increases."[71]

Rather than talk about "the violent American" or "the violent human," we need to face these facts and probabilities: A capacity for anger is inherent in human nature. When needs for expression are strongly thwarted, anger may erupt into violence, but violence is not essential to human personality or to human affairs. There are substantial alternatives, for example, to the position of the Algerian activist Frantz Fanon's statement that "decolonization is always a violent phenomenon."[72] Mohandas K. Gandhi's 1947 achievement in leading India nonviolently to independence from the United Kingdom is one of many examples contrary to Fanon's generalization.

Militarism, as the social analyst Cecelia Kirkman concludes, "affects everyone in American society. From children who play with war toys to students who learn the history of warriors but not of peacemakers, from teenagers targeted by military recruitment ads to adults who are constantly bombarded with new rationales for more military spending, we all live in a militarized society." She adds that women "are directly affected by both the economic violence created, in part, by our militarized national budget and the physical and sexual violence that is part of any militarized culture."[73]

Ideologies Change: Ideology Persists

The hopeful increase in popular sophistication in political and economic matters through expanded educational facilities is too often accurately described as increased brainwashing or homogenizing of an excess labor supply. In consequence, the numbers of manipulable voters, soldiers, and customers for mass political parties, armies, and mercantile operations continue to appear to be abundant and too unquestioning.

Thus one must speak of the persistence rather than of the end of ideologies as characteristic of human societies of a massive and literate sort in the world today. Ideologies are the intellectual and emotional patterns in terms of which groups and individuals are provided with ways to organize their cultural symbols for use in communication and action. Ideologies come and go, but the end of ideology is scarcely in sight. In the world's larger countries men and women with admittedly mixed motives continue to accept ideologies as reasons or excuses for participation in wars, in peace efforts, and in other social conflicts and competitions, the irrationality or rationality of which propagandas help to obscure and to justify.

When they are functioning as social scientists who care about society, people turn aside from the traditional roles of intellectuals. They refuse to be formulators, curators, disinfectors, interpreters, redefiners, and obfuscators of ideologies for those who employ them and whose social manipulations and exploitations benefit them. They try critically to see such social instruments as ideologies more nearly as they are and to help people generally to have that advantage.

5

Defenses against Manipulation

Social actionists take propaganda to be one of their key instruments. In our competitive society, they make tides of propaganda beat against our eyes and ears. Buy this! Join that! Fight for or against this! Vote for or against that! The messages are each supposedly clear, simple, and well intended. The volume is overwhelming. Some hopeful observers believe we are developing an increased immunity to these influences or are learning to balance one appeal more accurately and constructively against others. But are we? Equally important are the facts that propagandists do not mention or prevent from being reported.

"Propaganda" and "brainwashing" suggest manipulations of individuals and groups that are to many as mysterious and dastardly as black magic. "Mass culture" and "mass media" imply that we are all somehow caught up in mind-twisting webs of words, sounds, and pictures—that humanity is on its way to the human equivalent of ant hill like-mindedness and authoritarian control. Whether that prediction is true or not depends in a large measure on how quickly and accurately we can all come to understand those manipulations and to devise defenses against them.

What can we, as the objects of the propagandists, do about their efforts? What can we do about other techniques of the social actionists? To what extent can we wisely select the winners in the struggle for our minds? Into how many aspects of our lives do such pleadings and other manipulations for special interests now penetrate?

How should we react to the 1987 ABC-TV miniseries entitled "Amerika,"[1] one of the most expensive ever produced? It fantasizes the situation in 1998, a decade after an unopposed Soviet Russian take-over of North America. It implies that lack of resistance to the invasion was due to the influence of "liberal" ideologues of the women's, labor, peace, and civil rights organizations. Is it "only entertainment" or possibly a "civics lesson" about "freedom"? Or is it propaganda to nurture mistrust and fear, support for cold war and nuclear militarism?

In contrast, how should we evaluate the contention of Peter Clausen speaking for the Union of Concerned Scientists when he asserts that the "real truth of the matter, of course, is that the United States is not inferior to the Soviet Union and never has been during the forty-year history of the nuclear arms race"?[2]

As we saw in the previous chapter and as these and many other possible illustrations indicate, propaganda is ideology in action, given application. Propaganda is an ideology being expressed wholly or in part or by implication. It is current events being interpreted in terms of an ideology or associated with an ideology as a tactic in a manipulative effort.

Media spokespeople and media critics have long quarreled about the nature of the relations of propagandists to their audiences. Since any propaganda effort can best be understood as part of social competition and conflict, let us look at what is typically involved in purposive social manipulations that go into such struggles. Then let us discuss defenses available to us against such manipulative efforts and especially against misleading propaganda. Isn't the promise of an education in the liberal arts and sciences, among other things, the learning of wise ways to select the people, movements, symbols, and ideas that we should be able to trust and ought to distrust, what we should support and reject? Are our current offerings in high schools and colleges providing such wisdom? Are those educational procedures reaching enough people?

Social Actionists' Orientations

This is an effort to generalize firsthand observations of successful actionist entrepreneurs in business, labor organizations, politics, religious bodies, art, civic affairs, and academia. Since such orientations have much in common, the following description of the social viewpoint and tactics of such operators is given in the form of an ideal-typical model. Even though individual feelings, rationalizations, and façades differ, the patterns have much in common.

The actionist orientation set forth is a kind of basic *modus operandi* that the successful appear to share. If the portrayal appears harsh and even brutal, stripped as it is of protective rationalizations, please bear in mind that it is not a view that is being advocated here. Socially wise and humane actionists find ways to avoid strategy alternatives too costly to parts of their constituencies. At any rate, the following is what this observer has perceived as being overriding characteristics of social actionists' agendas.

Regardless of how sacrosanct we may regard any aspect of society, some social actionists *as actionists* look upon *everything* in society as a stockpile of matèriel more or less available for their use or for that of their competitors or opponents. To determine operational needs and possibilities, they may carefully and objectively study and assess special qualities, disabilities, and difficulties of society's constituents as implements or media. Thus the work of objective social scientists may intentionally or unintentionally become grist for the actionists' mills.

Actionists tend to look upon commitments to values, ideologies, and personal and social goals and relationships as employable, exploitable, and expendable. Similarly, people, organizations, laws, constitutions, and communications media are matériel. Such matériel, it is insisted, may include any thing, any person, any organization, any aspect of society's heritage or culture that might conceivably be useful for or against a project. Just as a military actionists expends fifteen thousand soldiers to gain a strategic position, so an industrial actionist readily consigns to the scrapheap a product, a factory, a town, or a category of employees skilled in a mechanical or intellectual specialty when it no longer serves a selected purpose. Members of the clergy, academicians, and journalists are often shocked at the self-interested ways in which their theories, symbols, and artifacts are so often employed. They often find it difficult to respond.

ACTIONISTS' GOALS

At the outset of an effort, social actionists focus upon personal and social goals they believe to be attainable. Since success is often facilitated by opportunism, actionists' goals are typically subject to modification, redefinition, or replacement. With these flexibilities in goal as a basis, operators seek an ideology and a strategy that will forward efforts to achieve the goal currently sought. These searches are seldom undertaken in the manner of a thoughtful and dedicated social scientist.

Scientists persist in being aware of the larger setting, not of just next steps. They respect durable social values such as commitments to representation, freedom of speech and of the press, and due legal process. A scientist is aware of the contradictions between a traditional ideology's idealizations and the opportunistic notions of an actionist.

Actionists usually count on ideological contradictions becoming lost in rhetoric. For example, does a "pro-family" position support or oppose birth control measures, including abortions? Does the United States's "democratic mission" necessarily include upholding existing undemocratic governments in so many other countries and supporting alleged "freedom fighters" against democratically elected regimes in such countries as Chile and Nicaragua? Social scientists try to demand much more substantial and consistent policy statements than actionists usually think necessary and to have them worded as specifically as possible. Actionists typically are obsessed with that to which their ideology is subservient — their own sense of direction toward their selfish or idealistic goal.

A PATCHWORK OF ENTICING IDEAS

Many times the search for an ideology thus results in a jerry-built, ill-defined, illogically stated rationale. It is couched in glittering generalities and name-calling terms that are interpreted to suit the interests of selected publics and power brokers. An ideology "works" so long as enough constituencies and power brokers accept it. The "ideology" may be just a group of vague pleasantries and caveats surrounding a personality, an institution, a group of commercial products, or an urban reform movement.

Successors to ancient tribal bards — plausible journalists, members of the clergy, speech-writers, advertising copy specialists, and public relations counselors — all do what they can to give even flimsy ideologies some appearance of coherence, consistency, and sincerity. Bards similarly served their ancient tribal chieftains. Their products were sagas rather than television spectaculars, but their purpose was much the same. Current minnesingers and counselors try to make personalities or aspiring powerful ones compel attention, attract support, and appear substantial wherever they are exposed.

The results of actionists' second search—that for a strategy—are again frequently such as to arouse no confidence in a methodical lawyer or banker or social scientist, but they may still satisfy actionists' principal criterion for their use: They are taken by them to be what will achieve their goals.

Entrepreneurs of social action have much in common in viewpoint with old-fashioned military actionists. The analogy is not being made with strategists of contemporary six-day or six-hour wars; that is a little too frightful to think about and too short to be useful for our purposes. For strategies, actionists constantly reconnoiter the terrain, as it were, in order to select or improvise tactics appropriate to changing conditions of competition, conflict, or unilateral aggression. Issues get used up. Personnel become outmoded. New issues, readaptations of old issues, must constantly be planned and then related to the actionist's alleged ideology, then stated as simply as possible, maybe even as a slogan or a joke.

Strategy involves especially ways to use (1) personnel, (2) organizations, (3) propaganda, (4) media of communication, and (5) existing opinion matériel in the light of (6) the changing social situation. Let us look briefly at each of these facets of a typical actionist's efforts in our society today.

1. To Exploit Individual Potentialities

In categorizing the types of personnel involved in social action, social actionists can be thought of as (a) leaders, (b) promoters, (c) manipulators, and (d) sponsors. They are all more or less in leadership roles, and they work out ways of using each other. Their principal tools are spokespeople, bureaucrats, rank-and-file volunteer workers, "just members," and sympathizers. These are not mutually exclusive categories. They are rough role types. Like other more or less specialized roles, they draw to their performance different emotional and intellectual personality types whose multivalence further complicates their use.

The principal spokesperson for a movement or organization or agitation may be a leader or a front, the boss or a puppet. In either case, this person is usually someone with a degree of charismatic quality who feels some sense of having a special mission. This person provides the individualized symbolism to spearhead the zeal and emotional drive of a campaign or program.

Because successful social action involves many technical problems today, the professionally competent promoter furnishes the arts of speech-writing, penetrating mass media, arranging public meetings and other events, and infiltrating programs of other organizations. Promoters usually specialize in one or more types of activity necessary for social action. They tend to bring an objectivity and a technical quality to an effort that help to stabilize it and give it more consistent direction.

Manipulators are more often prime maneuverers rather than mere employees. They tend to be power brokers who are privy to sources of funds and to terms upon which funds and other support may be obtained. Often looked upon as "necessary evils" in social-action programs—when they are not the boss—they are frequently experienced lawyers, politicians, or business entrepreneurs who quietly work themselves into power control positions.

Promoters and manipulators seek out sponsors and fronts upon whose status and influence their agitation can ride piggyback, as it were. Bureaucrats trail behind their employers into any movement or organization in which they are required. Their small talents and narrow aspirations make them helpful parts of the "machine." Rank-and-file volunteers and "just members" furnish impressive bulk and a degree of substantiality to religious bodies, political organizations, and civic societies. Fellow travelers are friends of any social action that carry its message or help to sanction it with other groups without being openly identified with the action in a formal sense.

Leaders, promoters, and manipulators develop shrewd senses of the personality characteristics and motivations to be found most dependably among given groups of people. Through experience, they learn how to use them. The more experience they have the less they have to depend upon loose formulas in order to exploit human potentialities.

2. To Control Social Structures

Organizations, like so much else in society, derive what influence they have from popular support and acquiescence. Their leaders are prone to forget this as they come to count on themselves being more and more shored up in their positions through their control of organizational decision-making, finance, and physical assets. On the other hand, leaders under attack find it expedient to turn to mergers, interorganizational deals, and especially propaganda to rebuild their influence. Mergers and deals are ways to borrow or buy acquired influence; propaganda is a return to a direct approach to gaining popular support.

Social power appears to be based upon many things. It includes the management of social networks and structures, money, physical resources, patents, know-how, communications media, and contacts. All such power and its domination depend ultimately upon popular concerns, acceptance, support, or acquiescence. Without morale, an army fails, and without a popular market, a commodity disappears. Without faith in the value of a currency, the credit structure based on it collapses. Without belief in the fairness of governmental agencies, subversive, vigilante, and even riotous procedures — terrorism — become possibilities. Disinformation (lying) can help maintain a group's control for a time, but it is a vulnerable device. A "Watergate," "Irangate," or "Contragate" revelation suddenly undermines such covert efforts.

Those who control established organizations often have a power derived from myth and submissiveness that bears little relationship to the current mobilizable social strength of their actual supporters. As the noted journalist Heywood Broun asserted, illustrating this point, "There is not a single New York editor who does not live in mortal terror of the power of this group [the officials of the Roman Catholic Church]. It is not a case of numbers but of organization. . . . If the church can bluff its way into a preferred position, the fault lies not with the Catholics but with the editors."[3] When a project of any powerful religious or other organization serves the interests of those who control media editors, the editors become quite cooperative!

ORGANIZATIONAL TACTICS

The chief tactics for dealing with organizations that are available to promoters and manipulators are: (a) controlling them through the employment, seduction, corruption, or capture of their trusted leadership, (b) gaining support of additional organizations by finding or successfully alleging common interests with organizations already dominated, (c) creating or capturing and exploiting "front organizations," and (d) boring from within uncommitted or even antagonistically committed organizations — in other words, placing agents in key spots within them.

The first of the above tactics is clear enough. Actionists first find it expedient to obtain a base of operations in one or more organizations that they can decisively influence.

The second tactic includes joint lobbying, joint efforts to win elections by citizens or by stockholders, the infiltration of committees, commissions, and bureaucracies, and joint money-raising schemes, such as communty-chest drives, political action committee (PAC) campaigns, and trade-association and joint trade-union war chests for politico-economic programs.

Public relations specialists have created or captured a whole range of front organizations for trade associations and corporations of this and other countries.[4] These are organizations controlled by or for their clients but apparently operated under other, reputedly "independent," auspices. They include university departments, institutes, and bureaus,[5] federal, state, and local governmental committees, commissions, and bureaus,[6] and a variety of societies, foundations, corporations, and trade unions.

The boring-from-within tactic is most often discussed publicly in connection with the infiltration activities of disruptive left-wing groups, such as communists,[7] but it has long been a device for extending the power of established social entrepreneurs and groups. Thus large financial, utility, and manufacturing firms find it expedient to stimulate "good citizenship" and "civic responsibility" on the part of their key employees so that they can participate in a wide range of community, state, and national projects. Some such employees even do this on leaves of absence with pay from their regular positions. One need not be a cynic to note the control implications of such operations.

So much for an outline of how actionists control and manipulate the groups available and potentially useful to them. What are the characteristics of the groups to which actionists give special attention? Groups are quite complex and have frequently been discussed, and they therefore need not be examined again here at great length.[8] Some of the principal aspects, in addition to size (human resources) and physical assets, that concern actionists are groups' cohesiveness, staying power and continuity, visibility or invisibility, adaptability, and intergroup relations. Organizational adaptability or flexibility embraces the potential to shift from long-term educational efforts, for example, to high-pressure political maneuvers, from the sponsorship of an exhibit or a conference to the infiltration of other organizations, and from serious efforts for a cause to entertainment.

The keen social analyst Willard Waller made some very telling comments on the nature of organizations in relation to their institutionalization of ideas. As he said, "Something happens to ideas when they get themselves organized into social systems. The ethical ideas of Christ, flexible and universal, have nevertheless been smothered by churches. A social principle degenerates into a dogma when an institution is built about it. Yet an idea must be organized before it can be made into fact, and an idea wholly unorganized rarely lives long. Without mechanism it dies, but mechanism perverts it. This is part of the natural flow and recession — the life principle in society."[9]

3. To Cast Nets of Symbols

Propaganda has a somewhat reciprocal relationship with organization. When a social actionist has adequate organizational support for current purposes, propaganda efforts can be routine. When he or she has problems with obtaining or maintaining organizational backing and control, she or he is wise to turn to propaganda in order to gain or regain impetus.

The basic ingredients of propaganda are omnibus words and the A-B-C pattern. Omnibus words are vague and glittering. They are emotionally charged symbols, both negative and positive, that might be called propaganda building blocks. They carry much of the burden of a message. The A-B-C pattern consists of the appeal, bond, and commodity, the ideological bridge that is implicit or explicit in one or many intertwined forms in all successful propaganda. The appeal is the come-on, the part of the message that strikes into the probable interests of the intended public. The bond is the tie-in that links appeal and commodity. The commodity is the item, idea, service, personality, project, ideology, cause, institution, or country that the propagandist is pushing.

Name-calling and virtue words — negative and positive symbols —

are used not only to construct A-B-C bridges, but also to put together a variety of other types of association. Thus, for example, a proposal may be associated with a revered or a detested institution (transfer technique) or personality (testimonial technique), with the masses, the common person, the silent majority (plain folks technique), or with what is the current trend, what "everyone" is or is not doing or avoiding, accepting or rejecting (band-wagon technique). To illustrate, one can constantly perceive efforts to transfer the prestige of religion, science, and democracy to special projects that may or may not have any legitimate relationship with those revered ideologies and their institutional settings. Similarly, individuals with wide reputations for any reason are in demand as endorsers of special projects, a use of the testimonial device. These four techniques are employed both fairly and accurately and also quite unfairly and inaccurately.

WHAT ABOUT LOGICAL FALLACIES?

Students of formal logic sometimes contend that the propaganda devices just mentioned—and others—do not go far enough in the analysis of such messages. They advocate the use of classical logical fallacies. The difficulty with those fallacies, however, is that they focus upon violations of a canon of logic rather than upon the nature and the content of the communication and the communication process.

Logicians say that a propagandist using an *argumentum ad hominem* (argument to the man) is discussing ideas in terms of the personality or personal relations of the spokesperson rather than in terms of their accuracy or relevance. They tell us to reject the propagandist's message because of its lack of propriety in the use of logical procedures as they see them. They do not face up to the practice as a common aspect of human intercommunication and do not weigh its use in that light.

When logicians call the testimonial technique's application an *argumentum ad verecundiam,* an appeal to accept modestly a view on the basis of authority, they have chiefly substituted a more complicated conception in Latin for one that is straightforward enough for anyone's understanding. They have also attached the notion of fallacy to a practice widely and sometimes dependably used in popular discourse.

Similar comments can also be made about such other logical "fallacies" as *argumentum ad invidium* (appeal to hate or envy) and *argumentum ad ignorantiam* (an allegation that something is correct if not proven wrong or false if not proven true). These "fallacies" are too absolute, too technical in an irrelevant sense, and too lacking in a recognition of moral and cultural relativity. Their definitions do not recognize the significance of their common use in social discourse.

MORE SPECIALIZED PROCEDURES

The techniques of identification or association mentioned do not exhaust the possibilities at all. They are types, not categories. They are really ideal types, and in practice they usually appear in more complex and mixed forms. One can reconsider the list given (transfer, testimonial, plain folks, and band wagon) and come up with more specialized procedures, such as guilt by association ("a bad lot," "a bad neighborhood," Joe-McCarthyism, Reaganomics) and guilt by heredity (racism, ethnicism, classism, sexism, "bad stock") and their opposites, virtue by association ("name dropping," "good connections," arbitrary accreditation procedures) and virtue by heredity (racism, classism, ethnicism, sexism, "good stock").

With this fairly simple armament the propagandist constructs and reconstructs the content of her or his communications to implement the planned strategies. Such communications are keyed to constant selection and definition, reselection and redefinition, in the light of current issues, case-making opportunities and necessities, and the production of simplified end-results often in the form of a slogan.

4. To Gain Access to Audiences

Media of communication set the potential size and character of audiences that propagandists can reach. They are also in effect controlled windows through which we receive much of our impression of current events. They even try to give the impression that they are accurate mirrors of what we are thinking about the passing scene.

Gaining access to the audience of a given medium requires an actionist to get her or his message past the medium's "gatekeepers" or, better still, accepted by the medium's own staff as their own. It is often easier to enter media with advertising than with materials intended to be treated as news or entertainment. Thus actionists employ both advertising—as a "medium sweetener"—and efforts to infiltrate non-advertising space or time.

As the sociologist Herbert J. Gans has it, the relationship between sources and media people is often a tug of war. This struggle for news-gatherers "is shaped by at least four interrelated factors: (1) incentives; (2) power; (3) ability to supply suitable information; and (4) geographic and social proximity to the journalists." He adds that, "in the end, power of one kind or another is highly instrumental, at least in the attempt to gain access."[10]

Even with access, a propagandist still has the problem of turning potential audiences into actual, receptive, and responsive readers, listeners, or lookers. Or, if such is the desired purpose, into inactive, unresponsive nonlisteners. Audience reactions depend largely upon the message itself, upon the manner in which it is "played" by media functionaries (reporters, copywriters, columnists, commentators, co-medians, programmers), and upon current social conditions, the general social context of climate of opinion. Statements or dramatizing events must demand attention. Proposals must be of a kind likely to be viewed with positive or negative seriousness.

When considered as a "window" or a "mirror," a medium is often filled with contradictions. As the political scientist Michael Parenti notes, "Seldom holding itself accountable for what it says, [a medium] can blithely produce information and opinions that conflict with pre-viously held ones, without a word of explanation for the shift." Never-theless, the media do create an "image of public opinion that often plays a more crucial role in setting the issue agenda than does actual public opinion and which has a feedback effect on actual opinion."[11]

TYPES OF MEDIA

The principal propaganda media can usefully be typed in a few simple categories. They can be distinguished as formal or informal, and in terms of their relation to an actionist organization or move-ment, as internal, controlled-direct, uncontrolled-direct, and indirect media. In addition, during World War II, it became customary in the Federal Office of War Information to talk about "white," "gray," and "black" propaganda media, types that may also be found else-where than in international struggles. Let us illustrate these three types of media quite briefly.

Formal media may occur to us more often than the informal media in our thinking about the activities of social actionists. In addition to established newspapers, radio and television stations and networks, advertising agencies, publicity firms, magazines, trade journals, book publishers, speakers, motion-picture studios, theaters, and other formal media, there are many informal or less formal ones that can play powerful roles in organizing public responses. These are rumor and gossip, direct mail, leaflets, pamphlets, marginal books, placards and small posters, handbills, speakers, pickets, and many more. Such a pamphlet-publishing organization as the nonprofit Public Affairs Committee becomes a rather formal medium when it issues more than eighty million pamphlets on over six hundred topics in fifty years, but pamphlets are ordinarily casual and separate publications rather than parts of a systematic series such as the Public Affairs Committee has developed.

The institutionalized and "responsible" character of formal media makes them routinely available only to publicists for established and "responsible" organizations. But agitators for radical and innovative programs can gain attention in almost any medium by exploiting the potentialities of the "news" conception. Louis Adamic summarized the extreme expression of that opportunity for agitation by reminding us that newspapers do "print the riots."[12] In addition, in periods of tension when formal media become even more fully the vehicles of orthodox social rituals (sports, sensational crimes, the waywardnesses of our youth, soap opera and comic types of entertainment), informal media take on power out of all proportion to their unpretentious character. Such periodicals as *The Progressive, The Nation,* and the New York *Guardian* even force their concerns into the news emissions of the formal media. For example, they sometimes can prevent the formal media from ignoring or treating as inconsequential such disturbing events as strikes, riots, and nuclear mishaps.

The formal-informal relationship is best seen as a continuum. At the more formal end are the relatively rigid and institutionalized media: the daily newspapers, block-booked motion pictures, mass magazines, and radio and television networks. Their tremendous financial commitments are largely met by advertising, but they must also have popular adherence in order to get that advertising. Thus they are vulnerable to discordant pressures, both financial and popular. Their operators attempt to anticipate or avoid controversial issues and other hazards. They follow a socially nonspeculative, conservative course. Only in that manner do they ordinarily assume that they can maintain or better their existing competitive or monopolistic situation.

To illustrate, the "patron saint of television news" Edward R. Murrow asserted in 1958 that his employers were operating a "money-making machine." He wanted and did what he could to make news important, helpful to vast publics, and not merely commercially profitable entertainment.[13] Richard Salant, for 16 years president of CBS News, observes that "the seeds of trouble Murrow talked about then have turned into forests."[14] In other words, as the journalist Jonathan Alter sees it, "the pressures Murrow described have intensified to the point where serious-minded CBS employees fear for the soul of their company." Soul? He states that CBS did have a spirit that "attracted talent and made it the prestige network for so many years."[15]

The formal media on the whole have done much to elect such presidents as Eisenhower, Nixon, and Reagan and to try to defeat F. D. Roosevelt, Truman, and Kennedy. When "their" presidents are in power, "What is amazing in this country is the speed and the enthusiasm with which the national media adopt official values and promote the consensus almost before it is put forth by the authorities." To this editorial viewpoint, *The Nation* adds, "The stuff in the newspapers and on the tube is for the most part beyond definitions of truth and accuracy."[16]

At the other end of the formal-informal continuum are such irresponsible and unorganized media as gossip, stump speakers, volunteer pickets, and handbills that are here today and perhaps untraceable tomorrow but all of which can also be somewhat organized. At least they can be stimulated and even created, given aid, and motivated. They cannot be made into highly controlled or monopolistic instruments in our society as it is now organized. The student, black, feminist, peace, and lesbian and gay activists since the 1960s have demonstrated that less formal media provide powerful recourses for democratic discussions and adjustments in our society.

INTERNAL, DIRECT, AND INDIRECT TYPES OF MEDIA

These are well illustrated by the propaganda roles of teachers and their organizations. Schools' and teachers' associations and unions use internal media to give directives and solicit reactions. Such media include convocations, institutes, and conventions, as well as bulletins and news letters. When outside interests can gain access to such media, they have a captive audience that may or may not be responsive. Critics of teachers and educational budgets keep careful watch over such media to spot unguarded statements and events that can be used for their purposes. Direct media are those through which messages are transmitted with admitted sponsorship to outside publics. In education these are textbooks, teachers' lectures, public statements and writings, and pronouncements by administrators and teacher organizations. Indirect media are legion. They carry endorsements or rejections of a program without the source of influence being indicated or obvious. In this area the compulsions toward cooperation range from news, facts, logic, services, and friendship to retainer fees, bribes, and coercion.

Broad changes in the relations of university teachers to social action during the nineteenth and twentieth centuries have altered their propaganda roles. At the outset of this period our colleges and universities were training schools for clergymen, lawyers, and other "gentlemen." Their professors were assimilated male members of a social structure in which the vested interests of those roles were to be accepted and defended. Sharp criticisms of theology, the church, law, and judicial process came chiefly from "radicals" outside the academic halls. Then with the addition of more and more educational assignments to the college programs, professors with traditions other than those of the "old professionals" became increasingly numerous. They are professors informed about the practical worlds of engineering, physical and biological science, business, large-scale government, mass communications, social work, and all the rest, and they and their students are no longer all males.

During the transition from colleges controlled by those defensive of "old" professionalisms to those trained to produce technicians and "professionals" for an integrating technological society, the descendants of the former fought a losing battle against the "profanation of the temple" by the latter. To illustrate, the American Civil Liberties Union discovered that during the 1920s "thousands of dollars were spent in universities for subsidies to schools of commerce, fees to professors and promotion work for text-books favorable to utilities. That there was 'a close connection between public utilities and the academic profession' was confirmed by the American Association of University Professors which undertook an investigation of charges against members of the profession in 1930." Then what happened? The Union adds:

It is significant that after this exposure of the prostitution of the schools and colleges to the Power Trust no teacher was dismissed or disciplined. Some of them may have severed their connections . . . but nothing happened remotely akin to the prompt dismissal of teachers or professors guilty of 'radical' utterances. The public furore aroused by the exposure of this propaganda has resulted in dissolving the [open] alliance between schools and utilities.[17]

What was then exposed as a covert form of influence through fees for speeches, consultations, and grants for research persists, has become more routine, and continues to expand in frequency. In others words, what was an indirect propaganda medium now is often a direct one, albeit still clothed in an academic disguise.

Thus, as the educator Paul Von Blum proves, "Grantsmanship has . . . come to play a crucial role in academic visibility." Since it "enhances prestige, . . . substantial faculty efforts are expended in this direction." The theory has emerged that "almost anyone can teach, but only first-rate professors can achieve national and international reputations. . . . Hundreds of thousands of university undergraduates, unfortunately, pay a lifelong price for their professors' collective short-sightedness."[18]

Why is it worthwhile for business and financial interests to subsidize and control very expensive, prestigious, and privately financed universities? Why do they also do what they can to control the character of tax-supported education? The private university provides a less complicated medium than the public one for obtaining research, development, and advocacy services on a tax-exempt basis. It is also thought to be somewhat safe to assume that the employees of the private institutions are more dependably selected to be congruent in biases or interests with sources of funds. Because of the plutocratic control of government in our society, a disproportionate share of governmental subsidies for university research goes to such institutions as Harvard, Yale, and Princeton. The resulting public image entices many of the "best and brightest" students to share in such universities' job market prestige and network possibilities.

Even for relatively small colleges, the entrepreneurial "research university" pattern has growing acceptance. Graduate academic departments now quite commonly sponsor bureaus or institutes that undertake subsidized research for branches of government, specific companies, industries, interested individuals, and trade unions. Professors and their undergraduate and graduate students thus get field-work experience and laboratory research training on what must be, in most cases, biased or narrowly technical projects and scarcely the greatly needed basic research to which academic institutions presumably dedicate themselves. The relationship of academician to sponsor is accepted so uncritically and has become so natural that in many cases the biasing influence is not apparent to either, nor is the social and professional damage. At the least, it confines investigations to uncreative repetitions or to inconsequential trivia.

This situation is now rarely exposed or discussed. There is no public furore about it. Graduate schools have thus often become direct mediums of propaganda among their own students and also, through that influence, among undergraduate and high school students. These practices are sometimes called *sponsor pandering* or *foundation panhandling*.

WHITE, GRAY, AND BLACK MEDIA

These types, as used by the Federal Office of War Information, differ somewhat from the ones called internal, direct, and indirect. In terms of the latter, the internal and direct are "white," the undisguised indirect is "gray," and the disguised indirect is "black." The use and the analysis of disguised indirect propagandas are slippery business. They create difficulties for many media. The alleged analysis has taken the form of Red-scares, Right Wing plots, and racist and ethnic distortions. It has led overzealous American "patriot" extremists, unacquainted with the actual writings of Thomas Jefferson, to assume that a Jeffersonian democratic position is radical, disturbing, and hence, communist!

As in the case of personnel, the social actionist does not accept traditional assumptions or allegations about media. As nearly as possible, he or she must know the details of their manner of operation in order to penetrate them effectively and to influence their audiences accurately.

5. To Find Compelling Appeals

Existing *opinion matériel* provides the basis for selecting the "A" appeal to be used in the A–B–C pattern of propaganda construction.

With an appeal, a propagandist can only attempt to manipulate what already exists in the minds of the groups of people she or he is trying to influence.

Simplifiers have worked out list after list of appeals and motives as ways to tap existing needs and aspirations, but such lists are merely caricatures or, at best, crude steps toward an understanding of this social psychological complexity. To synthesize the mental equipment of a person from another culture requires a degree of preparation, study, and care that emphasizes the complexity and inclusiveness of a society's, and also of group's, cultural patterns. In international psychological warfare, therefore, it has usually been more effective to employ a person who grew up in the enemy's culture than to attempt such synthesis. Even in intergroup — interethnic, interclass — communication, publicists and advertising people have found it expedient to obtain blacks to speak to blacks, for example, and similarly to depend upon other authentic ethnic and class specialists.

The influence of cultural patterns — of the predominant mores in groups and of the accepted morals in society — upon individuals gives the actionist an approach to the opinion problem. An opinion becomes public rather than merely personal not because of any group "spirit" or group decision, but rather because common cultural patterns and common access to facts, ideas, and events result in the emergence of similar opinions on a given subject in a given public. Statements by leaders succeed chiefly in crystallizing rather than in creating public opinions.

A public opinion differs from a common attitude or a more deeply held common sentiment in that a public opinion is expressed. An attitude or a sentiment is a mental pattern that may or may not resemble an expressed opinion.

OPINIONS ARE MULTIVALENT

As we grow up, our minds are "programmed" — to use a rough analogy to computer practice — by mother, father, siblings, friends, teachers, and mass media. This programmed or guided experience in social interaction etches upon our minds values and behavior patterns delineated in our society's culture and in the customary patterns of the various groups into which we are assimilated. In consequence of this and other personal experiences, individuals can express personal opinions, opinions of one or another of different limited groups or publics, and opinions of what is taken to be *the* public, all of which may differ in detail or even in entirety. This common social phenomenon, called multivalence, finds ready illustration in popular experience and in fiction, even though it is not often consciously recognized as such or is self-righteously condemned as "hypocrisy."

This matter of multivalence presents actionists with a basic problem when they try to use reports of public-opinion pollsters. The type of opinion people express, like their other behavior, depends upon the conditions under which a reaction such as an interview response takes place. Interviewers and other listeners ordinarily receive an expression of opinion customarily given to a stranger. It is usually an opinion thought by the speaker to be appropriate in a general societal context. This is especially so if the interviewer appears to fit into the stereotype of a schoolteacher, parson, or some other official representative of societal morals. If people interviewed feel some group identification with an interviewer, then they may state opinions typical of that more limited public. "Since you are a neighbor, I know I can talk more freely!" or "Now that I know you are a fellow trade unionist, I can tell you what I really think!" or "Why didn't you tell me that you are a fellow Vietnam vet?"

The question thus arises: In what context — or, more likely, variety of contexts — did interviewers gather the reactions reported in a given "scientific" survey? Astute actionists realize that they must go beyond such superficial data. They also understand that multivalence may present them with practical opportunities.

MULTIVALENT SENTIMENTS ARE BASIC

Actionists can learn about the opinions of certain publics and of the general public, but these are surface matters. Opinions change. Sometimes they appear to reflect societal morality. At other times, they seem to arise from opportunistic peer-group values. Thus the communications media can credibly interpret public opinions as focusing on certain morally righteous issues at times, even though those issues are quite inconsistent with other simultaneously popular concerns. The moral issue might reflect sexual prudishness, self-sacrificing patriotism, or a presumable obsession with law and order. At the same time, popular politicians may be successfully tempting the same publics with opportunities for commercial deals, tax cheating, sexual permissiveness, or access to drugs in a not too subtle manner. To what extent is there an "underground" untaxed economy? How great and entrenched are drug operations? What are the ties between the "underworld" and the "upperworld"? Multivalent sentiments help to create and maintain this inconsistent social structure.

To guide an actionist, a knowledge of common sentiments is thus much more useful than reports on opinions. Sentiments are basic patterns of emotion and thought underlying how people think and behave. They are deep, typically inconsistent, and largely unverbalized. Although powerful in the determination of opinion and behavior, sentiments are revealed only by analyzing what people say and especially what they actually do. We cannot approach the phenomenon more directly.

Through repeated analysis of the spontaneous statements and actions of leaders and members of publics as gathered by political scouts and media reporters as well as by "scientific" pollsters, propagandists can gradually build up dependable "clinical knowledge"[19] of the required accoutrements with which they can work. The political scouts may be employees of political actionists, or they may be salespeople for a corporation, union representatives, social workers, or others. They report background data that probes more deeply than sample opinion surveys. When compared and analyzed in the light of repeated polls and other data having to do with ethnic, occupational, and class patterns and behaviors, shrewd students find few surprises in the shifting of opinion reports, votes, sales records, or lists of voluntary contributors.[20]

Thus both propagandists and brainwashers attempt first to work with what already exists in the minds of those who are their targets. "Communications will be most effective—that is, will secure the response most in line with the intention of the communicator—when they are in accord with audience predispositions; when they tell people what they (most) want to be told." In other words, communications "are more effective in canalizing people's existing dispositions than they are in redirecting their responses into directions neutral or counter to their interests, social positions, and group memberships—in which case they encounter a good deal of resistance."[21]

That people do not always realize how their existing values are being used to exploit them is the basic problem of propaganda analysis. Many thoughtful psychotherapists contend that they cannot do more than aid their patients to understand better their existing sentiments (consciences, superegos) and thus to live more satisfactorily with them. The purpose of popular propaganda analysis can only be much the same. The highly successful Alcoholics Anonyous group therapy program depends upon substituting an equivalent but more healthful way of life for drinking and alcohol-related socializing.[22] Although they give up drinking, AA members admittedly remain "alcoholics." Once socialized, people have sentiments that can change but that have a high level of persistence.

6. To Utilize the Current Situation

The changing social situation, often called the changing climate of opinion, is ever present in the thoughts of the successful social actionist. What was impossible yesterday may become easy today with a change in the overall situation. War, depression, inflation, urban tensions, student unrest, growing evidence of environmental pollution, population pressures, black dissatisfaction and upward mobility, agitation against sexism, relaxed or raised bans against pornography, nuclear mishaps, and more can all figure strongly in what is currently possible for a given actionist.

Basic to the utilization of the current situation is the selection and definition of the social issues to be exploited in actionist propaganda. Is the issue drug use or "star wars"? Is it "terrorism" or international negotiation? The struggle over issues is endless and basic, the fundamental battleground of social action competition and conflict.

Intelligent and experienced actionists can serve as catalysts of social change, as temporary or prolonged stumbling blocks, or even as diverters or perverters of it. Here we do not mean struggles among relatively similar brands of cigarettes, perfumes, automobiles, or political candidates, but to overall efforts concerning cigarette use or automobile safety—or collectivism or private enterprise or state socialism. For affecting the course of change, many techniques and media are available. Let us discuss some of the devices that are often used.

Keys to Popular Propaganda Analysis

Our best defense against both brainwashing and propaganda contrary to our own interests could be education, but it is not the kind of education now often provided in our nation's schools. Our educational procedures are more often geared to the development of believers and technicians rather than of independent investigators and thinkers. But our closeness to our farming and urban-worker heritage has given even our middle-class intellectuals an earthiness and realism at times not to be found among their European counterparts. The tasteless trash associated with much contemporary mass culture is deadening, but popular culture also carries with it great literary and artistic productions. Often it exhibits a healthy distrust for the pretentious intellectual games of traditional academicians as well as faith in people's ability to test ideas against commonsense evidence, and especially against their own observations and experience.[23]

Some intellectuals call this earthy heritage in our mass culture an anti-intellectual one because it rejects the overly abstract and finespun theorizing used to support elitist social perquisites. It opposes going beyond what may be observed or otherwise experienced. It brushes aside opinions supported solely by elegance or expression or by allegations of societal or intellectual legitimacy. This is part of the Mark Twain heritage out of which realistic social science grew in the United States, even though many sociologists would now contend that it is anti-intellectual to look upon social science as a revolt against traditional intellectualism. Elitists try to carry about with them a baggage of philosophical footnotes and hair-splitting that is presumably useful to understand life but actually distorts or obscures it.

TACTICS TO LOOK FOR

After an actionist selects and defines a campaign issue and determines the most useful appeals to be used, attention is then given to tactics. Here are fifteen commonly employed tactics: hot potato, stalling, least-of-evils, scapegoating, shift of scene, change of pace, big tent, conflict, compromise, confusion, big lie, censorship, person to person, program of deeds, and leadership. Most of these are self-defining or have been discussed at length elsewhere. When one sees how actionists use them, the intent and probable consequences of their propaganda can become clearer. Here are brief comments on each of them:

Hot potato springs an event, a trap, a situation upon an opponent that forces the appearance of embarrassment or guilt. Hot potatoes are often statements torn out of context or made in a different climate of opinion, a different type of social situation. Mud-slinging political campaigns are full of hot potatoes.

Stalling, the use of delaying tactics, sometimes causes the opposition to lose vigor, interest, and support or to miss a timely opportunity. Many official investigations have this purpose rather than genuine fact-finding. Sometimes a lawsuit does the same sort of job.

Least-of-evils was Hitler's favorite. He asserted that his program's alternative would be a bloody Communist takeover and terror. Efforts to legalize traffic in marijuana and to institute state gambling systems are regularly supported by the least-of-evils argument. The tremendous expenditures for armaments throughout the world—typically at the cost of social services—are claimed to be the least-of-evils. Whether a given use of least-of-evils is delusory or a sound judgment of available alternatives depends upon one's conception of one's own interests and of relevant evidence.

Scapegoating haunts western civilization and is often a disastrous tactic. It may be used to picture a group or a person as the focal point of blame and dissatisfaction for selected or general social woes. The allegation can be, as in Nazi propaganda and persecution against Jews and Poles, cruelly delusory. Politicians and media spokespeople continually parade an assortment of scapegoats—terrorists, the Soviet menace, Communism, labor bosses, machine politicians, ethnic minorities (black, oriental, Latino), peaceniks or doves, hawks, and the military-industrial complex.

In some cases, it is not clear whether scapegoating is a deliberate tactic or merely develops as a useful happenstance. For example, while American revulsion mounted against the human wastage of the undeclared Vietnam war, First Lieutenant William Calley of the frightful My Lai massacre of noncombatants appears to have been seized as an army scapegoat, once a photojournalist had forced his crime to the nation's attention. By finding him guilty of multiple murders after a long and spectacular military trial, perhaps army commanders hoped to establish publicly their abhorrence of the wanton destruction of noncombatants. If that was the purpose, it was poorly calculated. "For reasons that seemed to spring from the natural human tendency to translate moral dilemmas into personal terms, the Calley case was turned overnight into a symbol of the entire American tragedy in Vietnam."[24] Instead of serving as a scapegoat's trial, the trial triggered vivid public reviews of war's inevitable degradation and brutalization of its participants.

Shift of scene, the moving of a participant's efforts in a struggle to a different arena, often can disorient the opposition. In politics it may be a shift from election fights to lobbying in administrative halls or in a legislature, to litigation in connection with a relevant issue in the courts, to appealing more directly to constituencies between elections in a propaganda campaign in the mass media. Parades, petitions, delegations, mass meetings, television programs, study commissions, investigations—each can help to shift the scene and perhaps to catch the opposition off guard. Commercial advertising illustrates this tactic when it shifts from emotional to factual appeals, from lottery-type inducements to ones stressing economy, from sex to mystery to mechanical know-how.

Change of pace can be equally useful to a strategist, and sometimes it is employed with a shift of scene. It is often a replacement of high pressure by dignified low pressure or vice versa.

Big tent, like a circus's many rings and side shows, offers many attractions, many possible appeals. It is an appeal of large organizations with extensive and varied constituencies. Thus a large corporation can dramatize itself as a benevolent employer, a sponsor of scientific research, a friend of education and of community social agencies, and a gilt-edged investment. Big tent can be a tactic of developing a more general social movement in such a way that a great many organizations will attempt to tie in with it, to come under its canopy. Instances of this have been Prohibition, Red scares, our various wars, antiwar programs, and ecological and anti-pollution efforts.

Conflict, compromise, and *confusion* are sometimes phases through which change of pace may go. *Conflict* refers to the actionist tactics of strikes, lockouts, boycotts, picketings, shows of official force, defiances of soldiers or police, riots, and even wars. While the more violent types of conflict often result in media attention and shock people into a consciousness of a confrontation, they are typically more costly than advantageous. Hence nonviolent confrontations—actually nonviolent conflicts—have often demonstrated greater utility in the accomplishment of social goals than has recourse to violence. Official nonviolent repression takes such forms as censorship and biased legislation, judicial decisions, and administrative acts. It can become excessively oppressive. Unfortunately, popular nonviolent uprisings in protest require far more extensive and devoted organization and support than do popular violent acts.[25]

Acceptable synonyms for *compromise* are conciliation, mediation, mutual concessions, give-and-take, and even "horse-trading." Compromise involves negotiation, arbitration, or adjudication. If the proposed tactic or its consequences are unattractive, a propagandist may call it appeasement or "selling out." It is a valuable tactic for nonviolently resolving differences when it proceeds without such distortions as bribed or otherwise unrepresentative negotiators.

Allegations that there is *confusion* may serve extremists of the left or right, or they may satisfy any in power who merely wish to muddle along. Allegations take such forms as the presentation of contradictory "evidence" or claims of being overwhelmed by presumably unforeseen developments. Any such confusing event or arrangement can become a smokescreen behind which activists can affect a *fait accompli.* "After all," they assert, "in such a confused situation, someone just had to do something!"

The *big lie* and *censorship* are frequently used, but they can be self-defeating in all but a short-run sense. Media rhetoric substitutes credibility gap or communications gap for the big lie in referring to differences in verity between public officials and their own commentators. American official or commercial censorship typically brings pressure to bear prior to the point of publication. Even in wartime, censorship's goals are usually obtained by controlling access to facts, by timing the release of news materials, by quiet agreements with media representatives concerning news treatment, and by trusting the "good judgment" of those typically conservative operators who own or control mass media.[26]

Censorship by any method breeds rumor, barbed antiestablishment humor, and disrespect for and lack of confidence in formal announcements and policy statements. The more effectively a country's public discussions are censored or controlled, the greater the extent to which people come to regard them as empty rituals divorced from the reality of flesh-and-blood situations. Censorship encourages establishment representatives to use the big lie as a means with which to denigrate opposition propaganda indiscriminately.

The *person-to-person* approach often attempts to create a tone of sincerity that can overcome public resistance to tired symbols and rituals or to otherwise unattractive proposals. This is the power of the empathetic actor turned politician or salesperson on radio or television. The appealing ability of a friendly and seemingly honest person "directly" to communicate to us may be convincing—at least until the processes of comparison and disillusionment shatter the spell.

A *program of deeds* is a stratagem utilizing dramatic events. Its aura of genuineness often arises from the apparent appropriateness or spontaneity of its happenings. The more such deeds characterize construc-

tive efforts, the more believable the message becomes. Dedication cere-
monies, parades, protest marches, and planned confrontations such
as picketings, strikes, shut-outs, and even street riots are examples
of events that might be fitted into a given program.

A person in a *leadership* role can give focus to a propaganda effort
through having a personality that inspires confidence and thus being
able to guide thoughts and activities. The role may be seized by a
charismatic person or be assigned to someone selected to serve as a
front for others in control. Struggles may develop over how much power
the leader controls and for what purposes. In any event, propagandists devote special attention to how the role is filled and how it might
be improved. It can be crucial to a campaign's success.

Struggles against Manipulation

So much for an outline of a social actionist's typical orientation,
methods of operating, and available facilities. How can we free ourselves enough from such a manipulator's spells to think thoughts of
our own about personal concerns and interests and about their interrelationships with local and international issues? How can we separate ourselves enough from the pall of orthodoxy to gain some understanding of that orthodoxy? How can we be less puppets and more
the rational human beings the traditions of democracy idealize? Is it
worth it? Why not just drift with the stream of humanity through
time and space and take what comes during our brief stay on earth?

Those who believe that we need not be puppets know that human
beings with a glimpse of human potentialities cannot just drift. We
need not be discouraged by the intricacies of modern mass society.
We can learn two major defenses against being manipulated: On the
one hand, we must discover as accurately as possible how social actionists do their work, for what goals, and with what success. The more
we know and understand about how actionists operate, the more we
can be aware of how our own interests are or are not served by their
manipulations. On the other hand, we must give up one common human preconception: We must sacrifice any faith we might have in certainty and realize that in life wisdom lies in examining probabilities.
In a world in which all is relative to all else and in which all is constantly changing, there is no certainty, no valid absolute or dogma.

For many this is a horrible thought, a nightmarish speculation to be rejected as quickly as possible. To a growing multitude of others who can face life without that mental crutch, it presents a breathtaking challenge to intellectual enterprise and endless opportunities for growth and welfare.

As John Dewey notes, a notion of immutable reality can only be a fantasy or an inculcated dogma. He sought to replace it with a knowing through participating that he related to a more durable and useful principle of indeterminacy.[27] This is similar to the theory of societal and cultural (including cognitive) relativity developed by such social scientists as Julius Lippert and W. G. Sumner and modified and refined since then.[28] This is not the doctrinaire type of cultural relativity. As Clyde Kluckhohn indicates, this scientific conception places each aspect of opinion, propaganda, or behavior "in the unique structure of the culture in which it occurs and in terms of the value system of that culture." This does not mean that such items are "so unique that comparative appraisals are ruled out."[29]

As Dewey said, "Intelligence in operation, another name for method, becomes the thing most worth winning."[30] This is intelligence as equipment and ability to deal with, and to participate in, reality. Only with this type of intelligence, of which liberation sociology is a part, can a more participatory democracy emerge.

If we will dare to teach this kind of propaganda analysis in our high schools and colleges, and if we dare to live up to its implications, we can be implementing in our society a basic promise of a liberal education.

6

Ideologies
among Sociologists

Philosophers like to think that they can understand the myriad complexities of human relationships, and they regularly articulate rhetorics and social theories supposedly supported by sources of authority. They then introduce their products to a market and defend them against those of competitors. The resulting ideologies are intended to enlighten and guide. They furnish symbols and formulas used in intergroup struggles in academia and society. Social scientists usually do not like to be labeled philosophers — even though they are "doctors of philosophy" — but they do carry on this ancient heritage, albeit elaborated by modern technology.

The current market orientation of sociologists often distracts them from functioning as students of society. It leads them to reify their rhetoric, theories, and research techniques as privately owned merchandise available for sale. It tends to push them toward allegedly apolitical or "value-free" stances rather than toward searches for knowledge regardless of how it might question the existing social power structure. The search of so many sociologists for validation of their saleable merchandise thus results in their adopting a methodological puritanism. The sociologist Franco Ferrarotti finds the "hustle and bustle" that is characteristic of sociologists "as pure methodologists" to have "a good deal of comic quality."[1] Instead of bustling, we need to preoccupy ourselves with lifting the veils that disguise or hide social manipulations. We can thus help to create a sociology that is emancipatory rather than one that is an end in itself.

The activities of practitioners in the social science disciplines yield multiple visions of "normal science." In his study of *The Structure of Scientific Revolutions,* Thomas S. Kuhn defines "normal science" as research activity "firmly based upon one or more past scientific achievements, achievements that some particular scientific community acknowledges for a time as supplying the foundation for its further practice."[2] Those past patterns, models, or plans shape up a paradigm — that is, a guide for research, the kinds of data to use, and the major outlines of theory to be pursued and applied. A "normal science" is thus the body of accepted precedent within a scientific community or school of which it is the approximate consensus at a given time.

At its outset, a paradigm is "sufficiently unprecedented to attract an enduring group of adherents away from competing modes of scientific activity" and also "sufficiently open-ended to leave all sorts of problems for the redefined group of practitioners to resolve." As the paradigm develops a following, research springing from it becomes grist at any given time for the efforts of writers of a community's textbooks to define its current character. Such normal sciences typically do not "call forth new sorts of phenomena; indeed those that will not fit the box are often not seen at all," as Kuhn contends. "New" scientific pursuits are often "directed to the articulation of those phenomena and theories that the paradigm already supplies."[3]

Paradigms are more influential in the physical sciences. Kuhn declares that "it remains an open question what parts of social science have yet acquired such paradigms at all."[4] As yet, sociology has had no paradigm domination at all comparable in extent or acceptance to Ptolemaic or Copernican astronomy or Aristotelian, Newtonian, or Einsteinian dynamics.

The chief paradigmatic influence upon sociology has been "the spirit of modern positivism, which in turn is closely related to the spirit of capitalism," as the sociologist Gertrud Lenzer points out. She adds, "Once successfully established . . . the social sciences tended increasingly to cut themselves loose from history . . . notwithstanding . . . the existence of critical analyses of the history of social theories and thought." Alternative viewpoints now include "neo-Marxist and critical theory and the widespread sense of unease among students and younger scholars."[5]

Positivism in its generic sense is a paradigmatic influence more limiting than science. In modern professional usage it becomes even more restrictive. Science is ordinarily conceived as any objective search among empirical data for generalizations, regularities, and possible systems. It may be either the inductive or deductive quest for knowledge among apparent realities. Positivists take a more narrow view; they contend that "sense experiences and their logical and mathematical treatment are the exclusive source of all worthwhile information."[6] They reject introspective and intuitional procedures, underrate random observation and historical data, and overrate mathematical methodologies. Their allegedly value-free pose makes their selected "truths" of value to vested interests in our society whose values they habitually respect and fail to criticize.

What about Social Scientists' Autonomy?

This theorizing about dominating paradigms suggests a lack of autonomy, a cultural patterning of scientific thought and behavior, that limits exploration and creativity. It also reminds one of the sociologist Alvin W. Gouldner's finding "that the development of sociology depends on a societal support that permits growth in certain directions but simultaneously limits it in other ways and thus warps its character." He concludes that "every social system is bent upon crippling the very sociology to which it gives birth."[7] And from which it might benefit!

The concept of autonomy for the individual or the group, like many other ideas used in the social sciences, is highly relative in character and degree. It is diverse in its manifestations. It is perceived (1) subjectively by the evolving socializing self, (2) socially by a person's individual associates or (3) by a group's members and associates in interaction, and (4) objectively in terms of behavioral consequences of individual thoughts, emotions, and actions or (5) of group interactions.[8]

This framework helps but does not suggest adequately the major facets of the autonomy problem. In addition, the individual has a collection of role identities or social personality stances, each keyed to the individual's understanding of a given type of social situation. For roles, people accumulate attitudes and behavioral patterns or "scripts" that they are led to believe are appropriate and useful in given situations.

One's sense of autonomy can vary from role to role. The criteria by which independence or freedom and lack of it are evaluated are embedded in contrasting societal and group cultures. To grasp the nature of role patterns, they must be observed in their social-historical and especially their life-historical contexts. Within all researchers are role conceptions and thus ideas of autonomy that were learned in childhood family and peer-group contexts and then adapted or given different interpretations in their adult lives.[9]

Behind differences in theory, methods of research, and rhetoric stand life-history contexts and resulting occupational postures that help to account for significant contrasts in the values, the degree of intellectual independence, and the creativity of social scientists.

Sociologists' Focal Points

Let us consider similarities and dissimilarities among notions of autonomy and among other related aspects of the ideologies and practices of sociologists. In doing so, let us look at four focal points of concern and involvement and their associated problems. These points are: (1) science as curiosity versus science as technology; (2) a general market for one's products and services or one consisting of students or clients; (3) the profession with its networks as seen by mainliners and marginals; and (4) an institution with its networks as seen by bureaucrats and the vocation-centered. These concerns carry with them problems associated with these terms: relative independence, authority, authenticity, identity, social values, politico-economic ethos and pressures, goals, tactics, occupational stance, work patterns, and communication.

Neither set of conceptions—the four focal points nor their associated problems—contains discrete categories. The items overlap and many times combine, but it is helpful to consider them all. Let us look at these lists of concerns and problems in a little more detail.

1. *Science as curiosity versus science as technology:* Sociologists are, as the foregoing suggests, intellectual descendents of ancient social philosophers and then of the participants in the "social science movement" of the nineteenth century. The latter movement attempted "to construct a single body of scientific knowledge which would be used as the basis of an intellectual and scientific solution of the welfare prob-

lems of mankind."[10] The effort proved to be too comprehensive and controversial for an integrated movement or organization. It gradually disintegrated into more specialized movements, disciplines, and associations.

The social science movement's most inclusive successor is sociology, but sometimes sociologists have difficulty deciding just how broad or narrow their section of social science might be. Nevertheless, as C. Wright Mills and many other humanist sociologists see it: "Whatever may be true in such disciplines as political science and economics, history and anthropology, it is evident that in the United States today what is known as sociology has become the center of reflection about social science," especially about social scientific research methods. He believes that "the sociological tradition contains the best statements of the full promise of the social sciences as a whole, as well as some partial fulfillments of it."[11]

This tradition is a challenge to those who are irreverent and curious-minded, but it contains problems for the technician. It calls upon sociologists to emphasize their search for novel research findings rather than to preoccupy themselves with such marketing problems as possible audiences, possible practical applications, and possible criticisms.

For technicians, science is more useful in its accepted "normal" form. This makes it a source for established and dependable symbols and formulas, of merchandise that is saleable.

Either science or technology offers a possible base for vocation-centeredness. Either can take precedence over entanglement in disciplinary politics or institutional bureaucracy.

Sociologists who are oriented entrepreneurially, bureaucratically, or technically often denigrate those preoccupied solely or principally with innovation, revision, and criticism. They often view the latter as irresponsible, negative, and, thus, unscientific, biased, and value-laden. The "irresponsible" devotees of curiosity and innovation in sociology, with their characteristic irreverence toward established authority, have not been numerous in American sociology, even though United States sociologists are the most numerous in the world.

Scientific innovators are not without their biases. Their predominant one is the drive motivating their quests. That drive usually overcomes at least some of the preconceptions to which they were subjected. In consequence, for example, Marxians tend to be dissatisfied and even disillusioned with many of the analyses of Mills.[12] Not to provide an exhaustive list but merely some examples, we have also such "irresponsible" social-scientific innovators as Charles Horton

Cooley, Robert E. Park, Thorstein Veblen, W. G. Sumner, W. I. Thomas, Willard Waller, and those imports, Pitirim A. Sorokin and Florian Znaniecki.

2. *A market* strongly preoccupies the vocation-centered. Technicians gear their efforts to attract attention from whatever markets they seek. They may try to influence a general or special public or to draw students to their classes, members of their discipline to adopt their texts, or clients—foundations, governmental agencies, or corporations—to contract for their research or advisory services.

Sociologists who focus their careers on the marketing of research techniques, facts and analyses, and policy guidance attempt to bridge gaps between academia and the people of the "real world." In doing so, they follow a kind of problematic-technical paradigm that early gained strength in British and American sociology and continues to flourish.[13]

The use of the problematic-technical paradigm was stimulated in particular by the early leaders of the University of Chicago sociology department.[14] In a sense, its adherents might be called investigative journalists or contemporary social historians, but their exceptional researchers go beyond the demands of such crafts. They deepen their perceptions and analyses by borrowing or developing increasingly sophisticated research techniques and theories based upon comparative investigations. They typically push quantification as far as appears practical for the purposes of reporting and analyzing data concerning actual problem situations, but statistical virtuosity seldom becomes for them an end in itself. What they have in common is chiefly a concern with using their research techniques and theories to shed understanding or to help society cope with its problems.

"Normal" vocationalists—the bulk of sociologists—are those who are guided in their thinking chiefly by others. They retail what they find available in such "warehouses" as graduate schools, sociological conferences, and publications. Some use it to liberate their audiences from restrictive intellectual controls and to help them find satisfying and viable life adjustments. Others are either fearful of being so constructive or are unaware of the extent to which they are serving as transmitters of outworn social myths and deliberate social manipulations.

3. *The profession.* As the sociologist Andrew Abbott notes, "So familiar are credentials, associations, and examinations that the organization of pure and applied knowledge seems incomprehensible without them."[15] His Rutgers University colleague, Irving Louis Horowitz,

discusses those who belong to the discipline's dominant cults, the main-liners, and their relations with the marginals and mavericks. As he points out, "One test for the extent to which 'mainliners' and 'marginals' are subject to differential treatment are the reviews of their work in the sociological journals — the respect accorded the most extreme 'insider' of the sociological community in contrast to the rejection accorded the latter." As a mainliner, Horowitz labels the vocation-centered as "anti-sociologists" if they exhibit "a functional allegiance to a source of authority, or to a set of ideas which is outside the control system of sociology."[16] He does not mention the independents who work on their own often as sidelines to other occupations and who have contributed so much to sociological knowledge. Such examples as Charles Booth and W. I. Thomas need to be remembered.

How autonomous and creative can a "normal" or mainline sociologist be who bows to the authority of "the control system of sociology," whatever that might be?

Horowitz's designations are confusing. For him, if a mainline vocationalist becomes unpopular among establishment leaders and thus "marginal," he or she is an "anti-sociologist"; if a professional falls from grace or fails to achieve it and is thus "marginal," she or he is an "un-sociologist"! What would our knowledge of society be without the contributions of such "marginals" as Thorstein Veblen, Pitirim A. Sorokin, and Robert S. and Helen M. Lynd among many others.

Many people find a way of life in professional and continued employment. It systematizes their life and gives a sense of security. By defining a field, professionalism limits competition. It provides an intellectual label or even a uniform. It defines the proposed scope for one's activities. It requires a choice among a limited number of methodological and theoretical paradigms. Major and minor professional societies help to strengthen these controls internally in the discipline in order to repel invaders and to lobby for privileges externally.

4. *An institution,* especially when it provides continuing employment, also helps decisively both to select personality types and to shape them further. The sociologist G. Robert Jackall, in speaking of engineers, summarizes this influence thus: "[Continuing employment] regularizes people's experiences of time by engaging them on a daily basis in rational, socially approved purposive action; it brings them into daily proximity with and subordination to authority; it shapes their measures of prestige and overall social status; and, in the case . . . of the managers they hope to become, it places a premium on a pervasively pragmatic habit of mind."[17] So far as sociologists are concerned, what Jackall is describing applies especially to the "normal" bureaucrats.

Within an institution, the vocation-centered work out compromises to minimize bureaucratizing influences. Some mavericks and marginals are usually tolerated.

Both in universities and in "real world" agencies, the enticements for the craftsperson to become a bureaucratic technician rather than vocationally centered grow stronger and stronger. A professor "is a member of a petty hierarchy," notes Mills, "almost completely closed in by its middle-class environment and its segregation of intellectual and social life. In such a hierarchy, mediocrity makes its own rules and sets its own image of success."[18]

In sociology, this bureaucratization has given birth to the managerial-bureaucratic paradigm for thinking and research. This pattern accepts the myth of an equilibrating social order, "the social system," as its basic conception of society. This systemic structure, with congeries of subsystems nested within it, is usually subjected to what is called functional analysis. This is a concern with how the system's parts satisfy the system's and its members' needs and maintain an adequate degree of integration and balance. This usually implies the indispensability of certain functions as they exist in order to maintain the system as an ongoing enterprise. Alternative social structures or cultural forms may perform functions necessary for the persistence of subsystems or of "the system." In other words, functional needs are satisfied by alternative social structures, a range of possible structures. If "the system" is to persist, these needs must be satisfied.

The school of adherents enthralled by this paradigm exhibits a pretentious display of systematic theory based particularly on the writings of Max Weber and Vilfredo Pareto and developed in this country by Talcott Parsons, Robert K. Merton, S. A. Stouffer, and George Homans, among others.[19] The dignity and possible autonomy of people generally does not appear to interest them nearly so much as does the welfare of the system. They are preoccupied with how people can be managed, led to preconceived goals, and with how the bureaucratized system can be maintained and made to flourish. This bias is taken by the school to support, not undermine, their contention of being "value free," of assuming strict neutrality in their scientific investigations.[20]

Parsons' version of this paradigm gained academic as well as some industrial prestige. This was through the acceptance of his contention that all manner of social-psychological and sociological theories are integrated or replaced by his evolving theoretical scheme. What he offered was highly abstract and, at any point in its life history, dogmatic.

This paradigm has also gained authority through its adherents' use of highly "sophisticated" (i.e., "impressive even when not relevant") and "unmanipulable" (read "resistant to popular reinterpretation") methodologies. With the aid of cybernetics and the digital computer, these followers have been able to interpret their systematic functionalism to the powerful. In doing so, they construct such gadgets as models that represent simplifications of the "social system" or an aspect of it or a "subsystem" with little attention to human constituents. Or they put together games that caricature a somewhat repetitious aspect of human interaction by reducing it to the proportions and relative importance of a chess or bridge contest.[21]

Those accepting a version of the managerial-bureaucratic paradigm could not avoid concern with social change, but they give the impression of trying to be ahistorical. For example, Parsons contends "that the crucial focus of the problem of change lies in the stability of the value system. . . . Empirically, forces making for change seldom operate neatly according to discrete analytical categories; their impact is diffused."[22] The users of this paradigm appear to be dedicated to preserving the bureaucrat's home, "the system," as intact and viable as possible.

Many allege or anticipate the demise of the influence of Parsons and his ilk. What is currently called "Parsonian" in a general way has had other labels in the past. It will probably be replaced only by something different in name and style, not in basic intent and character. Some tied intellectually to the managerial-bureaucratic paradigm are now playing with Erving Goffman's dramaturgy and Harold Garfinkel's ethnomethodology.[23]

The most convincing indication of the acceptance of this paradigm as a social-scientific tool by power manipulators was the setting up during World War II of a four-year study by the Research Branch, Information and Education Division, United States Army. It was co-sponsored by the Social Science Research Council. Some 134 civilian and military specialists labeled social scientists were listed as having participated in this project. The Carnegie Corporation of New York provided the funds for the publication in 1949–50 of the resulting four volumes of *The American Soldier* by S. A. Stouffer and others. "Sociology" of that kind had arrived. Given the goals of problems set by management, such studies offer promise of "enlightened" policy recommendations, but it is a promise often damaged in accuracy by the nature of the assignment and of its funding and by the commitment of researchers to the managerial-bureaucratic paradigm. Incidentally, the efforts to play down, distort, and "answer" critical reviews of *The American Soldier* volumes and to brag about praise from the bureaucratic and technique-oriented appear in a volume edited by two participants in the project, Merton and Paul F. Lazarsfeld.[24]

Another example of the same sort of thing—Project Camelot—reached a climax in the summer of 1965 that "revealed American sociologists as willing handservants of the United States Army's effort to throttle center-to-left political movements in a variety of sovereign states around the world." With headquarters at American University in Washington and guided by high-echelon Army officers, the Project recruited a prestigious academic staff from a variety of American universities. Its "scientific" mission was to spot situations in Latin America that might become insurrectional. In the work of the Project staff, "Two parallel but distinct vocabularies were maintained—one military with military justifications, the other sociological with social-scientific justifications." As the sociologist Robert W. Friedrichs notes further, this illustrates "the sleight-of-hand manner in which role theory is able to transform military intelligence work into value-free social research without the slightest change in the activity itself."[25]

Project Camelot died of exposure. J. William Fulbright, chair of the Senate Foreign Relations Committee, spoke of its "reactionary, backward-looking policy opposed to change."[26] But those who will do such work and call it social science are always with us.

The adherents of the managerial-bureaucratic or functional-systemic paradigm have been able to develop an inclusive, impressive, and thus vendable body of theory and method. They gain for themselves significant roles in government, business, and voluntary organizations as the dispensers of a kind of magic. They also help graduate students to become useful to the manipulators of power rather than merely to liberal-arts college students and to the critical and constructive pursuit of knowledge. These graduate students help with the details of managerial-bureaucratic assignments. They often "work out their doctoral dissertations" as spinoffs from a major research contract project in a manner not at all conducive to training in autonomous scientific research.

Ideological Problems

As is indicated above, these four focal points and their associated orientations in sociological identity confront at least eleven concerns, suggested by the terms listed. Of those terms, relative independence, authority, authenticity, identity, tactics, occupational stance, and work patterns are perhaps discussed enough for the present purpose in the foregoing and in parts of what follows. Let us therefore turn now to the other four problems listed: social values, politico-economic ethos and pressures, goals, and communication:

Social values: As Robert S. Lynd points out, the values held by social scientists are significant and are often in conflict with pressures from outside their discipline. "Social science cannot perform its function if the culture constrains it at certain points in ways foreign to the spirit of science; . . . it is necessary for social science to work directly to remove the causes of such obstacles."[27]

The critical stance that Lynd expects of social scientists worries those defensive of traditional formulations of value conceptions. C. L. McGehee, for example, asserts that sociologists often "take great pains to strip away the façades, the myths, and illusions about society which frequently serve vested interests." He claims that teachers "frequently destroy students' lives in that they, as persons, are left not only with nothing of value, they also are unprepared to deal with the world as it is." He wants teachers to focus on students' "spiritual needs," and this leads him, he says, to "speak in terms of God, or a Divine Being, or the Source of Consciousness."[28]

After graduation, my own students report that they have thrived on realistic sociological studies. They became constructive and socially useful, rather than cynical or defeatist. Students who remain or become trapped in narrow definitions of ethical imperatives suffer later when they discover how vested interests exploit their illusions. Maverick marginals dedicated to human welfare more than the conformist mainliners provide a great deal of the ferment and creativity needed in any social scientific discipline and in society. As C. S. Green, III, suggests, students should be taught "techniques by which they can become effective change agents — techniques such as whistle blowing, the organization of principled oppositions, resignations in protest, etc." Their ethical orientation can well benefit, as Green asserts, from a study of "the ethical imperatives in our religious traditions, Constitution, laws, codes of ethics, and bureaucratic rules." They need to inspect and compare these "imperatives" critically so that they can understand their uses and abuses.[29]

Pitirim A. Sorokin worried about the "internal cancers" in many social scientists' value commitments. He called some of them physicalism, thought phobia, quantophrenia, and testomania. Physicalism is aping the physical scientists. Thought phobia points to the fearful adherence to existing hypotheses and the common failure to do fresh explorations and daring analyses. Quantophrenia exaggerates "the prestige of the statistician, the pollster, the builder of 'mathematical models' or 'mathematical robots,' the numerologist and the metrophrenic manipulator of numbers," a "cancer" now further stimulated by the excesses of the "computer revolution." As Sorokin adds, "Being ignorant in the history, theory, methods, and other fundamentals of sociology and psychology," students can still "get their Ph.D. with high honors if they know elementary statistics." Testomania refers to "the doubtful validity of the artificial psychosocial tests" so commonly glorified, the rejection of which is now gaining more support.[30]

Politico-economic ethos and pressures upon social scientists are not illustrated only by McCarthyism and Red Scares, the subsidization of right-wing radical spies on campuses and right-wing radical college papers.[31] They also include subtle day-by-day experiences rewarding conformism and frowning on deviance. As the sociologist Theda Skocpol has it, "The social sciences have been inescapably affected by and implicated in political conflicts and in the vagaries of public policymaking on openly contested issues." She adds that "this situation has made it more difficult than in the case of the natural sciences to construe the social sciences as purely objective and autonomously cumulative forms of knowledge."[32]

What is taken to be respectable and thus pro-establishment propaganda makes more conservative both sociological vocationalists and bureaucrats, above all the "normal" ones. In 1986, for example, the editor of the British journal, *Sociology,* Jennifer Platt, worried that "sociology has a bad image." She says "that the components of that image include the ideas that it is not a serious discipline or is a soft option, that it is politicised/'leftish,' that it uses ugly and unnecessary jargon, that it is not 'relevant' and that it produces unemployable graduates." Whether these contentions are accurate or not, she asserts, "doesn't matter. In this context what matters is that they are felt to be true, or bad things, by people out there."[33]

Platt, like many upset by this dilemma, prescribes principally a stepped-up public relations program as the appropriate response. A part of this response, she suggests, is the "setting of standards," the writing of "ethical codes," the rigidifying of the discipline's professional façade and controls! What an unfortunate but typical solution! Whose standards and for what purposes? And aren't "codes of ethics" too often public relations gadgets? Dedicated social scientists do not need such reminders, and professional associations have notoriously overlooked ethical violations by respected insiders.

Goals: For what or for whom does the sociologist work? As Mills observes, the applied researcher "does not usually address 'the public'; he has specific clients with particular interests and perplexities." As he sees it, this "clearly undermines the idea of objectivity-as-aloofness."[34] This does not mean that the "applied" worker's goals are necessarily less humanist and emancipationist than the unsponsored or otherwise uninvolved in "particular interests and perplexities." The applied social scientist, to remain a scientist and to be something other than a tinkerer or manipulator for a special interest, needs to take care in selecting a sponsor whose goals are similar to his or her own and to place the work in hand in its larger human context. All clients can benefit from seeing themselves and their problems more broadly as well as more accurately.

In general, the goals of sociologists today are not much different from those of social philosophers and social scientists throughout history. Some are committed to contributing to human welfare through the liberating influence of more accurate social knowledge; others merely use a discipline to pursue their own selfish goals. A person who is an entrepreneur or a scientific innovator is characterized by Willard Waller as being "a little readier to act than his [or her] fellows, a little more determined to have his [or her] own way, a little more ruthless in carrying his [or her] projects through." He adds that for such leaders "social patterns are always more or less in the way; that is why the dynamic leader breaks precedents."[35]

One of the strong appeals of both the innovating Max Weber and the rationalizing Talcott Parsons is that both furnish academic bureaucrats with abstract, and consequently vague, "systems" of social thought that appear to order all significant aspects of society. Both have given bureaucratic aspirants pathways to career goals that are socially noncontroversial. They themselves apparently gloried in exemplifying the bureaucratic role model. During World War I, at the age of fifty, Weber "was commissioned as a disciplinary and economic officer, a captain in charge of establishing and running nine hospitals in the Heidelberg area." During more than a year in that capacity, Captain Weber took a "social apparatus . . . of dilettantes" and labored and "witnessed its transformation into an ordered bureaucracy."[36] Parsons exemplified similar routinizing talents and goals when, after serving as president of the American Sociological Association, he assumed the job of its secretary in a reorganization and became during

1965–67 the first editor of its "trade" journal, *The American Sociologist.*[37]

Communication involves problems of rhetoric, style, and the characteristics of available media. The sociologists of what Sorokin called the "mechanized research industry" with its "vast army of 'research factory hands'" do not need to concern themselves with communication to more than a limited market. When the publicizing of their products beyond the ranks of their customers appears to be required, commercial public relations specialists step in to do the job. But then this army "has not enriched our knowledge by many new discoveries or verities," as Sorokin adds.[38] But it has helped to give substance to special interest propaganda.

Rhetoric is defined as "the ability to use language effectively" and also as "the undue use of exaggeration and display" and "the art of influencing the thought and conduct of an audience."[39] When "effectively" means clearly and understandably, sociologists often lack that ability. A distinctive vocabulary and quantification are thought to be more useful for the building of professional stature than "journalism"! As Sorokin asserts, "the language of modern sociology has become a sort of jargon devoid of elegance, as well as clarity." He mentions especially "a blind transference of terms and formulas from the natural sciences," the "ponderously obscure description of platitudes" that gives them "an appearance of profundity and originality," and "the introduction of many neologisms which hinder precise communication and the understanding of ideas."[40]

The principal competing styles are those of literary clarity, stilted "scientific" terminology, and pretentious arrays of statistics. Of these, the second and third are usually regarded as carrying the greatest authority. C. Wright Mills[41] reminds us of the awe in which the 555 pages of Talcott Parsons'[42] *The Social System* are held. He then points out that its translation "into about 150 pages of straight-forward English . . . would not be very impressive." Mills also admits how imposing are statistics based upon "some thousand hour-long interviews, carefully coded and punched," but he observes: "If you have ever seriously studied [them] for a year or two, . . . you will have begun to see how very malleable the realm of 'fact' may really be."[43]

How convenient it is to hide unsatisfactory aspects of theory or research findings behind a precise-sounding façade of professional rhetoric! But in their writings, vocationalists have to remain reasonably flexible and adaptable and not become overly concerned with organizational security. Thus, as Irving Louis Horowitz points out, the vocation-centered look upon "the drive to build up security as in fact a move toward bureaucratization . . . a violation of the scientific ethos."[44]

Fortunately the discipline has had many creative and literate scientists and writers such as C. H. Cooley, Willard Waller, A. W. Gouldner, and Erving Goffman whose communicating skills do not compromise their accuracy or their wisdom.

Comparative Utility of the Four Focuses

The foregoing discussion may have given the impression that only those social scientists who are dedicated to innovation are to be considered seriously as sociologists and are to be emulated. In spite of this implication, sociology and other scientific disciplines require specialists with each of the four types of aspiration, identification, and autonomy, as well as a range of ethnic, class, national, and more uniquely personal differences in orientation.

Entrepreneurs develop support for novel types of investigation, for new trends in a discipline, and for new applications of scientific findings. They upset vested interests as well as support them and offer new inducements to productivity.

Bureaucrats make possible the programs of our academic departments, research institutes, colleges, and professional societies. They furnish necessary administrative and organizational knowledge, dedication, and stability.

Technicians, skilled in social-scientific procedures and findings, make possible the replications of research, the applications of findings, and the training of more technicians who become the principal media for the polishing, transmission, and use of a field's products.

The innovators not only develop the great bulk of fresh "merchandise," but they also share responsibility with the entrepreneurs for keeping a field somewhat shaken up and thus vital and relevant to the needs of society.

No one needs to feel downgraded by these labels. The labels can merely be brushed aside, as they constantly are in practice. At any rate, the lion's share of prestigious jobs, titles, and other rewards goes to the entrepreneurs, bureaucrats, and technicians in any social-scientific field. As in the churches and the arts, the innovators receive their rewards from the enjoyment of their work or in anticipation of later recognition.

In social science we need greater mutual understanding, tolerance, and recognition of mutual usefulness among the adherents of these four diverse value orientations — the entrepreneurial, the bureaucratic, the technical, and the innovative. This would eliminate a lot of unnecessary professional planning, would assure each discipline of more dynamic development, and would certainly serve better the interests of people generally. The intolerance among the adherents of these four viewpoints in any field is at times shocking. Recognition of a discipline's multivalent motivational and organizational needs could result in a greater sense of autonomy for members of the four groups.

Humanist Dimensions

The orientations of scientists, technicians, bureaucrats, and entrepreneurs can also be humanist-existential. This orientation calls for a people-centered sociology in the service of human needs and goals as they are popularly perceived and defined. Since it is not elitist and manipulative in its value adhesions, it is not attractive as an instrument to many power seekers and their eager assistants. The humanist-existential orientation is supported by those who justify and reward sociological research activity as an important allocation of energies for the guidance and enrichment of life in society. Its adherents find their rewards in the contributions they can make to formal and informal education and as technicians or entrepreneurs forwarding the work of socially constructive interest groups.

Humanist-existentialism characterizes the high road of social thought in our society. In relating themselves to it, sociologists come to terms with social philosophers, historians, and bellettrists as well as other humanist social scientists. It asks that all possibly useful contributors be looked upon as relevant regardless of the label on the contributor.[45]

Some of the sociologists whose work served to develop the problematic-technical paradigm did even more to nurture humanist-existential viewpoints. Contributors include many stalwarts of the past as well as contemporaries who tend to be relatively individualistic investigators and writers. Examples of the latter are Rudolfo Alvarez, Mary Jo Deegan, Walda Katz Fishman, Jan Fritz, Herbert J. Gans, Elliott Liebow, Joan Moore, Joseph Scimecca, and Jerold M. Starr. They also number authors of successful student-oriented textbooks, such as Beth B. Hess, Robert E. Kennedy, Jr., Elizabeth W. Markson, and Peter J. Stein. Important contributors also embrace the works of such nonsociologists as the philosopher John Dewey, the psychologists Gordon Allport, Erik H. Erikson, and William James, the cultural anthropologists Ruth Benedict, Franz Boas, Marvin Harris, A. L. Kroeber, Margaret Mead, and W. L. Warner, the economists Edward S. Herman and Don Cole, and the political scientists Frances Fox Piven and Richard Cloward.

This exuberance about certain promulgators of humanist-existential viewpoints must carry with it a caveat: Like all other terms in social science, humanist and existential are subject to a multiplicity of definitions, some of them far from the intent of the present usage. Just calling some piece of allegedly sociological erudition "humanist" does not make it potentially useful to human concerns. Just attaching "existential" to some philosophical gamesmanship does not make it an acceptable interpretation of events. Hopefully the discussion of the humanist-existential viewpoint offered here accurately communicates the concept as it is used in this work.

When confronted by embarrassing data involving the concerns of important vested interests, bureaucratic-managerial sociologists can retreat into lofty and abstract systems theory. Problematic-technical sociologists at a similar juncture can conveniently change their focus by referring to considerations of relevance and research technique. But the humanist-existential community among sociologists expects its members to face as fully as they are able the relevant implications —wherever they may be found—of social control, conflict, and exploitation. They need to probe the significance of degradation, degeneracy, creativity, and nobility. This also means trying to understand individual, group, and societal multivalences—related as they are to hypocrisy, the generation gap, the credibility gap in public affairs, sexism, racism, and mature adjustment.

Social pressures to meet such challenges arise, for perceptive sociologists who are existential humanists, from our society's idealistic definition of the moral behavior expected of our scholars, scientists, bellettrists, teachers, and other professionals.

At the present time in our society we do a rather good job of developing vast numbers of well-trained and well-motivated bureaucrats and technicians. They are considered "normal." As citizens in the vastly expanded Rome of our century, we need both bureaucrats and technicians in great quantities and in many disciplines in order to operate our huge and complex society. We also need entrepreneurs and innovators in our disciplines. Many of our spokespeople admit this, but we often get such deviants chiefly by accident, largely in spite of our efforts to make instruments rather than to nurture autonomous leaders. Our most dependable sources of entrepreneurs and innovating scientists sufficiently autonomous to succeed in their difficult careers are individuals and groups who have been wrenched away from their social matrices and forced to cope with new social situations, new cultural patterns, and new social challenges. Marginality, chiefly due to such forced cultural mixing, gives us much of the invention, novelty, borrowing, and thus adaptation to be found in society. At the same time, it needs to be added, it also stimulates less desirable and even disastrous individual and social deviations.

As long as our latter-day Rome produces creative marginal people and also siphons off the similarly creative from other countries and does not frustrate them, perhaps the stimulation of the kinds of autonomy that foster scientific, artistic, and other sorts of innovation may be left to chance and accidents. The time may come, however, as it did for ancient Rome, when — as Edward Gibbon tells us — we will realize how the transmission of systems of thought

> with blind deference from one generation of disciples to another, precluded every generous attempt to exercise the powers, or enlarge the limits, of the human mind. The beauties of the poets and orators, instead of kindling a fire like their own, inspired only cold and servile imitations: . . . and the decline of genius was soon followed by the corruption of taste.[47]

The growing pall of orthodoxy over course work in the social sciences suggests that we also may already have developed an uncritical deference to established methods and theories. We, too, are inspiring many "cold and servile imitations."[48] Our compilers and commentators create a sense of activity with their vast piles of books and papers. As Hans Mauksch indicates, our "educational institutions move toward bureaucratic format." This transfers "the control of teaching . . . slowly but persistently from collegial to administrative structures." The professors thus change from "an academic status to an employee status."[49] The education critic Paul Von Blum also demonstrates how our research-oriented institutions of higher learning have increasingly come to "care little about their educational mission."[50]

Why aren't we doing more to exercise the powers and to enlarge the limits of the human mind? If one delves into the many offbeat, radical, and critical periodicals in social science and related fields, one may feel at least somewhat encouraged.[51]

For all the efforts of established elites to maintain the hegemonies they have over their cults, pressures are democratizing social science as well as society. The vertical invasion of the masses, the shrinkage and integration of the world, and the many human and environmental threats of humankind's actual extinction are all joining to make the young and the young at heart realize more vividly than ever that it isn't even safe to "play life safe." The clouds of McCarthyism and of Reaganomics will pass, but the persisting social problems must still be met. To learn about the life of a society and its vitality, do not look to the easily available reports. Look to its focal points of ferment and stimulation. The people at those foci in United States society today echo the creative impulses of Jefferson, Thoreau, Whitman, and other idealists of nonconformity and individuality.

If a scientist can maintain a sense of personal integrity and succeed in jumping a few academic hurdles without losing curiosity, autonomy, imagination, and sense of humor, he or she can be at least as free and productive on the staff of an American university as anywhere in the world — if he or she really wants to be free and productive.

7

Perplexities
of Social Perception

Social science attracts people who hope to find in it some sort of answer or aid. What is the matter with society that I cannot fit it to me, or myself to it? Can anything be done about people's inhumanity to other people? Why do we have authoritarianism and wars? What can be done about degradation in our slums and social isolation in our suburbs? Is there some effective manner in which we can deal with the rising tide of drug abuse? How is it that our only answer to crime is to expand our prisons more and more? And why are their inmates — but not the prevalence of criminals — so lower class? Can anything be done about the pollution of our soil, our water, our atmosphere, and our media of communication? Why do we have plutocracy rather than democracy?

These and other questions about social problems may be easy to state, but to shed light on them requires determined and difficult probing. It becomes more than a desk-centered task, an intellectual exercise to be carried out in a calm atmosphere. It becomes controversial. Relevant facts are likely to be contradictory and infected with special interests, special pleadings, and emotional attachments. Socially entrenched prejudices and influences may prescribe "respectable" conclusions and policy recommendations. These conclusions may or may not be accurate.

Candid and searching descriptions of our social procedures in all their subtleties — how "the games we play" actually take place and for what goals — are not easy to put together. Perceptive social scientists discover that the size and importance of a social situation does not make it more or less obscure or disguised. Self-revelation is difficult. Accurate empathy with others presents a range of difficult problems.

Only those who participate intimately in interaction with children, women, or men can achieve a high degree of empathy with them. Only thus can one learn with some accuracy what takes place, for what alleged and actual reasons and goals, and in what context.

The bigger competitions and struggles in business, politics, professions, academia, churches, trade unions, voluntary societies, and neighborhoods may appear more complex than those of a kindergarten, but such a view chiefly reflects one's inaccurate preconceptions. The chief difference is the number of human units involved. And what one learns in a kindergarten investigation or in studying a teen-age gang can help to understand what such people think and do when they "mature."

If currently acceptable explanations of a social problem were providing an adequate basis for dealing with it, there would be no need for fresh investigation into its nature. As long as a social problem persists as a troublesome aspect of a social situation, continual investigations are needed. Its results are likely to be unsettling to those with vested interests who help to maintain the social problem and who may benefit from the problem's existence.

From all this it may appear that social scientists have chosen a frustrating profession. It may be. It depends upon their commitment and curiosity and their dedication to public service. Social discoveries require both self-liberation and social daring. This is discussed in other chapters in various contexts, especially in connection with sociologists' ideologies and their temptations to accept distorting influences. Given this background, can social science become — often enough — brash, young, vital, productive, unsettling, liberating, even revolutionary? Only thus can it serve people.

The Intimate Obstacle

The chief obstacle investigators confront when they dig deeply into a social problem is not vested interests or social pressures, as great

and powerful as these may be. It is not social resistance to new perceptions of society's character, as deep-seated as this surely is. After all,
there are frequently dissatisfied groups or influential individuals who
will support any given investigation or innovation.

Investigators' chief obstacle is their own lifelong social conditioning. To gain fresh and useful conceptions of any important social problem and its social setting, they have to find ways to overcome that
obstacle.

Many social scientists turn away from the rocky path of creative
investigation because they cannot endure the travail — the culture
shock[1] — of modifying their own intellectual orientation and equipment. In turning away from that rocky path, they may find themselves embraced in the lush appreciation and support given to those
who are called "positive" or "constructive." In this use, positive and
constructive are double-talk words; they refer to being traditional and
protective of vested interests or of the status quo — in other words,
subservient to established "truth" and "authority."

Our society needs to have its problems studied more fundamentally, freely, and accurately. Reference is made to the study of society's
problems rather than the study of society because our lack of accurate
perspectives on problems is most pressing. Learning about how policies do or do not yield social benefits reveals more and more about
the nature of society.

Even though you may not wish to join social scientists in their absorbing and highly important work, it is imperative that as many people as possible understand what they are trying to do and why they
should be encouraged or at least not unduly limited or impeded. Their
distrust of "final truth," no matter how "moral," should be seen as a
useful attitude in the context of social research. It may have more than
experimental value even though in a particular instance it may appear socially irresponsible. In addition, we must assure the socially
constructive uses of intellectual contributions by various professionals
— including physical, biological, and social scientists.[2]

Obstacles and Pathways to Perception

The three preceding chapters discuss social roles of ideologies and
their associated rhetoric or propaganda, their relationship with social
competitions and conflicts. The previous chapter describes ideologi-

cal involvements of the various roles performed by sociologists. This chapter turns again to the social roles of sociologists to examine ways in which their ability to perceive may be colored or clarified. The next two chapters then explore the closely related and enticing distortions of conception that we all need to understand and to avoid.

Personal obstacles and pathways associated with perception of social situations can feature (1) one's degree of alienation or marginality and (2) one's experiences with culture shock. On the social scene, stereotypes of (3) mental abnormality, (4) criminality, (5) social power, control, manipulation, (6) violence and war, (7) social legitimacy, and (8) social setting need to be brushed aside in order to get closer to a perception of realities. And finally, characteristics of available (9) data and of reactions to (10) criticism/innovation can raise crucial scientific problems. Others, such as sexism, racism, and classism are relevant here, but to avoid duplication in discussion, they are treated in the next two chapters as part of distortions of conception.

These are ten difficult perplexities in the sense that traditional conceptions associated with them are common and popular, but they interfere with accurate observation. Scientifically useful pathways past such stereotypes are unorthodox and controversial, and they require courage to follow them. Nonetheless, each of these ten confusing items, and many others not mentioned here, often has to be resolved by scientifically productive investigators in an unconventional manner. Only thus do they find their way past their own emotionally charged intellectual blocks to more tenable and useful social knowledge.

STRANGENESS

Alienation may mean "disenchantment" or "uninvolvement" or "isolation." Traditionally, and especially in legal practice, it is employed to refer to "estrangement" of an owner from her or his possession of real or other property. It also takes on the sense of people becoming separated from their reason, thus "insane." In a law court, a psychiatrist may still be called an "alienist."

In social-scientific usage, alienation refers to estrangement or separation within a personality, of a person from society, and among persons or groups. Karl Marx was concerned with how conditions of labor, including the class structure, alienate industrial workers to an extent both from parts of themselves and from the rest of society.[3] Others have analyzed the significance of contrasts between ethnic or racial groups' appearances and cultures and those of the "main stream," and between individual needs and aspirations and the conformist demands of social organization, of "civilization."[4]

Robert E. Park offered *marginality* as a related term for immigrants who came to share the life and culture of a people other than their own and for those with a cultural duality due to belonging to an ethnic minority or being of mixed racial backgrounds. They are people who find they must live in two societies and be somewhat alienated from both.[5] Everett C. Hughes[6] and others point to the cultural marginality of "mainstream" people that results from multiple group memberships and statuses, a consequence of our society being so multivalent.[7]

These are useful terms when they are understood to refer to actual attitudes and behavior. In addition, a degree of alienation or marginality upon the part of a social scientist can open pathways to more perceptive observation of social situations. How do alienation and marginality provide obstacles to social perception? It is through their transformation into stereotypes of an ethnocentric or class-centric sort.

Some take a sweeping negative position as does Erich Fromm when he asserts: "Alienation as we find it in modern society is almost total; it pervades the relationship of man to his work, to the things he consumes, to the state, to his fellow men, and to himself. Man has created a world of man-made things as it never existed before. . . . The more powerful and gigantic the forces are which he unleashes, the more powerless he feels himself as a human being."[8] A wide range of writings avers that modern society is "inaccessible because of its remoteness, formidable from its heavy structures of organization, meaningless from its impersonal complexity."[9]

These vague and speculative assertions suggest that alienation has now become for many the successor as well as the antithesis of faith in "progress," a notion held for several centuries.[10] Built upon "progress," alienation can be another vague and value-charged word. Popular writers become involved in such ideas. They color their perceptions. Hopefully, social scientists will try carefully to avoid enmeshment in popular fantasies labeled by such terms. They do not prejudge their data so optimistically as the progressivists or so pessimistically as the alienationists.

Many assertions of "alienation" are simply and accurately translated as contentions that members of some "problem" group are at odds with the spokesperson's value orientation or conception of societal legitimacy or ideas about appropriate social-action procedures.

That members of another group may have a value orientation that they look upon as satisfying or useful (whether it be "rational" or "irrational" by our standards) is not within the focus of "alienation" in many cases. This usage tends to carry a judgment from one social viewpoint. In other words, what is gained by cynical or blasé or even "professional" oldsters calling cynical or blasé youngsters "alienated" or "marginal" unless the term is used objectively and with understanding? Stereotyped people become quite different after one spends enough time with them to develop some perception of the way they act, think and live![11]

In contrast with the generations of work-enslaved rural and urban workers from whom we are mostly descended,[12] a great many people are now amazingly autonomous, perceptive, and sensitive to their needs, desires, and relationships. Traditional allegiances are more subject to test, examination, and possible modification or replacement. We do have a burgeoning underclass of deprived people, unemployed and underemployed, and this is a crucial problem, but the vast majority in this country no longer face a primitive struggle to survive. Many of us are learning under the stimulus of nuclear and other threats that our fate is social in the broad sense of being tied to the fate of humanity. It is becoming socially more pervasive and binding than the exploitative relationships of our worldwide market economy. "Alienation" or "marginality" does not inevitably and continuingly separate or segregate people. Either has its problems, but it also enriches us with more cultural diversity and social ferment.

IN REACTION TO THE DIFFERENT

Culture shock presents a dilemma in popular perception that most people try to avoid except as a titillating or annoying aspect of tourism. When faced as part of the price of migration, its impact may be softened by finding a like-minded community. In contrast, a social scientist in search of new knowledge about an important social problem has to be prepared to experience it — sometimes in difficult depth.

What is culture shock? In an extreme form, and one to be anticipated, culture shock is the emotional reaction of a person living in a society very different from her or his own. It is like being dependent upon a pair of glasses — the comprehensive culture of one's native society — and then losing or breaking them and trying to get along with someone else's pair. Suddenly everything is out of focus, and it requires continual effort to perceive everyday affairs with some accuracy. As the anthropologist Philip K. Bock says, "Genuine culture shock is largely an emotional matter; but it also implies the attempt to *understand* an alien way of life, by choice or out of necessity. Since human society began, immigrants, refugees, and all kinds of travelers have been subject to varying degrees of culture shock."[13]

One or more experiences with culture shock in an alien land are valuable conditioning for any social scientist, but experiences with culture shock are also possible in conducting social-scientific field research in one's own country. When we travel about the United States, we tend to conclude that the population is very homogenized. Whether in Beverly Hills, California, Chicago, or Garden City, Long Island, they are considered much the same, varied only a little by those who have recent immigrant backgrounds or a different color. This is largely because we tend to associate with our "own sort" as we move about the country. We do not get really different perspectives on human society unless we are looking for it or by accident.

When students from middle-class homes go into either less or more privileged homes to interview people at some length, they experience a degree of culture shock. Out of that confusing and even painful experience, whether or not the students intend to become professional social scientists, comes a new understanding both of other people and of themselves. When white students go into nonwhite communities, the extent to which they suffer from culture shock becomes a fair measure of their intellectual and emotional gain. Often nonwhite and other ethnic minority students have already had such experiences to an excessive degree before coming to a college.

This reminds one of Fiorello H. LaGuardia's being "forced to learn the ancient art of protective coloration . . . as a condition of survival" early in his life. The person who later became a spectacular mayor of New York City "was to be roughly transplanted, several times, and each time he was to flourish more strongly than ever before." He had "to adapt himself to new environments and to use in unfamiliar surroundings the experiences he had acquired elsewhere." Even though this became a "key to a successful career," it was "the hardest lesson any youngster has to learn."[14]

To perceive living conditions of the ethnically and racially different, of the occupationally contrasting, and also of the mentally retarded, damaged, and disturbed, should be part of everyone's education. It is an essential aspect of a social scientist's education.

Social scientists whose research is abstract and thus often superficial appear never to have experienced the confusing wealth of strange and exciting data from which culture shock can arise. A long list of the most distinguished contributors to our knowledge of social problems in particular, and of human society more generally, includes *only* those who experienced culture shock in their own society or through migration. To inquiring social scientists, culture shock presents no dilemma. They know they must seek it.[15]

TO LOOK BEYOND NORMALITY

Mental abnormality presents a related dilemma in perception, understanding, and research. Here the investigator has to face contrasts between popular oversimplifications and dogmatisms on the one hand and the infinite and subtle variability of human beings and their living conditions on the other.

In terms of popular stereotypes, mental abnormality is an absolute matter: One is either "sane" or "crazy"; one is either "normal" or "insane." That is a comforting notion for the many who are socially labeled as being sane or normal and who cling to that satisfying designation, but it is inaccurate. As social investigators Marjorie Hope and James Young see this stereotyping in the case of the homeless, "They are the reflection of our own insecurity. . . . They are the face of our loneliness. They remind us of how estranged we have become from one another."[16] Stereotyping protects people from such realizations.

With mental abnormality, as elsewhere, social scientists have to look beyond stereotypes. They have to try to face social realities more intimately, with less preconception, and more precisely. To call strange behavior "abnormal" or an "illness" may be a serious prejudgment that distorts perception.[17] From cross-cultural comparisons, we are learning how variable "normal" human behavior may be.[18] Psychotherapists attempt to interrelate and intercommunicate with unhappy and unsuccessful people who come to them. They do not assume that such people are "sick" and try to "treat" them. Psychologists have learned that great strides may be made in understanding through attempting to perceive and interpret accurately how the deviant person sees himself or herself.[19]

Detailed psychological study is not the task of the sociologist as such, but sociologists need a perspective on deviant and typical mental behavior that psychologists can make available. Sociologists can thus probe more adequately into the social contexts and significance of deviance. For example, they can explore why "the lowest social classes have the highest rates of severe psychiatric disorders in our society."[20] They need to approach the deviants curiously and perceptively and not blinded by popular stereotypes.

TO PROBE THE CRIMINAL STEREOTYPE

Criminality occasions confusion similar to that accompanying the foregoing. Once again the challenge to perception arises from the contrast between popular oversimplification and dogmatism on the one hand and the infinite and subtle variability of human life on the other.

According to popular stereotypes, crime is an absolute matter: One is either honest or dishonest, a dependable person or part of a "bad lot." Juvenile delinquency in a "fine family" is brushed aside as "wild oats," not to be taken seriously. Comparable delinquency—legally defined—among members of a "bad lot" requires police action, judicial process, and perhaps a reform school. The tendency to extend the "bad lot" stereotype indefinitely to members of underprivileged ethnic and racial minorities is part of the persecution to which such minorities are subject. It helps to build up a disproportionate number of police arrests and judicial records of juvenile delinquency and crime among the depressed.

Crime is an action or a negligence defined by law as injurious to public welfare or morality or the interests of the state. It is an offense against the criminal law as currently interpreted and implemented. This definition may be good enough for some legal purposes, but it presents great problems to the social scientist who is trying to learn about the nature of human behavior, whether or not the behavior is called "criminal."

Of those who commit criminal acts, who gets caught? Relatively few. Of those who are apprehended and charged with crime, who are convicted? Of those who are convicted of any given offense, who are not subsequently pardoned or paroled? What kind of sense do either the processes of our cluttered courts or our noncorrective prisons make? Those who actually serve time in a penitentiary and who are fairly well informed about the behavior of a circle of acquaintances are often bitter that they should be among the relatively few (guilty or not) "losers" and not among the many whose similar behavior did not—because of connived "good luck"—become the basis of conviction. Underclass and ethnic minority prisoners also brood on the class-ridden character of "the system." They know that "white collar" offenders get much different treatment.

Social scientists certainly do not apologize for antisocial behavior or try to justify it. They also realize they cannot approach the study of even the least consequential — not to mention the disastrous and obnoxious — aspects of human behavior equipped chiefly with simplistic popular stereotypes. Any adequate approach to what is called criminal or delinquent behavior has to be with as much unprejudiced curiosity and clear perception as possible. It must consider such a range of behavior as "wild oats," fee-splitting among professionals, the payment and acceptance of a variety of bribes under many guises, tax evasion, price-fixing conspiracies by merchants and manufacturers, deliberate or negligent mislabeling of commodities that cover up inferior or adulterated ingredients. It also can mean "quiet understandings" to deny access to jobs and housing on the basis of gender, ethnic, and racial background, "insider trading" and illegal manipulations of the stock and bond markets, spouse-battering, child-molesting, and use of governmental agencies or private operatives to dominate or topple a foreign government for private gain. Some of these and other acts are more costly to society than all the depredations of second-story thieves and other types of small-time burglars and pickpockets combined.[21]

In addition to the distractions posed by popular stereotypes and by legal definitions and decisions, social scientists also confront the enticements of the sensational theories making up media criminology. Plausible journalists portray that organized crime is largely in the hands of an international Italian conspiracy based in New York City, New Jersey, or Sicily and called the Mafia.[22] Myth-making about Mafia conspiracy has been damaging to Italian-Americans who have no connections whatsoever with organized crime, and it has not resulted in the kind of governmental action the myths appear to demand.[23] Above all, the involvements of "legitimate" business and political operators in organized crime rarely reach the mass media. Social scientists have to look behind and beyond journalistic red herrings in order to perceive the realities of organized crime with its *interpenetration* of political organizations and governmental agencies (local, state, federal, international) and legitimate businesses (local, state, national, international.)[24]

Aided and abetted by publicity-seeking officials, journalists can find crime waves, or waves of some particular kind of crime, almost any time they need a headline story. Really dependable and comparable statistics on crime are not to be obtained. One standard text contends: "Crime statistics are among the most unreliable and questionable social facts."[25] Another asserts that "they do not represent the total volume of crime."[26] Another notes: "People create crime and people produce information about it."[27] Even "alternative sources of information on the crime problem" developed by criminologists, according to still another text, are "subject to shortcomings and limitations of their own."[28]

TO AVOID A FAUSTIAN "COP-OUT"

Social power, control, and manipulation are elements in the biggest games played with the greatest seriousness and absorption for the highest stakes in society. Naturally, information about how such games are played is not readily available, and those who are pawns, or even knights, in such games usually have little knowledge of the larger contexts to which they contribute and which define their careers. An outline of how the typical social manipulator works is set forth in the fifth chapter and related there to how people can defend themselves against such operations. Social power, control, and manipulation are presented here as dilemmas to perception that social scientists have to face. To remain scientific, they cannot take the Faustian cop-outs discussed in the previous chapter on sociological ideologies. They cannot sacrifice their scientific ideals to achieve selfish goals.

The nature of social power, control, and manipulation is largely obscured behind the façades of institutions and other organizations. Social scientists thus face the dilemma of whether to accept the façades as definitions of reality or to probe behind them. To understand society's dynamics, and especially how efforts at social action succeed or fail, social scientists have to penetrate those façades as best they can. They proceed by observing and analyzing basic raw materials and procedures used by manipulators — public opinions, organizational structures, personnel, mass-communications media, propaganda content and context, and overall and more specific strategies. Where many people commonly consider such matters to be parts of the "going order" of society that are not to be questioned, social scientists may have to look at relevant aspects of society in the same manner as does a power operator. This enables the scientists to understand as fully as they can how such a person may achieve goals. This may mean to regard all aspects of society—for the sake of perception only—as *matériel* more or less available to manipulators and utilized by them.

The predicament here is whether to accept society merely as it appears to be, as do most human beings, or to come to a conclusion close to or beyond that of the great journalist Lincoln Steffens. As a young man visiting the California state legislature, Steffens was amazed at the contrast between what the legislature was supposed to be and what it actually was—a no-holds-barred arena in which people played for very high stakes. His immediate reaction was, "Nothing was what it was supposed to be."[29] With greater maturity, he realized that such social organizations had to be seen as fitting into many different contexts and interpretations, not just into one public and one intimate one.[30] It depends upon whether one looks at a legislature's societal façade, as described in public-school textbooks, at the political power game Steffens saw at Sacramento, at larger financial, industrial, political, and even criminal struggles in which participants are able to utilize legislators and the legislative process for their purposes, or at the bureaucratic struggles and conspiracies in government that depend upon legislative actions and contribute to them.

Plutocracy: As the literary historian Vernon L. Parrington points out, Charles A. Beard's *An Economic Interpretation of the Constitution* contains a view "that unsympathetic readers were quick to attribute to Karl Marx, but that in reality derived from sources far earlier and for Americans at least far more respectable." Beard described how the American government was formed and controlled by economic groups. This is a plutocratic conception that "goes back to Aristotle," Parrington notes, and it "shaped the conclusions of Madison and Hamilton and John Adams."[31]

As economic controls developed and concentrated, especially after the Civil War, liberal intellectualism did not crumple and disappear, but its dedicated adherents found themselves having to deal with more and more effective hirelings of vested interests. As Parrington adds, liberals had "the problem of the subjection of property to social justice," a struggle in which too often they "underestimated the strength of the enemies of democracy."

This recalls the realism with which William G. Sumner in the late 1880s assessed the ravages of plutocracy in our society. He said:

> A plutocrat is a man who, having the possession of capital, and having the power of it at his disposal, uses it, not industrially, but politically; instead of employing laborers, he enlists lobbyists. Instead

of applying capital to land, he operates upon the market by legislation, by artificial monopoly, by legislative privileges; he creates jobs, and erects combinations, which are half political and half industrial; he practices upon the industrial vices, makes an engine of venality, expends his ingenuity, not on processes of production, but on "knowledge of men," and on the tactics of the lobby. The modern industrial system gives him a magnificent field, one far more profitable, very often, than that of legitimate industry. [32]

Since the 1880s, the situation Sumner described has, as he predicted, become more disastrous. Plutocratic power becomes more concentrated and spreads multinationally. Colleges of engineering, business administration, law, communications, and the rest produce carefully honed and servile technicians. Think tanks, pressure groups and societies, and university research institutes improve the manipulative procedures and facilities of the powerful.

Charles A. and Mary R. Beard in the 1930s worried about "the struggle between the plutocracy and the middle class." If that struggle could not be delimited and "continued endlessly without resolution, what forms were the future relations of the two groups to assume, especially in the presence of labor pressures in town and country?"[33] The middle-class expands, but its members become less autonomous, more servile. The Beards placed their hope in the belief that the "humanistic wing" of American democracy would seek "to provide the economic and cultural foundations indispensable to a free society, by rational methods of examination, discussion, legislation, administration, and cooperation, employing the sciences, letters, and arts in efforts to fulfill the promises of its heritage and aspirations." In these struggles, such ideals do not remain unadapting. They absorb the dynamism of a more participatory and less legalistic sense of democratic process. They retain their central emphasis upon the dignity of the individual and the necessary autonomy of the socially active. As the Beards wisely add, our useful leaders cannot have "illusions about the peril of sheer force and cruelty, exalting the irrational, despising justice and mercy—despite noble professions on all sides."[34]

In speaking of the plutocratic drift in American society, one need not attribute to its operatives the kind of integrated conspiracy of a "power elite" that C. Wright Mills describes. He concludes that "the leading men in each of the three domains of power—the warlords, the corporation chieftains, the political directorate—tend to come together, to form the power elite of America."[35] What unity of viewpoint and operation exists among those in power in American society evolves among a shifting aggregate with sharp interpersonal and intergroup rivalries and conflicts. Whatever apparent or actual agreement prevails among them arises from common orientations bearing upon expedient solutions to current opportunities and problems. Only under the brittle and transient conditions of an authoritarian dictatorship can an elite temporarily appear to form a cohesive and unitary organization.

With the aid of muckraking journalists and disenchanted novelists and essayists, many existential humanists in all the social sciences gradually came to some realization of the seriousness of the maturing plutocratic crisis. If these existential humanists were to continue to accomplish anything substantial, if they were to avoid taking on some special interest's livery themselves, Parrington suggested that they would have to approach social issues "recognizing the masterful ambitions of property, recruiting democratic forces to overmaster the Swiss Guards, leveling the strongholds that property erected within the organic law, and taking care that no new strongholds should arise." Somehow, he hoped, we would achieve "the subjection of property to social justice."[36]

EXAMINING HIGHLY CHARGED ISSUES

Violence and war present social scientists with melodramatic confusion. The conditions are so fraught with emotional attachments and rationalizations that they have destroyed the objectivity of a great many.

Violence and war are so unthinkable to most middle-class intellectuals in peacetime that they do not permit themselves to perceive the extent to which both grow out of the nature of our present socialization processes and out of the general nature of our society. To work toward more adequate understandings of violence and war, social scientists must free themselves from popular prowar and antiwar stereotypes, as well as society's conventional excuses for accepting or rejecting violence. This doesn't mean that either violence or war is necessary in human society or that everyone is violent or warlike. The tremendous student, veteran, and general opposition to the Vietnam War and to United States military actions in Latin America and Africa are more than tokens of our resistance to war as an instrument of international policy and practice. As was mentioned in the fourth chapter, the many outstanding examples of successful nonviolent resistance in recent decades, even in the face of violence, indicate how strongly many people are coming to reject violence in social action.

Social scientists cannot go along with popular thinking that all unauthorized violence is uniformly evil and authorized violence is justifiable. They need to try to see violence — and all social behavior — in context. For example, how did a riot in an urban slum come about? What relationships existed among the slum dwellers and the police, social workers, merchants, employers, and landlords? What are the slum conditions of housing, education, sanitation, personal safety, employment, and racketeering? After police power is used to suppress the riot, will the controlling powers then mitigate the miseries that stimulated the riot, or will they count on the fear of force to prevent a recurrence so that they can forget about the woes of the slum dwellers?

Social scientists cannot go along with hysterical popular thinking about participation in war. They have many questions to ask about any war and especially about our constant preoccupation with war, about the extent to which our sciences, technologies, and education are oriented even in "peacetime" toward war.

WHAT DOES IT COST TO "BELONG"?

Social legitimacy is a term closely associated with social power and control, but it requires separate treatment because it presents sociologists with a separate perceptual dilemma. It refers to established rules, principles, or standards, the pattern of domination and control that a society appears to sanction at a given time. Max Weber suggests that there are "three inner justifications, hence basic *legitimations* of domination," the traditional, the legalistic, and the charismatic, and these types are likely to be mixed.

Traditional legitimacy is derived from "the authority of the 'eternal yesterday.'" It consists of customary rights, privileges, and controls long associated with certain social statuses and actions. It gives power to tribal patriarch or chieftain or king who presumes to rule by divine right. Shadows of such legitimacy persist in many democratic organizations.

Legalistic legitimacy depends upon the validity and reasonableness of existing legal specifications of controls associated with statuses and actions. Such legitimacy gives power to "servants of the state" who now commonly rule as a result of election or appointment. Such rulers are often also somewhat traditional or charismatic.

Charismatic legitimacy is the authoritative status given to some by their personal possession of an extraordinary "gift of grace" or merely by their assumption of a prestigious office. The gift or attribution inspires confidence and even devotion. Individually it may depend upon alleged revelation, heroism, or charm.[37] Charismatic legitimacy gave power to Gandhi, Eisenhower, and Martin Luther King, Jr., on the one hand, and to Cromwell, Adolf Hitler, and Ronald Reagan on the other.

Social legitimacy is much more than popular acceptance of a pattern of justified domination through which the head of a state or a corporation rules. It is the whole fabric of respected power and control relationships with which accepted members of society or of an organization or community identify themselves. It gives a sense of belonging and security and of identity. It is what outsiders often call the "establishment" and its hangers-on. Those who cannot make it into the "establishment" may try to achieve a degree of prestige and control in terms of a subsidiary or minority or even illegal identity.

What is the dilemma of social scientists in this connection when they try to study social problems keenly and precisely? Don't they want their work to be recognized as a legitimate part of societal endeavors? Shouldn't social scientists strive for the personal and professional influence that comes from acceptance as legitimate, as defining social problems as the established power structure sees them? These are difficult questions for a great many.

The perplexing problem here is that social scientists have to be as accurate and probing in their studies of the socially legitimate as they are when investigating the socially illegitimate and the unrecognized. They cannot let the reward potential distort their perception and their judgment. They can only build reputations for autonomous integrity, the basis of durable scientific contributions.

TO AVOID A LIMITING CONTEXT

Social setting influences one's perception of the nature of a given social problem. The complex and interrelated networks of society create social problems with a range of vested interests, some of them quite unanticipated.

As long as one sticks to superficial symptoms of a social problem, the relevant social setting can apparently be limited. Terrorist bombers in Belfast, Paris, or Beirut are killed or imprisoned, but have the law enforcement authorities solved the problem? What recommendations for public policy might come from a comprehensive investigation of those terrorists' social setting? Are the offenders evil individuals, or are they parts of a protest organization that will continue to endanger public safety? How justifiable are the goals, if not the methods, of a given protest movement? Do other groups of people exist who sympathize with and even support the "terrorists," yet utilize peaceful networks to accomplish the same goals? Would it be possible to take steps toward accommodating the protesters' demands? Would it be worthwhile to enough people?

What about activities of the "underworld"? Is the drug menace due to a growing demand for narcotics to be coped with through penalizing or educating the users? Or is the vast narcotics industry nurturing a growing market for its products? What would be involved in stamping out traffic in stolen goods? In the enlarging underclass of unemployed and underemployed people, what recourse other than illegal means do people have available in order to try to meet their needs and aspirations?

Social settings undergo continual change. In making an analysis of a conflict, is it being seen in relationship to its actual — not romanticized — historical setting? This often means placing current propagandistic contentions in a very different perspective.

HOW "HARD" CAN FACTS BE?

Data are the raw materials with which social scientists construct their theories or find ways to correct or modify them. Data include "facts," described popularly as anything taken to be accurate or "true." For scientific purposes, data include carefully collected and defined facts and their contexts — their changing social settings.

Traditionally, social observation has consisted chiefly of what has come to be called fieldwork or participant observation, together with surveys, in-depth interviews, and other documents. Both sociology and ethnology originally depended heavily upon firsthand observation of individual behavior and social situations. Since anthropology has exotic tribes and archeological remains to give it an unquestioned "scientific" label, ethnologists continue to depend upon firsthand field observations. Sociologists, however, lack that easy basis for a claim to scientistic "respectability." They therefore seize upon sample surveys based primarily on formula interviews to give them the quantities of statistical material needed to establish their resemblance to physicists and biologists. As the sociologist Jerold M. Starr notes, "The intoxication with the 'scientific method' has led social scientists to increasingly complicated analyses of increasingly trivial phenomena."

Censuses, social surveys, and controlled social experiments in "laboratories" are useful, and they will continue to be so, but, as Starr adds, "the participant observation method has left a rich legacy of community, organizational, and life history studies that have contributed substantially to the development of sociological theory. Moreover, students still receive training in this method in various graduate programs from Boston to Los Angeles."[38] The sociologist Herbert Blumer contends that "exploratory inquiry is not pinned down to any particular set of techniques." He calls for "direct observation, interviewing of people, listening to their conversations, securing life-history accounts, using letters and diaries, consulting public records, arranging for group discussions, and making counts of an item if this appears worthwhile." He urges that researchers "sedulously seek participants in the sphere of life who are acute observers and who are well informed." A discussion group of such individuals "is more valuable many times over than any representative sample."[39]

The statistician assumes that items grouped in categories are comparable, but to what extent does a given procedure ignore significant variations within each group? What happens to an observation when it becomes a unit in a summation, taken out of context? Blumer warns, too, about "the ease with which observation becomes and remains imprisoned by images," a problem that should surely haunt statisticians even more than it does fieldworkers.

The answer to this perception dilemma is to insist upon trying a variety of approaches, and, as Blumer suggests, "to ask oneself all kinds of questions . . . even seemingly ludicrous questions." This "helps to sensitize the observer to different and new perspectives."

The perception of data, as Blumer reminds us, demands "a high order of careful and honest probing, creative and disciplined imagination, resourcefulness and flexibility in study, pondering over what one is finding, and a constant readiness to test and recast one's views and images of the area." Data are not "soft" for the reason that they are not quantified or part of a "premapped scientific protocol."[40] As we have seen in connection for example with crime statistics, figures can be "soft," and considerable evidence exists as to the "hardness"—the verifiability—of conclusions based upon careful and critical participant observation.

Criticism/innovation are both sweet and sour. Social scientists critically evaluate the merits or shortcomings of widely held theories based on the facts they collect. When they are diplomatic and take a constructive viewpoint, they are praised; they are saying what people want to hear. But the grubbing for significant and more accurate observations and concepts does not always mix with diplomacy. A social scientist investigating ethnic segregation or the pollution of the mass-communications media needs to understand — without being seduced by — the feelings and vested interests behind real-estate salespeople's segregation tactics or bankers' ethnic biases, or television or newspaper operators' propaganda motives. Social scientists have to "tell things like they are." That sometimes means "whistle blowing" on social abuses. That is their job. Only in that way can they give us more accurate, less prejudiced conceptions of social life.

Innovation, as popularly viewed, is a similarly tricky problem. When most parents use the word creative at all, they identify it as success in material gain, secure position, and perhaps prestige. They want their children to excel by following a beaten path. But in the social sciences, as in the physical and biological sciences, the fine arts, and the humanities, success means to be innovative; creative means to be upsetting, waybreaking; to be highly creative means to be iconoclastic. Creativity in science demands having respect only for ideas that can be verified and by trying to replace other ideas with more tenable and accurate ones. In social science this may require the development and testing of remarkably extraordinary hypotheses about child-raising, marriage, crime, or about intergroup and interpersonal relations in a corporation, a school, or a church. These are rarely the sorts of opportunities or exploits that parents have in mind for their children. The scientifically creative can follow beaten paths only to move out to the edges of existing knowledge. From there, they set forth on their own. They are not mere scholars, elaborately schooled in what is already known. They are avid to go where human minds have not previously succeeded in penetrating.

Most of us have grown up being taught the virtues of diplomacy, of being constructive and positive, of not being offensive to others, especially to those in authority. Such teachings make for pleasant, noncontroversial relations with other people. Social scientists need to maintain a pleasant approach toward other people. But, at the same time, they cannot permit politeness and caution to color or obscure the results of their research. They must look with skepticism at all existing research methods, facts, concepts, and theories relevant to their work. They must be careful to explore theories or hunches that they may at first think are absurd. Their efforts consist of the criticism and modification, as well as the amplification, of existing knowledge.[41]

Two Hopeful Concepts

The consideration of these ten perplexities to social perception and of ways in which social scientists resolve them has hopefully demonstrated these two concepts:

Suggested on one hand is the extent to which social scientists must realize that they are their own most important instrument in the study of social problems. They must know that instrument as well as possible — not an easy job. And they must use it as precisely and as wisely as they can in their pursuit of scientific goals.

On the other hand are issues of broader significance among these perplexities. Must these sorts of intellectual and emotional experiences be of service only to the professional social scientist? The answer to that question recurs frequently in the writings of leading educational theorists. Liberal education should help all of us to achieve objectivity, sensitivity, and empathy with those quite different from ourselves. It should provide ways of penetrating social façades and other barriers as are suggested here and in the next two chapters. By knowing other people more intimately and accurately, we can come to understand ourselves better. By learning more about ourselves, we can discover how to use our senses more empathically in our effort to understand others.

8

Enticing Distortions

Families, schools, workplaces, and other social environments typically include confrontations, struggles, and conflicts as well as friendly and supportive relationships. All of these—together with public events, gossip, and presentations in the media—shape our attitudes toward life and living. From such experiences we accumulate accurate perceptions as well as enticing distortions that mold and tint our attitudes and behavior patterns.

When such influences are distorting, they can lead even trained social scientists to help perpetuate them. They can exaggerate the significance of such symptoms as "terrorism" and underworld or upperworld crime and can encourage the ignoring of their settings and causes. They can push researchers to take solace in noncontroversial theoretical abstractions and methodological routines.

The activities of humanist social scientists who do not yield to such influences are often quite different. They dig into society's destructive oppressions and manipulations, and they do what they can to help people live more satisfactorily.

Distorting influences simplify for some and complicate for others the ways in which they attempt to answer these questions: What is my "proper" ideological orientation? What is my actual personal ideological position? Do I have one? What items should a professional's package of tools and procedures contain? For whom should work be done? How do wise social action policies likely differ from social scientific analyses — when they do? Should there ever — as a practical matter — be any contrast between the two? In what respects?

Answers to these questions are often complicated or distorted by enticing notions social scientists acquired in their personal backgrounds. These are numerous enough. The ones I will discuss in this chapter are these: Those that glorify elites or utopias. Others that promise to change all or part of society in one swoop by making a new "social contract." Many that involve preoccupation with symptoms and ignore a search for causes. Finally are ones that call for pretentious exhibitions of virtuosity with research methods or abstract theories out of touch with adequate observations and other experiences.

A case is often made for each of these notions in terms of social expediency or even "scientific" procedure. The notions are said to help the promotion of a cause or of an ideology or merely of a career. All have been used to justify professional and popular cults. Upon (1) orthodoxy, (2) legitimacy, (3) elitism, (4) social contractism and utopianism, (5) symptomism, and (6) pedantry have been erected significantly useful as well as inconsequential and disastrous social agitations and movements. Products of orthodoxy, legitimacy, and pedantry include (7) technicianism, (8) opposition to popularization, and (9) resistance to updating. More intimate distorting influences are discussed in the next chapter.

1. Orthodoxy

Orthodox views are those apparently accepted as correct and proper by the people in a community or society who are looked upon as "counting," as having authority or prestige based upon traditional roles, legal status, or charisma.[1] A great many people, with pathetic earnestness, want to have the security of feeling that they are not only "right-thinking," but that they are certified as such through their open agreement with spokespeople for venerated institutions. This quest for respectability becomes both complicated and confusing in our multi-class and multi-ethnic society.

To what extent are orthodox patterns useful and to what extent are they a set of blinders with which to oversimplify life's complexities? Which ones are valuable and which ones overly costly?

The sociologist Patricia Wilner made a revealing analysis of what she called the "consensus bias" or orthodoxy in the articles published in 1936 to 1982 in the *American Sociological Review,* the principal research periodical of the American Sociological Association. She found its authors did not focus "on momentous events such as the Depression, the Cold War, McCarthyism, social movements between the late 1950s and early 1970s, or the decline of the U.S. national economy and global hegemony." In contrast, the orthodoxy of participation in World War II made it "an appropriate topic for sociologists." She presented a detailed account of how "consensus bias . . . dictated which topics were safe, researchable, and publishable." In short, she concluded that the *"ASR* has earned sociology the reputation of being irrelevant."[2]

Fortunately that reputation is offset by books that are reviewed in another ASA periodical, *Contemporary Sociology,* and by articles in the publications of other societies, such as *Social Problems* and *Humanity & Society,* as well as in popular magazines.

Orthodoxy is cluttered with myths, "the value-impregnated beliefs and notions that men [and women] hold, that they live by or live for."[3] Myths are popular, treasured, traditional memories, scenarios, and theories. They carry sanctions derived from religion, family, state, business, science, or merely frequent usage. They may persist long after they have lost whatever social or personal utility they may have had. They may be costly distorters of experience and thought. Propagandists for special interests find some of them useful and some difficult to brush aside.

Life without myth is unthinkable since many myths help us deal with the complexities of life. Some are beautiful; some, ugly and scary. We can talk condescendingly and amusedly about the myths of other people or of our own grandparents, but we prefer not to look critically at our own myths. We rarely examine and sort out our own myths so that we can decide with some objectivity which to keep and which to replace. It is much more comfortable to rationalize and romanticize the retention of outworn myths than to reject them.

Let us look at three examples of orthodox myths that are widely held and are disastrous to teaching and learning: "peace through war," "education through rote learning," and "freedom through subservience." Those who have read George Orwell's novel, *1984,* will note parallelisms between these three tyrannous myths and the three slogans that that author predicts for a dictatorship of the future: "War is peace"— spokespeople for our ever-expanding military-industrial complex allege that their chief concern is peace—albeit quite possibly by way of aggressive military actions. "Ignorance is strength"—don't ask questions; just memorize orthodox "facts" and "principles." "Freedom is slavery"—be "free" through subservience to the people "who get things done."[4]

Peace through war. This is the contention that we can develop a more peaceful world through converging more and more of our energies nationally into the combined military-industrial complex. This is the far-flung international plutocratic imperialism underlying what Henry R. Luce of *Time* newsmagazine once called "The American Century."[5] This network, according to media critic Ben H. Bagdikian, "to a dangerous extent is now the military-media-industrial complex" in consequence of the growing ownership of press, radio, cinema, and television units by some twenty-nine multinational corporate giants.[6] And mergers are diminishing this number!

This network provides enticing opportunities for many who label themselves social scientists. In consequence, as the late President Eisenhower asserted, "the free university, historically the fountainhead of free ideas and scientific discovery, has experienced a revolution in the conduct of research. Partly because of the huge costs involved, a Government contract becomes virtually a substitute for intellectual curiosity."[7] In the social sciences, this led to a decline of social criticism, a rise of interest in counseling the established power-manipulators.

On this point, the academically sophisticated and constructive Senator J. William Fulbright took the same position as do dedicated social scientists. He contends that

> Pentagon-sponsored field [policy] research in counter-insurgency [is not] an appropriate activity for social scientists who ought to be acting as independent and critical commentators on their government's policies. Far from being victims of anti-intellectualism as some of these scholars complain when their activities are criticized, they themselves are perpetuating a virulent form of anti-intellectualism. They do so by contributing to the corruption of their universities, the militarization of American society, and that persistent degradation of values which goes by the polite name of "credibility gap."[8]

Too many social scientists now want to be of service to generals or corporate executives rather than to students, soldiers, housewives, and other rank-and-file citizens. We used to ridicule this tendency among Nazi, Soviet, and Japanese intellectuals. Now we too often embrace it ourselves. We would do well to remember Eisenhower's statement in a speech to the American Society of Newspaper Editors in 1953:

> Every gun that is made, every warship launched, every rocket fired signifies, in the final sense, a theft from those who hunger and are not fed, those who are cold and are not clothed. This world in arms is not spending money alone. It is spending the sweat of its laborers, the genius of its scientists, the hopes of its children. . . . This is not a way of life at all in any true sense. Under the cloud of threatening war, it is humanity hanging from a cross of iron.

Many scientists of all sorts agree in one way or another with the implications of Eisenhower's statement. To illustrate, in 1985, three hundred scientists from thirty countries made a projection of the probable consequences of a post-nuclear-war world under the sponsorship of the Scientific Committee on Problems of the Environment. In it, they point to starvation as the primary cause of death from such a war. "This vulnerability is . . . not currently a part of the understanding of nuclear war," they state, and they add: "Not only are the major combatant countries in danger, but virtually the entire human population is being held hostage to the large-scale use of nuclear weapons."[10]

Education through rote learning. This second myth is that science is the cookbook subject taught in most schools. That it is not the potentially radical and even revolutionary search that it can be to help make our knowledge and our society more youthful, flexible, and vital.

We teach the natural sciences — whether physical, biological, or social — chiefly as systems of established principles. On the contrary, such findings should be seen for what they are — collections of the more or less accurate and inaccurate relics of past research. We need to teach science as an approach, an attitude, a process, a quest for greater sensitivity, for keener perception, for new jumps into reality.

In "science," entrenched or orthodox principles can function as doors locked against innovation and innovators. The personal reminiscences of a black social scientist, Charles V. Hamilton, vividly illustrate this point: "I graduated from Roosevelt [University], I got a law degree from Loyola University and I got a Ph.D. from the University of Chicago. And I am going to tell you very clearly that my education over that twelve- to fifteen-year period was geared toward making me a middle-class black Sambo. Nothing devious in that, and I'm not blaming my professors. It's just that that was their orientation."[11] The principles and pressures that Hamilton resisted effectively shut doors for many who wanted to develop their scientific curiosity.

How many white graduate students are as perceptive? How many ever notice that they are being shaped into mere instruments of academic reproduction and aggrandizement, into white-Sambo technicians? How many fight against that distortion? The difficult experiences of such well known innovators in science as Charles Darwin, Albert Einstein, and Sigmund Freud in trying to revise or replace established principles need not be recited again here.

Freedom through subservience. A third outworn but dependable myth that tyrannizes many minds is this: That we need people of action in leadership positions. Stated thus, it can be a useful idea, but in "emergencies" it can uncritically result in quite immoral surrogates "getting things done." Uncritical subservience to a leader is a dangerous gamble. Leaders who demand subservience often reject the lessons of history as well as the counsels of wise intellectuals and the niceties of human rights and human dignity.

Such leaders assure us that they are not Girl or Boy Scouts! They put themselves forward as knowing how to play in the Biggest League! In the short run, they at times gather substantial followings in this as in other countries. Their costs often become apparent when it is too late.

As the preceding chapter points out, the social theorist Max Weber spoke of three justifications or legitimations of domination: the traditional, the charismatic, and the legal. The pervasive second type rests on "the authority of the extraordinary and personal *gift of grace* (charisma), the absolutely personal devotion and personal confidence in revelation, heroism, or other qualities of individual leadership."[12]

We tend to follow and even to worship such charismatic individuals — such Caesar-like figures — both in war and in peace. They are as diverse and Americanized as Theodore Roosevelt, Woodrow Wilson, F. D. Roosevelt, Dwight D. Eisenhower, John F. Kennedy, and Ronald Reagan. We permit such leaders to misuse the teachings of religious idealists as well as the utterances of those latter day instruments of revelation — the scholars, scientists, and artists presumably dedicated to humanity.

In attempting to explain why the United States "spent a thousand billion dollars on arms and men-in-arms" during the first twenty-five years after World War II, the seasoned television commentator Eric Sevareid stresses "the brass's positiveness, their unending *certainty,* as they present their plans and estimates. They are trained that way.

Civilian officials must summon the courage of their doubts; the military may be frequently in error but are never in doubt. This is a large reason why they have constantly carried the day in their presentations to wondering, doubting congressional committees."[13] Domestic programs for health, welfare, and education, for integrating underprivileged groups into our society, lack such Caesar-like lobbyists—and the corporations and campaign funds to back them up.

A report in 1984 from United Nations University indicates the global ramifications of this enticing distortion of governmental and private finances and of the efforts of scientific personnel:

> It is estimated that at the present time some 25 per cent of the world's scientific manpower is engaged in military-related pursuits.
> Out of the 3 million scientists and engineers employed worldwide in scientific laboratories, approximately HALF A MILLION were specifically engaged in the development of new weapons systems.
> . . . Of the world's total spending on research and development since 1945, an estimated *40* PER CENT has been directed to military-related objectives.[14]

There is evidence that many human beings will continually try to be more than Orwell's faceless and mindless party members. More and more people become disenchanted with such distorting myths of orthodoxy as the three outlined above. More social scientists need to treat the myths as data to be placed in social-historical contexts and reviewed critically rather than as "truths."

2. Legitimacy

The preceding chapter discusses how legitimacy can influence perception. It is so pervasive that it is desirable to discuss it further here as a distorter of theorizing.

For an orthodoxy to be legitimate depends upon wide acceptance of its relationship to the myth that an objective "mechanism" exists that is called "the social system." This latter myth lives in the minds of millions, but what does it label? It labels many different conceptions with little in common other than certain obvious bits of material such as streets, power lines, buildings, and sewers and also certain symbols such as a somewhat common language, moral and legal vagaries, and institutional figures and façades. All of these, too, are seen and understood in different ways in the various segments of the population, but those in power try to make their version of what is legitimated by "the social system" to be regarded as *the* orthodox one. They only partly succeed.

School textbooks on the various levels offer a simplistic and idealistic model of "the social system." Their writers overlook the contrasting perceptions and conceptions of people in various groups and classes and the extent to which they are writing apologies or even propaganda for a limited class view. Whatever "the social system" might be to any person or group, however, it is looked upon as a dominant social instrument even though its definition varies and related beliefs and actions with it.

How instructive it is to mingle for a while, as unobtrusively as possible, with groups of migrant farm workers, police, bond salespeople, or convicted criminals! Or with clergypeople, urban ne'er-do-wells, industrial managers, or assembly-line workers! It is useful also to bridge as completely as possible gender, age, and ethnic gaps.

In our society, only investigative journalists, some politicians, and a limited number of artists, social scientists, and others working with and for people undergo such experiences. They are thus given culturally unsettling and creative opportunities.

The one-actress play, "The Search for Signs of Intelligent Life in the Universe," by Jane Wagner and featuring actress Lily Tomlin, provides a rich product of such experiences. In reviewing it, Marilyn French tells about "Trudy, a bag lady who has been 'certified' mad, but whose madness is really a perception of society from the underside." She points out that "what is most extraordinary about the Tomlin show is the degree of truth about American society that it dares to present on a public stage to an audience educated by the artificial sunshine and artificial violence of most television and movies."[15] Only with the experiences Tomlin and Wagner had can one come to perceive and try to understand the shocking contrasts between what is considered right or wrong, expedient or unwise, legal or criminal, mad or sane in various parts of our society.

It is easy to use a version of a moral code to justify the legitimacy of politico-economic proposals or to denounce as illegitimate versions unattractive to those in power. Temporary plausibility rather than theoretical consistency characterizes much of such efforts by think-tank gurus, politicians, and media writers.[16]

Social scientists necessarily face relativity in studying society and culture. They have the task of trying to understand — not brush aside — striking differences in conceptions of "facts," beliefs, and behavior. How can such different notions of legitimacy and orthodoxy and thus of society exist? They demand understanding.

3. Elitism

Many theorists find elitism satisfying and defensible, especially an elitism that allots prestige and thus social power to such folks as themselves. What an enchanting set of opportunities such a proposal for social reorganization presents to merchants of ideas! For example, in his *Republic*, Plato urged the creation of a self-perpetuating power elite made up of those who could excel in a prescribed educational process. [17] That such a procedure, even if it were a wise one at a given time, might disastrously resist adaptation to changed life conditions apparently escaped the keen analyses of the ancient Greek. Few secular documents have been so widely acclaimed and admired by winners in various intellectual accreditation sweepstakes.

Elitist intellectuals often speak with horror of "vulgarization." Somehow a cult's writ, methods, and initiation requirements must be protected from infection, often even from adaptation to changed life conditions. Above all, they distrust vesting decision making in the "common man," in the "masses." As one such intellectual put it in the late nineteenth century, "One of the great divisions of politics in our day is coming to be whether, at the last resort, the world should be governed by its ignorance or by its intelligence." The former "assuredly reverses all the past experiences of mankind. In every field of human enterprise, in all the competitions of life, by the inexorable law of Nature, superiority lies with the few, and not with the many, and success can only be attained by placing the guiding and controlling power in their hands."[18] Such a simplistic, monovalent conception of "superiority" leaves a great many questions unanswered even in that author's own terms.

In *Science*, the weekly of the American Association for the Advancement of Science, an editorial by the anthropologist Nancie L. Gonzalez, takes a similar view. Under the title, "In Defense of Elitism," she is alarmed at the "public loss of faith in academia and schooling generally" and at "the lowering of Scholastic Aptitude Test scores across the nation" with "grade inflation rampant in colleges." Surely, she says, "a republic cannot remain both ingnorant and free." Few would disagree with that point, but she then pleads: "Elitism has been out of fashion in America, but laudable though that may be in political and economic matters, in education we should remember the values espoused by leaders such as [former Harvard University president] James Bryant Conant."[19] Her concern is one widely felt, but dealing with the problem she mentions does not necessarily call for embracing intellectual elitism. That, too, is a restrictive course. The creation and maintenance of such an intellectual elite — with its typical charisma, cultishness, and other rigidifying tendencies — should not be our goal, as attractive as that goal might be to some intellectuals.

Serious questions have been raised about the class-centeredness and ethnocentrism of the tests to which Gonzalez refers. Education and motivation to become educated should be more generally and more freely available. Useful contributors and leaders can come from any class, any ethnic or religious group. All intellectuals are also human beings, and they should be regarded and treated as no more than that. To attribute charismatic qualities — such as prestigious labels can stimulate — to individuals or to a group or class may be an enticing procedure, but it is distorting. Social history includes many examples of creative individuals who defied elites to report deviant observations of importance and to offer novel and useful theories and artistic creations.

Personality types attracted to philosophizing contrast sharply with the wheeler-dealers and Caesars who seize control over social power. At best, the politico-economic entrepreneurs find it desirable to represent popular sentiments, needs, and experiences. When they do so, they are often aided by the more earthy social scientists who dedicate themselves to serving people.

Democracy as liberation: Such examples of social disaster as the Weimar Republic, the Kerensky Russian regime, and the Spanish civil war are sometimes used as arguments against democracy. Yet Hitler's Germany and Mussolini's Italy can scarcely help make elitism appear attractive. Arguments of such extreme cases yield little on either side, and we do have many examples of benefits of more democratic participation. In the words of the political scientist Jack L. Walker, "The theory of democracy beckons us toward an ancient ideal: the liberation of the energies of all our citizens in the common pursuit of the good society."[20] To make more steps in that direction, the ideal must penetrate as many facets of our society as possible and give rise to an urgent demand for its implementation.

Even a "dictatorship of the proletariat" gets defined, as a practical matter, as a dictatorship in behalf of the proletariat. After successfully leading the revolt of the Chinese people, Mao Zedong spent the last twenty years of his life trying to guide that country through a "cultural revolution" toward an egalitarian, communist society. This effort had extensive results, but since Mao's death in 1976, under the leadership of Deng Xiaoping, a pragmatic "socialist commodity economy" became the goal. He had the Communist Party's central committee declare on October 20, 1984: "General prosperity cannot and will never mean absolute egalitarianism or that all members of society become better off simultaneously or at the same speed." On November 2, 1984, the Chinese public security ministry removed the label of "class enemy" from "landlords, rich peasants, counterrevolutionaries and bad elements."[21]

A dismissal of elitism in social proposals does not deny the existence of structural and individual inequalities. It treats the charismatic appeal and authority with which so many vest the more prominent and powerful only as phenomena to be studied and dealt with. Social scientists with extensive field experience as media reporters, political workers, salespeople, or first-hand research observers are those least influenced by charisma in their thinking and writing.

Although structural and individual inequalities are to be perceived, this does not imply an over-simple acceptance of their genetic determination. It does not justify genetically extremist theories of class and race superiority. The extent to which the class-based and racist theories of Cyril Burt, the English psychologist, influenced both British and American educational and immigration policies as well as psychological thought is still an open disgrace. Burt's dishonest "findings" were used in England to justify the class-oriented and racist tracking system in education and in the United States to enact anti-southern-European immigration policies. It is only since his death that his manufacturing of evidence and of admiring reviews of his work has been revealed.[22]

4. Social Contractism and Utopianism

Many believe that social arrangements can be changed dramatically — even to revolutionary degrees — by what amounts to a new social contract. They say that entrenched life conditions, customary social structure, and culture have been and can now be altered substantially and even drastically through contractual arrangement. They rarely examine in detail and make provision for all that needs to be modified in order to make a new collective dispensation work. In consequence, we have naïve disillusionment with socialism because the Soviet Union now represents a substitution of a different type of autocracy, of class stratification, and of intellectual and political repression — albeit a more benign and beneficial type — for that under the czarist regime.

The probability that humanity has to struggle forever with problems of facilitating social change is a prospect much less enticing than one of finally solving all human problems with one great utopian contract. The probability that human cupidity, distrust, and selfish shortsightedness will forever infect human society is looked upon by many theorists as unthinkably cynical, but what other conclusion can a social scientist tenably offer for social guidance? Social problems are entrenched in social process and need to be seen and acted upon as such.

What should be said about such great "social contracts" as the United States Declaration of Independence, Constitution, and Bill of Rights? How about the Emancipation Proclamation of 1863 and the implementing amendments to the Federal Constitution that soon followed it? What should be contended about the efficacy of the United Nations Declaration of Human Rights of 1948? These are great social action documents, but how long has it taken and will it still take to implement them? Those who "rested on their oars" after the enactment of any one of these documents placed too much confidence in the "one fell swoop" theory of social change-by-contract.

The Declaration of Independence's assertion "that all Men are created equal" is still a hope. Efforts are constantly being made to enforce and to abridge the prohibition against the establishment of religion by the first and fourteenth amendments. The blacks and other minorities have struggled, with modest success, to implement the Civil War amendments to the Constitution. Women have gained voting rights, but the Equal Rights Amendment has yet to be adopted. And the United States has yet to give its ratification to the United Nations Declaration of Human Rights, a declaration far more idealistic than most governmental practice around the globe.

Social contracts are useful in social action. Social scientists can assess them in the light of human experience, but they should not give them more weight in their thinking than they warrant. Nor should they overlook their significance.

Because of the enticements of utopianism, enticements so effectively exploited by religious as well as political leaders, many widely accepted social theorists make sure to end their writings on an upbeat and hopeful note. They promise that their proposals, based upon their "scientific findings," will bring a better life for the individuals they enlighten or even a better world.

As an example, on the individual level, the psychoanalyst Erik H. Erikson[23] offers the rewards of an "accrued ego integration" in his ultimate stage of developmental maturity, a triumph of ego integration over despair through renunciation and wisdom. It sounds great and is a useful goal for therapeutic purposes. He states it, appropriately enough, in vague generalities. In an objective sense, it is scarcely a scientific generalization that summarizes actual case materials.

On the societal level, Karl Marx and Friedrich Engels pledge: "The proletariat will use its political supremacy to wrest, by degrees, all capital from the bourgeoisie, to centralize all instruments of production in the hands of the state, i. e., of the proletariat organized as the ruling class; and to increase the total productive forces as rapidly as possible." They even promise: "In proportion as the antagonism between classes within the nation vanishes, the hostility of one nation to another will come to an end."[24]

These projections stimulate imaginations and wishful thinking. They have proved to be useful in individual therapy and in social action propaganda. Their resemblance to accurate predictions of individual or social consequences is doubtful. The political scientists Barbara Goodwin and Keith Taylor conclude: "A purely analytical account of existing society, even if that account is highly critical, can never suffice as a framework for formulating a constructive, imaginative picture of a desirable alternative society."[25] Let us explore further this significant and perhaps crucial ambiguity in human affairs.

Bridges to popular goals. Even though cases can be made against their quality as prediction, do not social contractism and utopianism — like some other enticing distortions — have their social utility? They are not always wholly delusory. Do they not also contribute inspiration and provide some continuity in social thought? This brings us again to ask: When do wise social action policies necessarily differ from social scientific analyses? As has been suggested, they may or may not, and this possible split needs to be faced fully and constructively by both social scientists and social actionists. It is useful to perceive and to maintain this division, this contrast.

Social actionists use as tenable social expedients as possible to deal with their problems. They benefit by having accurate social knowledge, but they also need to make projections or predictions, to use fantasies for which there is likely to be a high level of acceptance and belief among possible constituents.

Social scientists can help constructive social actionists more accurately to predict the chances of such a venture as a campaign for the Equal Rights Amendment. They can also provide similar information as ammunition against destructive projects, such as the short-sighted disposal of chemical wastes or planned deforestation. They can examine popular aspirations and dreams like "a home of my own" or "Medicare for everyone and for every health need" or even "a job for everyone." Even though these may appear to be utopian objectives, they are possible bridges to more modest and realistic goals. At any rate, social scientists can help evaluate all such bridges in terms of available social experience with comparable cases.

Even though it may be something too remote or idealistic to achieve, an expedient actionist goal may help produce movement in a direction useful to people. Social scientists should not advise against fantasies useful to a constructive movement only because they might have an illusionary character. At the same time, they should not permit such considerations to disorient their own perspectives on social processes.

5. Symptomism

A preoccupation with the symptoms of a social disorder rather than with its causes is especially enticing. Delinquents, addicts, terrorists, rapists, and murderers are more easily considered as individual problems than as products of both individual and social factors. Why do people become addicts? Why do people riot against authority, and why do police brutalize and even murder suspects? What leads to rape and murder, often among close associates? Why does the United States have the highest incarceration rate in the West? Why does our crime rate mount more rapidly than suspects can be caught or prisons built to hold convicts?

As one young slum dweller puts it: "When you grow up down here, you look around and all you see is nothing. Kids wander off in their own world. You get frustrated and angry. If you don't have a car, you get a bus. And you start taking your frustrations out on the first person you see, the driver." As another summarizes it: "If you give us no place to go and nothing to do, if you treat us like dirt, then we'll act like it."[26] If policy makers would empathize with such human beings in their settings, our ways of dealing with them could be based upon more accurate and humane diagnoses. Few policy makers are willing to take that scary step. It would mean, among other things, an attack on the existing power structure.

The superficiality and propagandistic advantages of symptomism are well illustrated by our handling of the "drug crisis" and of underclass delinquencies. The 1986 "drug crisis," involving chiefly cocaine, furnished President Reagan with a sparkling propaganda weapon with which to be a popular hero again and to divert attention from international tensions and the shaky domestic economy. Cocaine-related deaths of some popular athletes and related revelations led the White House to announce that the "full power of the presidency" would be employed "to remove drugs from schools, the work place, athletic programs and from all elements of society." This was to be achieved principally through individual drug testing, some to be required and some "voluntary." The journalist Hodding Carter III, in a "Viewpoint" column in the *Wall Street Journal,* attacked "the weird lack of proportion" in this panic. He noted that tobacco deaths are estimated to total as many as 350,000 a year and that alcohol-stimulated death figures range from 100,000 to 350,000 a year. While the cocaine threat is serious, it currently takes only about 3,500 lives a year. What Carter then discussed was the significance of the billions in illegal drug-dealing profits. Those funds "submerge and then absorb banks . . . buy judges, businesses and the ears of the politically powerful — if not their souls." The solution he demands is to "eliminate drug-trade-generated corruption" through decriminalizing drugs. He claims that that would "narrow the problem to its health component."[27]

Anti-drug educational programs can possibly be even more successful than anti-tobacco instruction, but the perversions of business, political, and police power mentioned by Carter should be the most pressing concerns.

Similarly, opening adequate opportunities for education and employment to the underclass — white, Black, and other — would attack their basic problems directly, but it would mean a shift in priorities by the politico-economic establishment. It would require changing from greater mechanical productivity using fewer and fewer workers (fewer customers/consumers), from irresponsible exploitation of the Third World for cheap labor and natural resources, and from the manufacture and use of armaments. It would call for emphasis upon the intelligent and comprehensive employment of human resources. Our society has not yet learned that it needs to make this transition from superficial symptoms to basic causes in policy-formation in order to persist. How far will we permit the underclass to expand and to suffer?

The racism and class-centeredness of symptomism in policy-implementation in our society is well illustrated by statistics for jail and prison populations. Prisons train the indicted and convicted in criminal rationales and methods and help assimilate them into underworld networks. They provide informal services for the underclass similar to those offered formally to the more successful by schools of business administration.

In 1978, 43 percent of jail inmates were nonwhite; 61 percent high school dropouts; 43 percent from the unemployed; and 40 percent under 24 years of age. They had a pre-arrest median income of $3,255 a year.[28] Adults in jails increased 42 percent in 1978–83. The males per 100,000 in state and federal prisons rose from 149 in 1925 to 217 in 1935, then continued at roughly that rate with 220 in 1975 but mounted to 395 in 1985! In 1983, the rate for white males was 225, but for blacks it was 1,445 and for Amerindians, 504! Inmates of such prisons were 48 percent nonwhite! Inmates of all correctional facilities were similarly 48 percent nonwhite![29]

In contrast to these figures are estimates of the largely undetected, ignored, or underpenalized white collar criminals who cost society far more than the underclass offenders mentioned above. Such folks are typically more privileged whites over 30, college graduates earning substantial incomes.[30]

6. Pedantry

Think of the plight of the student who engages in a fresh search for social knowledge. After selecting a problem for investigation, she or he can well feel overwhelmed by the tremendous bulk of pertinent literature that exists. Add to that the potential danger of revealing or advocating ideas offensive to the powerful or to societal morality as currently interpreted in the media. The would-be searcher many times also must first find a subsidizer or an employer who grants freedom to observe and to think and provides time for the exercise of that freedom. Too often, one devoted to creative intellectual exploration may feel bogged down by all of this.

Often at a price of freedom and creativity, professionalization of social science simplifies these problems. It narrows one's focus and thus the relevant literature to be explored. It suggests expedient operational procedures. It often diverts one from the uncertainties and interpersonal problems of the direct study of human affairs. Methodological and theoretical exercises in a time-worn academic tradition can be absorbing. Even more practically, too, professionalization indicates how to gain access to social networks influential in obtaining employment and grants or research contracts.

As a comfortable bourgeois adjustment to intellectual life in our society, professionalized social science builds directly on the common social class commitments and personality types that its images attract. Such a professional instrument as a prestigious graduate faculty furnishes allegedly legitimate criteria for limiting the range of literature that is relevant to the concerns of budding social scientists. It may identify a profession with the respectability of a physics-modeled "science" and with some such orthodoxy as functionalism, structural-functionalism, ethnomethodology, survey research, symbolic interactionism, or marxism. Vast library stacks of books and periodicals may thus thankfully be ignored. The most common labels given to rejected works are "journalistic," "humanistic," "radical," "popular," or just "unscientific," but sociologists can learn much from writings so labeled.

In that connection, I am reminded of the statement of one of my post-doctoral professors at Yale who once said: "It is outrageous that I could go clear through for the Ph.D. in what was called sociology and not be exposed adequately to the teachings of Karl Marx and W. G. Sumner!" His Ph.D. was from the University of Chicago. At Yale, the chief difference in my own pre-doctoral work was that Sumner was carefully misrepresented as a "social Darwinian" and not as a critic of capitalism by his successor, A. G. Keller.[31] Marx was lightly passed over as a propagandist.

The cult-making potentialities of the foregoing six enticing influences can be distorting to efforts at social scientific research and thought. Orthodoxy, legitimacy, and pedantry in particular can stimulate competitive and bureaucratic atmospheres that emphasize technicianism, opposition to popularization, and resistance to updating.

7. Technicianism

Formulas tend to invade the curricula of such fields as business administration, law, engineering, government, medicine, computer operation, and mass communications. On the promise to fit students for specific, existing jobs, they draw more and more students from a shrinking pool to absorb their cookbook methods. On the promise of doing subservient technical investigations, the faculty of such fields are also obtaining a larger share of available research funds. Teachers of sociology, anthropology, literature, composition, and foreign languages perceive this and conclude that specialized technical research is the resource they have to grasp to contend with declining support. Computers are therefore invading all such fields. "High tech" is a saleable façade whether it is applicable or not!

This reminds me of several Brooklyn College colleagues who wanted to launch a curriculum in mass communications with an emphasis on advertising. They were delighted to be given an opportunity to discuss their plans with the executive vice-president of the largest advertising agency in New York City. However, they were then a good deal less than delighted when they heard him say: "We only hire as dead-end clerks college-trained technicians of the sort you have in mind. For our responsible jobs with a future in our organization, we try to get broadly educated men and women who are alert and adaptable and can find ways to cope with any specific problem with which they may have to deal."[32]

An overemphasis on the technical promotes rote performance in any field, and that quashes imagination and creativity. In attempting to provide dependable round pegs for round holes, it ignores the fact that such holes are constantly changing, that society is in constant flux.

Our "idiot machines": Americans used to be highly amused at caricatures of the robotlike English clerks and butlers and Prussian bureaucrats and militarists in our periodicals who could only behave in terms of precisely memorized formulas. With our growing glorification of technical specialization in employment, in so many universities as well as in our more obviously labeled trade schools, we appear to be emulating the rigidification of the English and German burlesques. But we now compound that tendency to an extent only recently made possible by "idiot machines." We are permitting useful tools to dominate our lives. We should control computers, not become their dependents.[33]

Admittedly, it is a distortion to call complicated contraptions with electronic circuits "idiotic." Some of those machines have even been termed electronic "brains," but, of course, they are far from being such. Any human brain has the mystery, magic, and majesty of the human spirit at work within it. A human brain, given a chance, is flexible, adaptable to changing facts and conditions. A machine is just what it has been programmed to be, and nothing more or less. When an electronic date-processing outfit makes a mistake, one hears it said: "Garbage in, garbage out!" The machine can process only what has been put into it, marred only by imperfections in programming and by mechanical gremlins over which our technology has not yet gained complete control. The programming, too, is sometimes weakened by the kind of people who like to work routinely with machines. They tend to be relatively less autonomous, less imaginative, and less flexible than the more competent.

Have you ever had a debate by letter with a large merchandising organization that depends upon computerized records? It takes patience, but, like other clinical experiences in our society, it can be instructive. It does not take many exchanges of notes until the human representative of the machine, or the machine itself, gets completely bogged down. The buck is then passed to higher and less routinized powers. On one occasion, a friend of mine ordered and paid for twenty $100 bonds from the federal government. He received in the mail twenty $1,000 bonds and had the greatest difficulty convincing the representatives of the government that he had received them in error! They contended that machines could not possibly make such an error.

Some even claim that humanity's salvation in finding its way through an increasingly complex future rests in the use of computers. A frightening possibility is that the prestige of "science" and of computers may give vast power to those controlling the solution of complex problems. That such omnipotent machines could and should remain utterly impersonal and objective is absurd. In addition to the biases of their owners, computers have a narrowness of focus and lack of adaptability built into them.[34]

If we continue to place more and more faith in the dehumanized technician and in machines, we can look forward to substantial catastrophes in the future triggered by formula-ridden programming and dull-witted machine-tenders. There is no substitute for the broadly and fundamentally educated human being, with all of her or his imperfections yet boundless potentialities.[35]

8. Opposition to Popularization

When a journalist or other media expert approaches a social scientist or humanities specialist, the latter often exhibits a sense of outrage at being forced to prove oneself to a "crude" or unsympathetic functionary. To illustrate, the former editor of the *Humanities Report* expressed his disgust at having to cope with popularizers by asserting: "Many newswriters, in conformity to the sovereign cynicism of their profession, believe that the humanities are not news."[36] He forgot that journalists have produced much of the most memorable literature of this country. What would our literature be without the writings of Walt Whitman, Mark Twain, Willa Cather, H. L. Mencken, Sinclair Lewis, and so many others, all graduates of newsrooms? What would our social sciences be, too, for that matter, without the writings of such former journalists as Robert E. Park, Robert S. Lynd, and C. Wright Mills as well as of that foreign correspondent for a New York newspaper, Karl Marx?

Many social scientists have looked with envy at the success of the late Margaret Mead in interpreting cultural anthropology through the mass media and even in producing best-selling books. Robert S. and Helen M. Lynd made a similar contribution for sociology with their Middletown studies. Such social scientists and others dealt with socially significant issues and problems in clear and interesting English. They faced the reality that uncomplicated and understandable expression is at least as valuable a disciplinary instrument as statistics.

The exemplars of the social sciences and the humanities may treasure their prestige, their authority, and their ability within their disciplines to say something newsworthy, but the rendering of it into common parlance is their responsibility in such a society as ours and not that of the media.

Many questions can be raised about the desirability of current definitions of news, of existing mass media operating policies. Prior to 1921, the media paid slight attention to developments in the physical and biological sciences, and that attention was often inaccurate. The editor of Science Service at its beginning in 1921, E. E. Slosson, put it this way: "As seen through the medium of the popular press the scientist is apt to appear as an enemy of society inventing infernal machines, or as a curious half-crazy creature talking a jargon of his own and absorbed in pursuit of futilities."[37]

The chain newspaper owner, E. W. Scripps, had recognized this problem and furnished a subsidy to start the service. As Slosson continued: "To the journalist there is something saddening about a great university. He is distressed to see so much good copy going to waste all the time. . . . Every doctor's dissertation contains a good newspaper story concealed in it." Science Service initiated a new era in popular interpretation of the physical and biological sciences, but its example has not been followed to any great extent for the social sciences other than psychology. Newsworthy social scientific developments are often controversial. If they serve "establishment" interests, they may be publicized. Despite some successful sporadic experiments in media relations by sociological society representatives, no effort resembling Science Service has as yet been attempted.[38]

As the sociologist Charles Tilly admits, "No one, so far as I know, has stood up to defend the quality of sociological writing as either better than advertised or necessary for its objectives. Sociologists often try, of course, a conventional defense that other people write just as badly, but critics single out sociologists because they study controversial subjects on which critics have strong, if uninformed, opinions."[39]

The sociologist Howard S. Becker has written a text on how to use understandable English to write a thesis, book, or article in social science.[40] Tilly looks upon it as useful, but he calls for "similar manuals on giving talks, teaching classes, qualifying for tenure, and preparing grant applications." All this is needed, he contends, so that "sociology's lucidity level would rise and its tension level would decline."[41] As the writers of another useful text on writing add: "No one can write decently who is distrustful of the reader's intelligence or whose attitude is patronizing."[42]

9. Resistance to Updating

Intellectual disciplines — whether they be medicine, law, literature, or social science — have a tendency to crystallize, to routinize, to develop vested interests in existing formulations and ideas. The updating of philosophy and history has taken the form of the creation of "new" disciplines, those of economics, political science, sociology, anthropology, social history, and many more. In turn, each of these is being fragmented further to meet the demands for particularization, for application to special concerns, and for providing new opportunities to the ambitious. The tendency to ignore social history in so many of these fragments often permits participants to pride themselves upon their inventiveness as they in effect concoct new labels or restatements for well-worn ideas. In addition, the rising boundary walls among these intellectual fiefs encourage special jargons, a shrinking of perspectives, a lack of communication, and a duplication of effort.

To update a discipline or a profession is a gargantuan task. It confronts the resistance of some of the most sophisticated, successful, and entrenched bureaucrats in society. Yet somehow it must be done if these occupations are to continue to service our changing society more positively than negatively. Many have pointed to such needs in law and medicine, especially to their routinization and their exploitative abuses, but updating is constantly urgent in the social sciences and the humanities. The latter still retain too much of the characteristics given to them by their male, aristocratic, clerical, and upper-middle-class ancestors, but all this is rarely acknowledged or discussed in many circles. Sociologists for Women in Society actively contributes views and findings to offset the male bias, and other organizations confront other of the prejudices mentioned.

Some tendencies toward change appear to serve principally special interests. This is illustrated by the relatively uncritical and intensely capitalistic stance of such a body as the American Marketing Association and the scientistic and commercial emphases of the American Statistical Association. These bodies are, in effect, efforts to update applied social science concepts and methods from limited viewpoints. On the other hand, such a prim organization as the American Sociological Association (founded in 1905) grudgingly confronts the rise of a variety of competing general and special interest bodies that fragment the sociological field.[43] As in economics, political science, anthropology, education, and psychology, sociology has sprouted specialty organizations. Specialized sections within the ASA have not succeeded in preventing this fragmentation into autonomous societies.

Updating the social sciences and the humanities through such separations is probably the most practical and constructive procedure available. Its success depends upon the influence developed by the new organizations to encourage more free and creative work and also more wholistic and integrating perspectives. These are pressing needs in the social sciences.

9

More

Intimate Distortions

The previous chapter is a discussion of nine alluring distortions of a more professional or technical nature that pervade social science. The present chapter takes up more intimate and permeating distortions of social thinking. These are: (1) sexism, (2) tribalism, (3) classism, (4) intentionism, (5) life events, fads, and fashions, and (6) the personality types each discipline attracts.

1. Sexism

A statement by the late Martin Luther King, Jr., applies to many of the distortions discussed here and especially to sexism, classism, and tribalism. He said: "There is little hope for us until we become toughminded enough to break loose from the shackles of prejudice, half-truths, and downright ignorance."[1] People are often unaware of their sexism, their class-oriented values, and their ethnocentrism and racism, but those biases are costly to us all. The sexologist Alfred C. Kinsey and his associates warn how "the human mind invents categories and tries to force facts into separated pigeon-holes. The living world," they add, "is a continuum in each and every one of its aspects. The sooner we learn this concerning human sexual behavior the sooner we shall reach a sound understanding of the realities of sex."[2] *And so, too, of the other distortions mentioned.*

In our society, sexual identity remains a problem for both females and males from childhood. It is a problem exacerbated by modern technological and employment developments. Both sexes become insecure as they observe the dissatisfaction of role models with their own social images and careers. The young try to improve on those "old fashioned" models, sometimes with costly experiments. The adults in turn have difficulty understanding the problems and challenges with which their children are faced.

Maturing females observe the greater opportunities for males to enter careers that society presents as being exciting and financially attractive. They also now tend to resist the belittling of their own economic and social worth and social pressure which results in female dependence and for an overemphasis on sexual attractiveness. Must they be like their mothers and not be given personally satisfying goals like their fathers and their male associates?

Women face many more choices today than the once relatively simple one between marriage and a career. They can now opt for a single life with or without children, one (or more) relationships with or without children, or marriage with or without children. Any of these may be combined intermittently with paid employment on a part- or full-time basis that is carried on briefly, sporadically, or on a lifetime plan. Presently, too, they must assume that, quite probably, separation, divorce, or widowhood may alter their circumstances and their choices. Thus young women now ask themselves: What enduring values other than cash are available to them? What is a husband worth? What are children worth? If there is something more in life than marriage and a family, what is a career worth? How many roles can a woman be prepared to perform? What is happening to the children?

Males often feel a continuing need from childhood to assert their male sexual identity—somehow to differentiate themselves—in a world they see as largely dominated by females. Father figures tend to be remote and often flawed as models. Must a boy and then a man try so hard to be a male among males? Of what does maleness consist? Must it be so ignoring or rejective of femaleness or so exploitative of it?

How can men react to women's increasing range of choices? What do men gain or lose by having a home with a legal wife or an unlegalized companion, with or without children? How do men balance the advantages and disadvantages of having a career-involved wife? To what extent can a man take on household duties and child care? What about the children?

New York Times reporter Gloria Emerson is optimistic about the future of maleness. in *Some American Men,* she describes her extensive, in-depth interviews during the Vietnam War and how they revealed to her the imprisonment of men by their macho image. She tells of a young woman, however, with whom she apparently agrees, who "saw the possibility that many more men were capable of change and that someone her age might just live to see it."[3]

This social categorization and stereotyping of gender roles continues to distort social life, sociological theorizing about it, and the character of the sociological profession.

Sociologist Harry Elmer Barnes introduces a history of sociology with the admission that the "largest group of sociologists are what are usually called 'social economists' or 'practical sociologists,' namely, those chiefly interested in social work and amelioration." The "well-known personalities" among these specialists he says include Jane Addams, Edith Abbott, Mary van Kleeck, Mary E. Richmond, and Jessica Peixotto. "Here the emphasis has been progressively shifted from amelioration to prevention, though the 'uplift' attitude is still strong in many quarters."[4] The implication is that the latter attitude is not "scientific." His book contains no further reference to any of these outstanding female contributors to social thought and action! Barnes' collaborator in another extensive treatment of sociological history, Howard Becker,[5] notes that Richmond's[6] *Social Diagnosis,* published in 1917 and republished in 1944 and 1965, "still remains one of the best systematic treatments of social case work as a scientific procedure."

Jane Addams' Hull-House, founded in Chicago in 1889,[7] and Albion W. Small's Department of Sociology, founded at the University of Chicago in 1892, had related interests, but they were also separated, especially by male sociologists' need for "scientific respectability" unsoiled by the "uplift" attitude. Small sponsored a "drive toward objectivity," assured by the importation of European theorizings. Thus sociology became male dominated not only in personnel but also by stressing theory and methods rather than participant observation and social improvement. Social work, in contrast, was hospitable to female workers (especially volunteers) and had a "feminine" image because of its humanitarian orientation.

When the University of Chicago organized its own settlement in 1894, Mary Eliza McDowell became its first head resident, but she was not a member of the sociology department.[8] One of the department sociologists, Charles R. Henderson, was said to be a more "humanitarian" than "objective scientist," and his successor in 1916, Ernest W. Burgess, did make contacts and send students to study in social work and other community agencies. This was excused by the more pretentious because it made possible "great data-gathering efforts."[9] W. I. Thomas and Robert E. Park in 1913–18 and then Park and Burgess on into the 1930s humanized the department and gave it great days, but it remained short of women.[10] A historian tells how the sociology department at Columbia University was similarly distorted by the "old boy" network and scientistic emphasis.[11]

Elizabeth Briant Lee studied the life histories of 949 American women who achieved eminence and died before 1960, 33 of whom were social scientists.[12] The barriers that these exceptional women surmounted emphasize the discouragements, exploitations, and degradations so many others of their peers suffered. Those who succeeded usually combined unusual talents with pressing economic needs.

With sociology — like so many disciplines — controlled by "old boy" networks and thinking, it has taken dedicated organizing and agitation by women to expand their roles in the profession, to focus research on gender issues, and to protect their dignity and interests. As recently as the academic year 1968–69, the Women's Caucus reported at a business meeting of the American Sociological Association "that women were 30 per cent of the doctoral students in graduate school . . . but only 4 per cent of the full-time professors in graduate departments; . . . that women were 39 per cent of the research associates in the elite graduate departments but only 5 per cent of the associate and 1 per cent of the full professors." This statement, read by Alice C. Rossi, then calls it "outrageous that a custom persists whereby a woman research associate or lecturer with a Ph.D. and ten years or more of research experience cannot apply for research funds as a sole principal investigator, while a young man with a brand new assistant professorship but no prior responsibility for conducting research can readily do so."[13]

The Women's Caucus became transformed in 1970–71 into Sociologists for Women in Society. As Arlene Kaplan Daniels recalls, the SWS name "was hit upon as one which would best express our desire to use our expertise to help improve the position of all women in society and not just our own middle-class positions as professionals." As a practical matter, however, Daniels adds, SWS "focuses most of all on the problems of our sister colleagues."[14]

Pauline B. Bart summarizes women's most pressing problems in sociology at SWS's start thus: "undergraduate women and graduate women were discriminated against in the awarding of scholarships and fellowships and in job placement, and faculty hiring, in tenure line positions, and in the awarding of tenure."[15] Joan Huber recounts the usefulness of SWS to individuals: "Nasty secrets that women students had typically kept to themselves could be exposed to the fresh air of collective evaluation." She mentions how a male professor told her: "We reserve some fellowships just for women students. But the women just don't stay. They get married or something and leave." She replied: "It certainly is true that some women leave for reasons that are really unfortunate. Why, . . . a bunch of us compared notes on the way some professors make passes at women students and proposition them — some women get so ashamed and depressed they just leave."[16]

Rossi, the first SWS president and later president of the American Sociological Association, spoke in 1985 at the SWS 15th anniversary about the status gains by women. She pointed out that they had by then reached a point where they should concentrate on participation in the general professional societies in order to make themselves "more visible." SWS meetings should focus, she said, "on topics of very special concern to SWS members." She recognized the problems still remaining, but she hoped SWS would "achieve the goals for which it was established, close its books, and quietly fade into history after one last stupendous celebration!"[17]

2. Tribalism

This is a tyranny we inherit from the peoples of many lands, but its American pattern owes much to the class-snobbery and racism that is called White-Anglo-Saxon-Protestantism or WASPism. The English developed it throughout all parts of Great Britain and then brought it to their overseas colonies in Ireland, the Americas, and around the world.[18]

That tribalism is an outworn tyranny is not to be interpreted as belittling other aspects of the cultural heritages we have received from our disparate ancestors and through borrowing. Our composite

American culture is and should be a mélange of the cultures of all lands, forever invigorated by the complexities and contradictions of its segments.

Distortions arise out of both *ethno*centrism, that is closely related to *ego*centrism, and the exploitation of ethnic and class identities in a tribal manner to obtain for a group special competitive advantages. Even when such an exploitation has not existed, myths about the tribal conspiracies of other groups are often developed and used to justify a counter-conspiracy as a "defensive" measure. Separatist WASPism has made other ethnic groups more separatist and militant.

In peacetime we sometimes become aware of the extremes to which we carried ethnic propaganda against wartime enemies. We are not nearly as sensitive to our common deprecation of other ethnic and class groups within our own society. In selecting business or political associates and employees, neighbors, and fellow club members, we too often enter into what is really an unspoken conspiracy against those different from ourselves and in favor of those with similar identities — "our own kind of folks." In consequence, for example, some blacks react to white racism by becoming openly tribalistic. They thus dramatize the fraudulence of their alleged opportunities in our white-dominated society. They help to drive home how tribalistically the whites treat each other as well as the blacks.

For small isolated groups in a primitive world unjoined to other groups by modern means of transportation, communication, and trade, tribalism was the basis for organized survival. In today's highly complex and interrelated world, tribalism pushes us along pathways toward national disaster and international chaos.

One small corner of the English-speaking world, Northern Ireland, provides one of a vast number of vivid illustrations of calamitous uses of tribalism. Since 1921, the six northeastern counties of Ireland, with a current population of 1.5 million, have been a somewhat autonomous province of the United Kingdom, at first under a local government but since 1974 under more direct rule from Westminster. Formed as an ethnically Protestant-controlled enclave, leaders of the Protestant majority — three-fifths of the population — use a variety of techniques to retain their dominance both of the province and of its business enterprises.

With constant charges and countercharges of ethnic conspiracy, the Protestants preserve and strengthen their separatism and tribalism, their access to jobs, housing, and other facilities at the expense of the predominantly nationalistic Roman Catholics. Children attend church-oriented but publicly supported schools, play different types of games, affect different dialects, and join different scout troops and clubs. When they are grown, those on each side contend that those on the other side plot to monopolize the province. Although both ethnic groups derive roughly from the same highly mixed racial stocks, extremists on both sides recite racist myths with which to flatter their own identities and to belittle those of the opposition.

Frequently since 1921, armed conflict has broken out, with the Royal Ulster Constabulary (the provincial police) and British soldiers usually showing partisanship against the Roman Catholic minority. A respected moderate Roman Catholic leader said: "It's hard to believe, but this is tribal conflict now, and as far as the Catholics are concerned, the police are just part of the other tribe. There's no credible authority left."[19] Another North Irishman—who could have been either a Protestant or a Roman Catholic—asserted at that time: "We've all been stuck in our ghettos for so long that we don't quite know what to do without them. When the barriers are up, we all know where we are, and who we are. But when they come down, we're a bit lost in the new landscape."[20] They do not know how to face a society of competing human beings free of conspiratorial tribal ties.

Unemployment typically, as a consequence of the exploitation of the tribal conflict, runs higher in Northern Ireland and wages average lower than elsewhere in the United Kingdom. The conflict serves as a distraction from more basic issues. If deprived Roman Catholics and deprived Protestants were to combine forces, there would be a dramatic and democratic shift in political and economic power. Hopefully, international tides of secularism, of education, and of closely related ecumenicism, as well as of trade, will continue to bring a broader and more tolerant spirit.[21] As one commentator notes: "The important new middle-class of all denominations finds it advantageous to be broadminded. Younger-generation leaders are showing their impatience with the old shibboleths." He reveals a class bias, but even though the struggle continues, he points to a hopeful symptom.[22]

Cultural pluralism is a useful ideal for our heterogeneous society. When cultural pluralism implies tribal pluralism and tribal conspiracies, however, we have to remind ourselves that the segments of a tribally divided society never enjoy equal rights.

Too many students of class stratification or of ethnicity appear to be trying to solve a personal identity problem rather than to develop more accurate conceptions. They even go so far as to declare, as do two Northern Irish scholars, "Unless you're from the place you can't start to understand it."[23] In contrast with this view, one of the most perceptive and widely read novels about Northern Ireland, *Trinity*, was written by Leon Uris,[24] a person not of Irish background but one who did adequate field and library research there and elsewhere.

3. Classism

James Madison asserted in the *Federalist* papers in 1787 that special interests "grow up of necessity in civilized nations, and divide them into different classes, actuated by different sentiments and views." He touches upon two of social class's most significant factors, concerns and life styles, but discussions of the subject now make it much more complicated and controversial.[25] In common usage, class is sometimes looked upon as (a) a *statistical* category, families on a similar income level, (b) an *occupational* category, those supported by relatively similar types of employment (unskilled, skilled, professional, managerial, entrepreneurial), or (c) a *political* entity, those sharing similar actionist needs and goals.

These conceptions lead to rather different notions of how people are distributed, of their social positions, and thus of social organization. The use of statistical categories based upon income is convenient for market studies, but it tends to place in similar categories people with rather different ways of life and senses of identity. Occupational categories come closer to placing people in population segments to which they feel that they belong, but they include people with contrasting values, friendship networks, and social concerns. Political or politico-economic similarities do more to give people a sense of class consciousness. It takes time, sometimes a generation or more, for people to adapt intellectually and emotionally to an upward or downward movement in terms of income or occupation. Family backgrounds as well as personal struggles have much to do with establishing politico-economic class consciousness.

Critical events or situations focus attention on the politico-economic and thus raise class consciousness realizations of identities of interest.[26] John Stuart Mill illustrates this by observing: "The concessions of the privileged to the underprivileged are so seldom brought about by any better motive than the power of the underprivileged to extort them."[27] This class picture in the United States is further complicated by the caste-like divisions of race and of separatist ethnicity.

When people are viewed in masses, the uniqueness of individuals tends to have less significance than the similarities within smaller and larger aggregates that have a continuing hold upon their members. Within those groups, people endlessly repeat routines that resemble those of their fellows. This culturally defined repetitiousness permeates all aspects of social life. It provides the background for class-oriented distortions that appear in sociology as well as in judicial, political, and business decisions and policy statements. This point has been mentioned elsewhere in this book, but it needs to be emphasized. A lot of the value conflicts in sociology arise from efforts by established professionals to stick to rationalizations for their own conception of the status quo, decorated with some face-saving cosmetic recommendations for change, rather than to probe the character and needs of all class groups.

4. Intentionism

About 322 B.C., Aristotle asserted: "Let injustice, then, be defined as voluntarily causing injury contrary to the [written or general] law."[28] In other words, "intention makes the crime." Attorneys for plaintiffs and defendants have juggled that concept ever since. It often takes the form of the legal maxim: "Every act must be judged by the doer's intention."[29] But intention from whose perspective, in terms of whose interests and of what evidence? When one takes into consideration all the possible variations in thought and behavior, one is faced with the haunting generalization of George Bernard Shaw: "All men mean well."[30]

In some cases of interpersonal relations, this use of "intention" makes sense and reasonable public policy. Was a violent death an accident or a murder? Was a person discharged from a position for reasons of incompetence, malfeasance, or a prejudiced decision? Lack of proof of malicious intent, not an easy case to make, has provided a convenient defense for public speakers and the mass media against suits for libel.[31] It has also been an excuse for behavior that "unintentionally" results in racist, ethnic, or sexist discriminatory situations and practices.

Another ancient statement, this one by the playwright Plautus about 190 B.C., furnishes a contrasting viewpoint: "To mean well is nothing without to do well."[32] This thought is relevant to the disputes that arise out of the U.S. Supreme Court decision on school desegregation, *Brown v. Topeka Board of Education,*[33] and in connection with many other controversies over intent versus behavior. Does desegregation mean integration? Or does desegregation merely call for an end to intentional discrimination? Wouldn't it require racist discrimination in order to force de facto desegregation and thus integration?

The Supreme Court's 1896 decision, *Plessy v. Ferguson,*[34] had established the doctrine that "separate-but-equal" facilities were permissible under the federal constitution. In its unanimous 1954 decision, the Court decided: "Separate educational facilities are inherently unequal." It said that "such segregation is a denial of the equal protection of the laws."[35]

To implement such a justified reorientation of constitutional interpretation meant a redistribution of power and privileges. It placed possible burdens on all segments of the population to correct an unfair and oppressive situation. As those burdens took forms leading to the mixing of pupils from different racial, ethnic, and class backgrounds, rationalizers volunteered avoidance patterns to powerful resisters of the movement. For example, the historian Raymond Wolters welcomes *Brown* as "a landmark that separates Jim Crow America from modern America," but he then laments that "education has suffered grievously from naïvely liberal court orders, from the influence of progressive education, and from the defiant and irresponsible behavior of some students." Little wonder then that he calls for the federal courts to keep their hands off schools that do not intentionally "discriminate": "Management of the public schools would then be returned to local school boards and superintendents, and racial policies would be fashioned through the give-and-take of the democratic process."[36] Thus actual segregation is acceptable so long as it is not intentional!

The political scientists R. A. Pride and J. D. Woodard base similar conclusions on a study of school busing for desegregation in Nashville, Tennessee. They tell how busing created "conditions by which dissimilar subcultures with divergent lifestyles come into conflict." This conflict becomes "no longer about skin color *per se,* it is about values and attitudes toward work and play, good and evil, and 'us' and 'them.'"[37]

This disturbed Pride and Woodard. The situation opened windows upon a bigger world. It made people see "them" as people rather than as stereotypes. It is, like all significant educational experiences, an opportunity rather than a burden.

Meanwhile, rural families have long gained from their children being bused into integrated public schools that often bring representatives of many subcultures into contact. Roman Catholics and some other religious denominations use publicly supported buses to send their children, often for many miles, into their own sectarian schools. These two types of busing are rarely mentioned in discussions of busing to achieve racial integration even though they do share some of the integrative problems.

From my own studies of segregated and integrated schools, I am convinced of the value to pupils and to society of mixed classes and of teachers from a variety of backgrounds. Spectacular evidence of the evils of segregative education exists in Canada, England, and Northern Ireland as well as in many parts of the United States. Somehow social scientists themselves have to avoid empty intentionalism. What counts is what can happen and does happen.

5. Life Events, Fads, and Fashions

Social scientists are creatures of their times and environments. Wars, cold wars, riots, "terrorism," depressions and recessions and booms, women's rights, youth problems, lesbian and gay rights, sexual freedom, drugs, nuclear energy, the aged, suicide, death, illegal and legal migrations, underworld gangster activity, white-collar crime, multinational corporate activities, and political scandals come and go in top billings not only in the mass media but also in professional convention programs, periodicals, and textbooks. Adaptable and penetrating social scientists grow with such waves of experience. As a result, they try to transcend the immediate, to look behind current symptoms, and to discover and formulate more radical, critical, or basic knowledge.

Wars, riots, and international and domestic imperialism point to central characteristics of society that require more than the sporadic investigation social scientists have given them. Attention to anti-feminist and anti-minority discriminations and exploitations has not held the continuing attention that is needed to help clarify and counteract such inequalities.

Distorting mirrors. The prevailing conception of news is dangerous to social scientists as well as people generally because it involves tyrannous entrapment. In the guise of furnishing the people "all the news that's fit to print," the mass media try to give the impression that they mirror objectively the day's most important developments. On the contrary, their staffs select and present material "in the belief that by so doing [the media] . . . will profit," to quote a leading writer on journalistic practice, Curtis D. MacDougall.[38] Newspapers, like radio and television, are operated to attract and to hold the attention of consumers so that advertisers can sell them merchandise, services, and ideas. The media do not risk boring customers or offending advertisers. Thus, news reports are only as instructive and representative of popular interests as appears to be expedient at the time. The daily *New York PM,* during its 1940–47 period, without advertising, furnished a striking contrast to the ordinary commercial conception of news. It was made possible by the creative journalist, Ralph Ingersoll, and by the enlightened generosity of Marshall Field of the Chicago mercantile family. This experiment became too costly, and it died.[39]

As a result of his comprehensive study of world communications media, the journalist J. Herbert Altschull contends that neither in the Soviet Union nor in the United States "is censorship necessary." He concludes:

> Only in the rarest circumstances are challenges raised to basic goals and values. Three factors contribute to the absence of challenges. First, there is the educational system under which the journalists learn to adopt those goals and values as their own. Second, the hiring process weeds out nearly all those who might be likely to raise challenges. And third, those rebels who make it through the first two screening processes are pressured into conforming, either by their colleagues or by their own wish to rise up the ladder.[40]

Thus, most journalists in whatever country tend to be "true believers" in the establishment unless they invest their talents and efforts in alternative or experimental media. When such people as Ralph Nader do that, they—like autonomous social scientists—can make memorable contributions.

What does the mass media concept of news do to our daily picture of the world? It seizes upon exciting antics of extremists—warmongers, black nationalists, student rebels, women liberationists, hippies, yip-

pies, yuppies, users of marijuana, LSD, and heroin, domestic murderers, battle scenes abroad and in our streets, small-time thieves, and
members of the so-called Mafia. News accounts build them up. Reporters typically bring into focus only superficial events, not the conditions out of which they arise, and they like running stories about
glittering individuals. The latter are much like episodes in comic strips
or TV serials, except that they deal with the Presidency, the very
wealthy, the English royalty, astronauts, and figures in entertainment,
sports, and the underworld.

Think of all the excitement the media develop in connection with
"communism" and such other undefinable conceptions as isolation-
ism, internationalism, the Third World, keep the world "safe" for "democracy." News makes us think that we are in touch with the "world"
and equips us to talk entertainingly and knowingly about the same
things other people can also discuss in an entertaining and knowing
manner. Those who quote alternative or experimental periodicals are
often greeted with annoyance or silence in such discussions.[41]

News helps build interest in fads — often irresponsible fads — by de-
nouncing or praising them in instructive detail. It unnecessarily stirs
the anxieties and antagonisms of overprotective parents and flag-waving
officials. It distracts attention, for example, from big-time thieves and
conspirators, from collusions between legal and illegal operators in
business and politics, from manipulators of government on behalf of
powerful special interests, and from wheelers-and-dealers using United
States power to exploit people and resources in foreign countries.[42]

If media recounted war stories more as the events occur, we would
be able to perceive all too vividly that wars are senseless to humanity.
They appear to mean something in the short run for those with a stake
in their immediate operation or outcome. Too many people are led
to believe that they have a stake, whether large or small, in war as
a method.

When students, blacks, Hispanics, women, lesbians and gays, industrial workers, and other activists see their events reported in the
mass media, they have evidence of how those media distort and attempt to trivialize disturbing efforts.[43]

A few excellent newswriters and newscasters transcend the dominant concept of news and thereby reveal its general shabbiness and
corruption. Notable examples are Lincoln Steffens (1866–1936), George
Seldes (b. 1890), I. F. Stone (b. 1907), Edward R. Murrow (1908–65),
and Ralph Nader (b. 1934).[44] Some publishers, such as E. W. Scripps
(1834–1926), William Allen White (1868–1944), Marshall Field III

(1893–1956), and Ralph Ingersoll (1900–84),[45] have demonstrated the utility of mass media dedicated to public service. They have exhibited unusual courage, imagination, and persistence in their efforts. They are discretely idolized but not extensively emulated.

6. Personality Types That Disciplines Attract

Perhaps one of the least considered distortions of scholarly disciplines arises from the ways in which a discipline's public images select the personality types attracted to it. This came to my attention through my undergraduate participation in the contrasting worlds of mathematics and chemistry majors and of student journalists. My interdepartmental teaching experiences and my non-academic activities since then have underscored the gross differences among those attracted to various types of employment. Since the dissimilarities are gross and imprecise, they do not reflect a single, simple characterization of any one discipline's single public image. They are not homogeneous categories.

People drawn to a social science by concern with macro-social problems such as class stratification and war can have rather different needs, emotional characteristics, and ways of expressing themselves from those attracted to it by concern with such micro-social problems as wife-beating, child abuse, or the use of drugs. Those enticed by the intricacies of methods or theory do not share the orientation of those enamored with participant observation or clinical social study or a clear literary presentation of findings. Still others do not enter social science primarily for such topical considerations. They see opportunities to pursue such a life style as that of a professor, a researcher, a social actionist, an author, or an administrator. To do so, they accept whatever ideological orientation and methods of work appear to be expedient to gain their end.

In consequence of these personality variations, among other factors, the various social sciences each tend to be exemplified by loosely integrated aggregates of specialists with different visions of what they want to do and what they think their discipline is or should be. A given academic department or research institute often avoids personality variation and thus fails to benefit from stimulating personality contrasts.

The personality type situation is further complicated by *individual multivalence*. Social scientists are in general acquainted with the fact that any given individual has complicated relations with a variety of other persons and social groups. They are likely to accept the generalization "that the more roles in an actor's repertoire, the better prepared he is to meet the exigencies of social life."[46] The word, "actor," refers here to any person, not just to a stage professional, but the label can scarcely be divorced in the usage of many—as it should be—from its dramaturgic connotation.

The individual person visualized as an actor is somehow thought to retain a monovalent consistency. This self is assumed to be separate from its roles and to manage in a controlled and voluntary manner its participation in a variety of roles and of group contexts. But when the individual is seen to be multivalent, the more or less contradictory social selves are recognized as becoming habitual, expressed automatically in appropriate situations. In consequence, we often formulate and state opinions and policies, even descriptions of "reality," somewhat differently in different social contexts.[47]

Social scientists who confront this multivalence perceptively in themselves and in their research do not give the impression—as do many others—that their subjects are monovalent. They realize how noncomparable interview data might well be unless they so arrange their interview personnel and situations as to make them comparable, so that they will result in a comparable type of role response from each subject. They also comprehend that a broader visioned survey, possibly with open-ended extensive interviews, would yield a much more accurate but complex set of responses. To an extent not generally recognized and implemented, multivalence greatly complicates social interviewing and especially opinion surveying![48]

The fact that social scientists themselves are also multivalent presents them with an even more profound problem. If they have not managed somehow to transcend their multivalence in their scientific work, which of their social personalities speaks in a given research report? How influential is the putative audience in determining what is said? A diplomatic statement to one audience—a statement others might label deceptive—can differ greatly from a speech made before another audience. Any such effort at diplomacy can contrast sharply with a candid presentation, one more likely to be scientific. Sometimes such a contrast is made apparent to students by the differences between a professor's classroom and conference discussions and the same individual's publications. Sometimes a social scientist assumes that this many-faced nature is expedient because of the controversial character of the topic under consideration, but constructive innovators find ways and take risks in order to report their findings accurately and in full.

Organizationally prominent social scientists expediently maintain and exploit exceptionally varied repertoires of roles. Because of their lack of focus, their lack of an obsessive monovalent quest for more accurate and useful knowledge, the reputations of such persons for intellectual leadership depend upon their political influence during life. After death, their contributions may be quickly overshadowed by those of candid offbeat innovators whom the politically prominent may have tried to brush aside in life. The monovalent quest for more precise knowledge of society for an individual is a highly speculative course, but it is the kind of career that has at times yielded great social gains.

The fifteen enticing distortions of social thought outlined in these two chapters are all related to deepset social doctrines labeled in popular discussions by catchwords. As W. G. Sumner concluded in 1903, "Doctrines are the most frightful tyrants to which men are subject, because doctrines get inside of a man's own reason and betray him against himself." People give their lives for them, but: "What are they all?" To which he replies: "Doctrines are always vague; it would ruin a doctrine to define it, because then it could be analyzed, tested, criticised, and verified; but nothing ought to be tolerated which cannot be so tested." Their catchword labels take hold through "popular mythologizing." Thus: "If you allow a political catchword to go on and grow, you will awaken some day to find it standing over you, the arbiter of your destiny, against which you are powerless, as men are powerless against delusions."[49]

More college graduates should be able to recall their educational experiences, as does the sociologist Howard Elterman: "The sociological perspective which I learned fascinated me because it never lost sight of the distinctions between images and reality. Or how ideologies, those belief systems which legitimize certain interests, could be used to disguise the actual nature and behavior of individuals and governments."[50]

It is hoped that this effort to define and analyze some enticing catchwords and doctrines helps to offset their tyrannical hold upon so many of us.

10

How Sociologists
Serve People

Sociology is portrayed in the foregoing chapters as an arena in which ideological struggles reflect those to be found in society at large. Sociologists try to understand and describe the complicated human dramas, and their findings can be significant for society as a whole or for those who seek to control it. Struggles within the profession are conducted as much as possible in terms of rhetoric, access or denial of access to opportunities for employment, research grants or contracts, or publication, and discrete disputes over organizational controls. Only occasionally do such dealings get media attention.

Let us turn now to a further consideration of how sociology and sociologists, whether humanist or not, enter into these struggles and in doing so serve themselves, others, and society more generally.

How does one launch an interesting and rewarding career in sociology, especially in liberating humanist sociology? This question takes us behind the de facto expansion of opportunities for literate and society-wise sociologists mentioned in the first chapter. How did they prepare themselves for the positions they obtained?

Similar preparation is required for a traditional college teacher, a full-time researcher, or an applied humanist sociologist. In view of tightening academic budgets, employment possibilities other than teaching now deserve consideration.

The most salable types of training for a sociologist outside of the academy, in terms of their attractiveness to potential employers — to judge from the experiences of my students, my colleagues, and myself, are the following: (1) ability to communicate clearly orally and in writing; (2) firsthand knowledge of the behavior of a variety of social groups; (3) competence in analyzing current events and developments in terms of available evidence and social-historical tendencies; (4) mastery of the methods of sociological research, with an understanding of their potentialities and their limitations; and (5) a good background in sociological theory and in the humanities. These five qualifications are needed both by "sociologists out in the world" and by academicians. As the sociologist Charles Horton Cooley insisted, "The more involved with human life is the material of a science the more is breadth of humane culture a *sine qua non* of the student."[1]

The ability to speak and write English prose simply and accurately is one of the easiest skills to sell to almost any employer. It is needed in government, business, private agencies of all sorts, and academia. It is a rarity and is well worth taking the time to learn. In my estimation, it should be a requirement for any academic degree in sociology. It is a much more important subject than the usually required social statistics training. What is the point of learning sociologese as a private language without being able to translate your findings readily so that others can understand you?

Concerning the second mentioned salable quality, field experience, intimate work in a variety of social class, ethnic, and social-cause groups, makes society, sociology, and the sociologist come to life. Such field work gives human affairs new and important dimensions. As the sociologist Glenn Jacobs has it, we look at the social world "first by the most direct means possible — ourselves — and then parsimoniously develop extensions (methods) to the degree that our existential involvement needs supplementing." This is "a radical empiricism in place of scientism, a disciplined skepticism about any substitute for man as his own measure."[2] Cultural anthropologists wisely require for the doctoral degree one or more years of participant observation in a different cultural setting, experience that often lends a sense of reality, vividness, and comparability to much anthropological writing.

It was often said of the great humanist sociologist, Robert E. Park of the University of Chicago and Fisk University, a former daily newspaper reporter, that he had learned about sociology primarily through walking the streets of the world, talking with the many sorts of people he found there, and observing their behavior. As the sociological historians Howard Becker and Harry Elmer Barnes point out: "Park represents the unusual combination of literary ability, wide range of experience, insight into personality, keen appreciation of empirical evidence, and a gift for systematic thought."[3] Through his formal training in this country, in Germany, and later and less conventionally in many other countries, Park developed a sophisticated grasp of statistical and other sociological methods as well as of the theoretical literature of the discipline and related fields. But Park never let methods, terms, or theories stand between him and real people. His basic research technique and the one he inspired his students to use was participant observation or what might more technically be termed the field-clinical study of human behavior. There is no substitute for what it can teach.

The third quality mentioned, competence in analyzing current developments in terms of social-historical tendencies, is not so academic a matter as it may sound. It depends as much upon first-hand observation and accumulated experience as it does upon background reading. Fads and fancies sweep through the commercial and political fields, often orchestrated by the mass media, and they surely penetrate the universities as well. The sociologist Everett C. Hughes indicates that this "interaction of sociologists with the public, or more exactly, with the several publics of a given society, is the interaction of universes of discourse, of whole systems of concepts which express, respectively, the sociologists' culture, and various lay cultures."[4] To place such matters in some sort of coherent social-historical perspective — a reasonably accurate one and not at all necessarily a conservative one — can be helpful in building the reputation of a rising humanist sociologist who is serving as a guide to sound strategies in public affairs and in social action.

The fourth and fifth places in the list of salable qualities include the "nuts and bolts" of sociology. This position in the listing is not because methods and theory are unimportant. Rather, from a standpoint outside of academia, they are back-ups for the first three items mentioned. You have to know sociological methods and theory to succeed in many a job, but your employer might not even know that you use them or what their names might be. They are not the items most specifically sought by employers in most cases, even though associates will come to value your use of them. If you have the first two competences mentioned — literacy and field experience — and an adequate training in the rest, the employer is likely to hire you.

Let us look at several general types of career that attract the sociologically trained. They are treated under these headings: brick-layers and trivia-makers; technicians, clinicians, and therapists; and nurturers of liberation sociology.

BRICKLAYERS AND TRIVIA-MAKERS

"Not philosophers but fret-sawyers and stamp collectors compose the backbone of society," asserts Aldous Huxley.[5] Even though this can also be said about those who call themselves the scientists of hu-man relationships, it should not be taken as a putdown. Fret-sawyers as elaborating artisans, with their scrolls and spirals, ornament social life. Collectors of many sorts of social data do more to advance our knowledge of society than do the too-speculative social philosophers. Unfortunately, too often favored today are those of slight curiosity, no courage, and a penchant for ritual. Our profession provides many ways for them to achieve a respectable status without prying into con-troversial matters, the matters more likely to concern a scientifically motivated sociologist. Thus collectors may be either useful bricklay-ers or mere trivia-makers.

Social science is a vast complex of findings and theories. It is con-tinually taking shape. Every researcher believes that his or her "hod" of facts (to continue the bricklaying metaphor) will somehow, some-where, sometime be found helpful to someone else in clarifying and extending social knowledge. Our profession being what it is, we or-dinarily think it impolite to remark that an ornate hod, carried well, is empty. Trivia-makers are ritualistic hod carriers who go through elaborate and even elegant motions but carry nothing useful. In con-trast, facts assembled by probing collectors can be controversial, even embarrassing, but they are what we most need.

Writers of trivia are most often "approachers" or contributors to methodological or other theoretical bric-a-brac. They make sweeping generalizations based on small but pretentious samples of possible data. Their grasp of the efforts of others is confined within a cult and a ten-year limit on hindsight. They resemble ardent fishers who spend their spare time throughout the year creating artistic trout flies of only ca-sual interest to trout.

They also bring to mind the preoccupation of so many university presidents with the extramural funding of research by governmental agencies, foundations, and corporations while their students face "dis-organized, uninspiring, and boring teaching, sloppy or non-existent advising, and a general disregard for the academic and other pursuits of undergraduate students." To this the educator Paul Von Blum adds: "Mediocrity characterizes the state of education at most large American research universities today."[6]

The sociological approachers expend endless research grants and fill many volumes with refinements of semantics, methodology, and theory which—like the angler's dry flies—are for the purpose of conspicuous distinction rather than the expansion of social knowledge. They always conclude their reports on the high note that they have made a ringing case for further research on the subject—that is, for more research grants. As the psychologist A. H. Maslow points out, definition and refinement of proper methods for research often lead "to voluntarily imposed self-limitations, to abdication from huge areas of human interest"[7]—in short, to that contradiction of terms, a "scientific orthodoxy."

Methodological purists contend that scientists should not call any conclusions "scientific" short of near certainty—as they define "certainty." The sociologist George A. Lundberg, for example, called for "undivided faith to science, . . . a faith more worthy of allegiance than many we vainly have followed in the past."[8] Another sociologist, Harry Alpert, notes that "partly as a result of Lundberg's influence and partly as a result of the noble convergences in sociological theory" Lundberg identified in the works of many others, "sociology has become more scientific," but "it seems to have become more irrelevant to the social issues of the day."[9]

Especially on publicly controversial matters, these scientific purists insist upon silence until they are overwhelmed with evidence, evidence they themselves would rather not collect. What is the growing class-stratification of schools doing to American society? How is increasing class segregation in living arrangements narrowing policymakers' perceptions in government, business, and non-profit organizations?

This protective negativism of the well-placed scientific purists easily aligns itself with establishment prejudices against social science as a competing source of intellectual authority. Negativism gives a cheap and heady illusion of dispassionate courage. It glosses over the unconnectedness, insignificance, and irrelevance of so much that they do. It makes it too easy to brush aside significant factual materials of a controversial nature that the more daring find and offer for consideration. The purists ignore the fact that social knowledge is never absolute. Social scientists serve by providing probable projections of social tendencies and of possible reactions to changes in social policies.[10]

TECHNICIANS, CLINICIANS, AND THERAPISTS

Sociologists develop practical applications of their findings and skills along many lines. Some continue interests in social case work, group work, organizing, and organization management. Some bring a greater degree of sophistication to market research — to product design and projections of a product's use, possible customers, and advertising appeals. In league with communications specialists, some help give an almost scary effectiveness to some public relations strategies. Some contribute to the propagandistic influence of public opinion pollsters by helping them make more accurate the one popularly visible check on poll accuracy: their ability to predict an election outcome.[11] Some help a variety of organization managers to perceive more accurately personnel problems and defects in social structure and ways to deal with both. Some offer new perspectives to clinical psychologists, psychiatrists, trial attorneys, and judges of criminal and civil courts.

Some of these sociologists might be thought of as social engineers in the sense that they are skilled in social planning, organizing, and managing. Some are technicians who provide guidance in applying sociological findings, methods, and theories. Others like to be called clinical sociologists or social therapists because of their involvements in interpersonal and group counseling.

The engineer and technician types sometimes lament in print about being grouped as sociologists with those they call do-gooders. Some even reject the sociologist label. But the shared identity offers some unintended services both ways. Scientific humanist researchers and professors tend to be do-gooders, but their creativity lends authority and even prestige to the professional designation that can then increase the apparent worth of engineers and technicians. The latter and their administrators in turn acquire respectability with the powerful in our antideviationist society. They therefore provide a kind of practical social standing for sociologists as a whole among power seekers and holders. This even gives some protective coloration for socially critical scientists once they have obtained a position with tenure. In addition, under the leadership of courageous popular writers in the mass media[12] and among educators,[13] more people in public affairs and even in industry are coming to understand what may be gained from giving attention to what some unconventional and unpredictable professionals in the physical and social sciences are telling us.

Whatever harm may come to the development of humanist sociology from the overweening claims of commercial market researchers, opinion pollsters, personnel managers, and policy consultants is in part counterbalanced by society's increased interest in whatever the term "sociology" may be thought to mean. The contradictions within the field of sociology help to give it its vitality, its searching quality. Sociology gains from the independent critical appraisal of commercial technicians' products.[14]

Pressures to be "practical": Previous chapters discuss aspects of managerial and manipulative social technology in connection with distortions of social thought by the news conceptions of the mass media and by the claims of therapists and reformers. They also describe the managerial-bureaucratic paradigm for sociology developed for social engineers and the roles of sociological technology in social manipulation. As these considerations suggest, significant problems arise in the relations between sociological scientists and social engineers chiefly within our colleges and universities. These problems concern the involvement of faculties and students of liberal-arts colleges and graduate schools in special-interest social-engineering projects. As the social analyst William H. Whyte, Jr., said in *Fortune* magazine: "The more quickly our bureaucracies grasp at the new 'tools' of persuasion, the more will the legitimate social scientist be pressured for 'practical results.' Those who would indulge in pure inquiry instead would find themselves 'deviants' from the integrated society they helped to fashion; only as lackeys would they have a function. In sheer self-defense, if nothing else, the social scientist must keep an eye on ethics."[15] It is noteworthy that it is the commercialized social engineers rather than the sociological scientists who clamor for ethical *codes*. Ethics are part of the way of life of humanist social scientists, but ethical codes are too frequently found useful as façades to the exploitative and denied as defenses of the idealistic.

Such considerations led the economist Thorstein Veblen to state that a "stale routine of futility" might "overtake the universities, and give . . . foolish results, as fast as the system of standardization, accountancy and piece-work goes consistently into effect." He placed his hopes to the contrary in "the continued enforced employment of a modicum of impracticable scholars and scientists . . . whose unbusinesslike scholarly proclivities and inability to keep the miner's-inch of scholastic credit always in mind, must in some measure always defeat the perfect working of standardization and accountancy."[16]

Rationalizations for converting sociological graduate departments into social-engineering institutes become rather precious, and at times downright cynical. The principal contentions are as follows: Outside subsidies from special interests, whether cloaked as foundation grants or not, make it possible to finance the expensive research now "necessary" for the "development of knowledge." Financing includes stipends for graduate students, technical assistants, and secretaries as well as funds for complicated computer operations and possibly also to pay report publication costs. Even though the immediate problems of such projects are technical rather than scientific, the data gathered are said to bear as well upon more "basic scientific issues." Donors (as they are often called) pay for social engineering, and they get what they pay for or do not subscribe again. The faculties also presumably get data related to their "scientific interests," as well as facilities and funds with which to recruit and train graduate students in big-time procedures "essential" to current sociological research. But instances pile up that do not bear out this line of reasoning. Soap manufacturers and television entrepreneurs, asbestos and tobacco industrialists make professors work hard for their subsidies. "Scientific interests" can be put aside indefinitely.[17]

How much do commercial pressures succeed in modifying the value position of academic solicitors for research funds in sociology? In a proposed misadventure, social engineers associated with a prestigious university institute outlined a series of investigations to determine how to carry on research more efficiently in an organizational or team setting. The proposal for the program quotes a "prominent research executive" as follows:

> We must know what we want and what we expect of the research worker. We must understand his motivations and characteristics. Based on our understanding of these things, we must provide environments conducive to good results. We must use creative imagination in the administration of research. We must follow this by sound engineering and good business planning. This is effective research. This is the kind of research which means position and control of destiny tomorrow.[18]

To these ideas, that sound so much more like those of industrial managers or advertising hucksters than anything worth being associated with scientific sociology, the academic social research institute says amen in these words: "It is toward such goals that the . . . proposal is directed."[19]

This example is extreme only in its frankness. In this project, as in many other social-engineering "research" proposals examined, precise ideological conditions are set at the beginning that define the kinds of facts to be gathered. These conditions, in effect, command certain conclusions. A much more fundamental problem than the one stated is whether or not scientists can best do sociological work under a research administration and as part of an organization consisting of one or more teams. Even more fundamental is the question: How does creative scientific work actually take place? For that matter, how does creative work of any kind take place? By what sorts of people? Under what kinds of conditions?[20]

Is it any wonder that academic social engineers take on the cultlike characteristics so common among business technicians, with security found in hierarchy, a full-blown "company" ideology, a patter, a few well-worn techniques and gadgets, and a narrow routine of life? The sociologist Daniel Bell notes the pride these people exhibit in what they call "strictly empirical research" with its "formidable statistical apparatus," and he adds, "Yet while researchers in this field often display a parvenu arrogance toward theory, a great deal of pretentious, senseless, and extravagant writing fills their own work, much of it inspired by the theoretical system they have taken over from [Vilfredo] Pareto." These technicians' ideology typically accepts a depersonalized view of less fortunate humanity. Bell observes: "The belief in man as an end in himself has been ground under by the machine, and the social science of the factory researchers is not a science of man, but a cow-sociology."[21] As Whyte concludes in his study cited above, social engineering "is profoundly authoritarian in its implications, for it subordinates the individual to the group" and provides "a highly appealing rationale for conformity."[22]

Intentionally or not sociological researchers and theorists have thus begun to develop as one of their major products a technology that engineers and technicians are placing at the service of special interests with little or no regard for broader and more humane concerns. At the same time, as the sociologist Everett C. Hughes observes, "A good deal of industrial sociology is a reporting of the news of industrial management and organization and of labor relations and conflict in a given series of industries in a given time and place." He adds that the critical use of such data can make helpful "generalizations come *from* the special or applied sociologies as well as being applied *to* them."[23]

Social therapists: How can any society persist without therapists of many sorts? Many therapists, especially those engaged in interpersonal consultation on personal and organizational problems, have long had as their ideal a nonmanipulative stance toward their clients. Their roles would be more easily perceived if they were more often called consultants, facilitators, or resource persons. But many of them function quietly and effectively without being too clearly identified as such. They provide clients or friends or associates with data and facilities with which those counseled may solve their own problems as autonomously as possible in their own ways.

Constituents, clients, inmates in all sorts of institutions, and members of many social groups are now organizing to achieve self-determination and to address their own problems. Prisoners, ex-offenders, alcoholics, tobacco users, other drug addicts, people in mental institutions and in other types of hospitals, people on relief, the physically handicapped, the overweight, and other people with special needs — all are claiming the right of self-control and self-guidance. [24] Women, blacks, Spanish-Americans, Amerindians, other ethnic minorities, lesbians and gays, schools pupils, college students, dropouts from school and from society, the socially experimental, and a vast array of other groups and social categories are all finding bases for joining in the general trend of the times toward self-determination. [25] Members of political factions and parties, professions and vocations, trades and industries, and religious sects and denominations had long preceded them. All are questioning policies to which they have been subjected. All are insisting upon policies that they formulate or negotiate themselves and that represent, as they see them and as nearly as possible, their own interests and needs more accurately and more authentically.

These many groups, factions, and categories of people are not at all averse to the use of facts and summaries of other people's experiences on which to base their views and procedures, but they do not want specialists to take one group's need for data or service as an opportunity for its manipulation or exploitation.

Such groups make mistakes. They and their leaders may be quite unprepared as yet for participatory democracy. They want to find believable and dependable answers to their own questions as much as they can for themselves, with or without trained aid. If therapists can convert themselves adequately into consulting resource persons whom clients can trust, such specialists in all their variety can weather the changes we increasingly face. [26]

Even self-organization of the socially rejected — prisoners and inmates of mental institutions — promises long-sought dividends for themselves and for society. The story of prisons as training schools for criminality and for sexual perversion, as brutalizers of guards, trusties, and other inmates, is well known to social investigators. The story of mental institutions, except for the notable examples of some constructive ones, is all too similar. They institutionalize staff and other inmates on a basis of persistence or even mere survival. The "cures" after inmate-assimilation are few. Irresponsible discharges without adequate aid have become a growing problem. Organizations of prisoners and ex-prisoners are beginning to bring a new realism to demands not only for the reform of prison living conditions, but also for improving the reassimilation processes available to such persons for their reentry into the "world outside." In thinking about such activity, we need to realize that only a small percentage of those who break any criminal law ever even see the inside of a jail![27]

Humanist sociologists who are field workers or clinical researchers or consultants have done much to stimulate this self-help type of individual and group therapy.[28]

Policy modifiers: Relationships among sociologists and public policy-makers for government, business, or voluntary organizations are complex and often problematic. The reception of research findings on housing and urban redevelopment, mass communications, and intergroup relations, especially racist evidences, illustrate failures and successes of sociologists in contributing to public policy formation in recent decades. In such work, as Irving Louis Horowitz notes, "What is at stake as a result of this newly acquired influence [in policy formation] is not the feasibility of social science, but the credibility of social scientists."[29] Even more at stake is the well-being of the people who are or are not being helped. In the following discussion, one outstanding example — race relations — is offered.

Sociologists, psychologists, and anthropologists have educated many thousands of high school and college students with regard to race, racism, interethnic relations, and other aspects of intergroup conditions and problems. This educational work is one of our greatest contributions to social welfare, but we have not done nearly as much to combat the growing pall of orthodoxy in mass communications. We generally give much less attention to the latter in our college texts and in our research. Our "researchers" have done more to solve technical problems in psychological warfare and for advertising and public-relations purposes than to help students understand propaganda and other aspects of social manipulation that directly affect them. In other words, we have done more to promote than to dispel the growing pall of orthodoxy.[30]

The social psychologist Kenneth B. Clark and his associates for the first time had scientific findings of sociologists and psychologists admitted as evidence and used as the major basis for a decision of the U.S. Supreme Court.[31] The resulting unanimous decision in *Brown v. Board of Education of Topeka*,[32] read by Chief Justice Earl Warren on May 17, 1954, has had sweeping consequences in school desegregation throughout the United States. This is especially so following a second *Brown* decision[33] in May 1955 that helps implement the first. As the journalist James Reston commented in the *New York Times* with regard to the first decision, the "court's opinion read more like an expert paper on sociology than a Supreme Court opinion."[34]

The educational work done by social scientists since 1896, plus the changed international status of the country, combined to provide the foundation for the elimination of the previous U.S. Supreme Court *Plessy* doctrine of "separate but equal."[35] This reference to historical preparation is not meant to belittle the hard-won accomplishment of Clark and his associates and of the National Association for the Advancement of Colored People. Instead, it is to help place it in a broader perspective. These court decisions constitute a formal recognition of participation in policy-making beyond anything previously achieved by sociologists in public affairs in this country.

From this instance, it should be clear that sociological findings make their greatest positive impact upon public policy when they are simultaneously moving through educational, popular, and policy-influencing channels. Such a success as that in the desegregation decisions does not arise from little social engineering manipulations. It comes from wrestling with a major issue in human existence.

This is not to imply that success with the desegregation decisions was more than a battle won in a long, continuing, and much broader struggle: the struggle for no less than equal opportunities for all without reference to race or color. While the struggle continues in our schools, it currently has other crucial focal points in employment and in housing through urban and rural redevelopment. For sociologists, schooling, employment, and housing can scarcely be treated separately. They are all integral parts of individual, family, and neighborhood life.

Sociological research, teaching, and counseling are contributing to this broader struggle both substantively and evaluatively. Substantively, sociologists continue to find and interpret evidence that verifies and emphasizes the contributions to social health of desegregation in all aspects of social life. On the evaluative side, sociologists produce articles and books that point time and again to contrasts between the alleged purposes of programs to improve employment or housing for the underprivileged and the actual consequences that follow. As the sociologist Mel Ravitz sums up such findings, "Despite the millions of dollars of federal grants, state aid, and local funds we have spent over the past twenty years for urban renewal, public housing, delinquency control, anti-poverty efforts, we have little tested evidence that all this money has made a significant impact in improving the lives of the mass of urban citizens."[36] When two other sociologists first revealed that housing segregation in Detroit "had increased steadily since 1930," and then that "Detroit was fast becoming a city of dependents —dependents who must be supported on a constantly shrinking tax base,"[37] they were fired from their positions in a state university institute. Their generalization applies just as well to a great many other American cities.[38]

As to the gains from such struggles with interracial policies and practices, Kenneth B. Clark gives this "down-to-earth" view:

> Every time a Negro sees a group of secretaries —white and Black— chatting over lunch; or children —white and Black—walking together to school, he feels that hope is possible. Every time his white friend shows he is not afraid to argue with him as with anyone else, he sees that freedom is possible, that there are some for whom race is irrelevant, who accept or reject a person not as a Negro or a white, but in terms of himself. Only so can the real confinements of the ghetto be broken. The Negro alone cannot win this fight that transcends the "civil rights struggle." White and Negro must fight together for the rights of human beings to make mistakes and to aspire to human goals. Negroes will not break out of the barriers of the ghetto unless whites transcend the barriers of their own minds, for the ghetto is to the Negro a reflection of the ghetto in which the white lives imprisoned. The poetic irony of American race relations is that the rejected Negro must somehow also find the strength to free the privileged white.[39]

Here are some of the questions of public policy with which sociologists are now dealing: How can society best adjust itself to psychological deviants —criminal, sexual, deficient, and other? Is police brutality inevitable, even defensible, something the busy and anxious world cannot help but permit the defenseless to suffer, or can the police gain a new and more mature understanding of their social responsibilities? What about the atomism and anonymity of urban life? Just what does rural decay mean to human beings and their families? How abstract and unrealistic — distorted by unbridged social distances — are the politico-economic views typically fostered in our suburbs? Can we have community planning for living and not just for commercial purposes? How can we achieve more satisfactory marriage and divorce patterns? Can lonely men and women of the latter twentieth-century decades learn enough about propaganda and social manipulation to take active and useful roles in their community's political and social life? How can sociologists contribute more to international understanding?

These questions suggest some of the major policy areas to which sociologists are now making research contributions. To the extent that they are devoting themselves to such problems as humane concerns, their work is useful. Too many still prefer fancy methodological footwork and dehumanized engineering. The latter contribute too much toward the tendency in this country to fall into the formalism and abstract speculation to which so many European and American colleagues are prone.

NURTURERS OF LIBERATION SOCIOLOGY

From what can sociologists liberate or emancipate us? Is such a freeing from customary intellectual preconceptions and controls a useful and a socially defensible step?

Nurturers of liberation sociology try to resemble in their aspirations and work the critical questing for humane knowledge that characterized the ancient Greeks and the Europeans of the Renaissance. They profess to have a better way to learn about human affairs than through the uncritical acceptance of traditional wisdom, religious inspiration, logical deductions, or speculation. In doing so, they assume an obligation to provide tenable criteria with which to judge inherited social and moral teachings and to help build the relevant findings of scientists into an altering perspective on people in society. This obligation is carried out through the critical acceptance of relevant findings from the humanities as well as from scientific literature.

In speaking about the competitive situation of sociology among intellectual disciplines, a sociologist points to how sociological debates often confuse "nonsociological academic folk, whose bewilderment is brought about by a field that sometimes appears to strive to be at once scientific fish, humanistic flesh, and reformist fowl."[40] It apparently does not occur to this sociologist that it is possible to be all three.

Liberation sociologists face audiences who think they already know a great deal about society and human interrelationships. Young men and women gain this from their parents, home community, religious precepts, friends, "sociological" novels, and "sociological" exposés on television, in newspapers and magazines, and in books. Sociologists thus deal with subjects often discussed in sermons, in peer-group "rap" sessions, and in union meetings and corporate board rooms. The vast complexities of people, groups, and society make this confrontation a highly tentative process either in a classroom or in a book. The views of a sociologist are part of the discussion process of Western society in which findings are weighed, interpreted, and related to those of cultural anthropology, history, social philosophy, psychology, literature, and the mass media.

There are at least four ways to look at writing about sociology for a general audience: (1) You can insist that all sociology of any consequence is for specialists. It has to be precisely written and only inaccurate and superficial reinterpretations can be presented to the general public. (2) You can say that sociology is much too complicated for interpretation below the level of college freshmen or sophomores. (3) You can state that it should be done, that it can be done, and then sit and wonder what in the world we have to say to people in general. Publishers inform me that any number of popular books about sociology have been unsuccessfully attempted. Finally, (4) you can take the position of professional writers for general audiences that any major idea can be translated into simple enough English for the understanding of readers of *Time, Newsweek, The Atlantic Monthly,* and the *New York Times.* When you tell such writers that popularization has rarely been attempted successfully in sociology, they try to raise what they consider to be embarrassing questions about whether or not sociologists really have something of importance to communicate, whether or not they merely put ordinary ideas into a pseudotechnical language.

The situation may partly be due to what the sociologist Peter L. Berger refers to as the "grim humorlessness" of social scientists.[41] More likely it is because of the touchy nature of the materials with which social scientists deal: We do critically examine mythic beliefs about the fabric of society and our relations with and within it.

Media for popularizing social scientific findings for larger audiences include Public Affairs Pamphlets,[42] the English weekly *New Society*,[43] and the American monthly *Society* (formerly *Trans-Action*).[44] In addition, since 1938 the American Sociological Association, the Society for the Study of Social Problems, and other organizations have somewhat systematically made convention papers and proofs of forthcoming publications available to media representatives for reinterpretation.[45] In another manner, the inclusive *Sociological Abstracts*[46] facilitates dissemination by providing libraries and periodicals with exhaustive sets of summaries of sociological contributions suitably indexed for quick reference. It is available both in print and "on line" by telecommunication.

Is liberation sociology vulgar? The elitist sees no virtue in the crude *demos,* the common mass of humankind. "No art form, no body of knowledge, no system of ethics is strong enough to withstand vulgarization. . . . At its worst, mass culture threatens not merely to cretinize our taste, but to brutalize our senses while paving the way to totalitarianism." Curiously enough, these are statements by a professional sociologist.[47] He ignores the intimate and reciprocal relationships between creative intellectuals in any field and their time, place, and culture. Intellectuals are embedded in mass society by derivation, kinship, and routines of life, regardless of the extent to which they may have been able to separate or even alienate themselves from it. Many intellectuals come from deprived social segments. They repay their privileged place in society by focusing attention on artistic and scientific accomplishments, by staffing educational and research institutions and activities, by criticizing and preserving the cultural heritage, and by using their educations to seek solutions to society's problems. Their tastes and senses always owe debts to others.

A cultured elite or one preening itself on being such has no monopoly on creativeness in any society. It may be able to control and even to discourage the less powerful, but those sneered at may produce ideas or art forms that will become fashionable before long. Look at the influence now of black and Latin music and dance! Think of the reactions of the "cultured" to such writings as those of Walt Whitman and Mark Twain!

Often those with both sufficient natural endowment and adequate motivation to be creative appear in depressed and exploited pockets of the masses rather than among the assimilated ranks of a cultured elite.[48] Some of the more conservative sociologists, interestingly enough, developed rather democratic views of innovation. For example, W. F. Ogburn concludes that "the existing culture is the mother of inventions."[49] A. G. Keller regards the great person as "the product of his time and place, and his greatness consists in his insight, or luck, in producing a variation—in anticipating some massive movement [in human affairs, social structure, art, science, ideas] that is about to take place anyhow."[50]

Thus sociologists need to understand especially the nonelite of our society. The lower classes are sources of discontented and, thus, innovative people and of insights about how so many of us live, strive, and die. Vulgarization, better called popularization, is an end-product sociologists should seek.

Sociologists Serving People

Mass education, mass suffrage, mass marketing, and mass warfare — hopefully, mass peacemaking— insistently focus the attention of intellectuals, regardless of specialty, upon non-elitist challenges. In this, class-biased errors in public opinion polls and other sample-survey investigations have done much to undermine elitist certainties. In a sense, one can paraphrase Karl Marx and Friedrich Engels' *Communist Manifesto* and say that the specter haunting the world of the intellectuals is not so much the communist ideology as it is the common people, the rising masses. This specter even haunts communist elites who allege that they can accurately make policies that represent the proletariat. Whether one speaks of the common people in terms of public opinion, the labor force, the electorate, the market or even culture or society, that bulky aggregate becomes an increasing threat to all holders of power, control, and authority based upon special privilege. The outcome of this tendency is not at all in sight.

More and more people as they now grow up in our society are learning that subservience is not necessary. People are learning that they do possess and can express autonomous human dignity. It is theirs to keep, to nurture, to use. It involves risks, experimentation with techniques and etiquettes, but the spirit of the times is providing opportunities for mutual reinforcement in autonomous participation that have not existed so readily and so widely before.

The awakening and rising masses are fragmented, diverse, confused, and often poorly motivated and led. Mass media mythmaking often misleads them. Their ferment and their efforts at self-direction and self-organization, however, are giving people ways to express themselves and to participate in cooperative self-determination. They are exhibiting autonomous human dignity to an extent hitherto not thought possible.

When reference is made to the kind of society we might have, there is no thought of furnishing a static blueprint for what we might achieve at some future time. All societies change. Societies are social arrangements in process, not fixed edifices. The concern here therefore is with directions of change and with leverages that may be exploited to achieve more humane social relationships. Admittedly, it is a struggle in which there can be no clear-cut victory, and in which only eternal vigilance can protect human gains from the selfishly aggressive and manipulative. There can be goals, nevertheless, and social assets can be assessed and employed for human gains rather than for the gains of antisocial elites.

Revolts against Dehumanized Social Science

The foregoing mentions individual revolts against growing bureaucratic-managerial control of social science. Such individual efforts are useful, but they have limited influence in significant policymaking circles (controlling research grants, book publishing, periodicals, and academic jobs) until they are able to obtain an organizational medium through which to indicate in a more concerted manner their professional and popular strength. To outsiders, professional social science societies may appear fusty and irrelevant, but they are crucial market places for ideas and personnel in each discipline.

Prior to the depression of the 1930s, sociologists and social psychologists were mostly academicians, teacher-scholars. The chief conformist limitations upon us were those typical of the bourgeois ethos and the conditions of employment in colleges and universities. Then came the struggles for survival during the 1930s. The established tried to protect their privileges in academia and commerce by defining as narrowly as they could the qualifications of those who should practice. In contrast, many of those fresh from graduate schools and in search of employment visualized needs for the expansion of their services to society. Some of these controversial idealists, led by such people as David Krech and Goodwin Watson, organized in 1936 the Society for the Psychological Study of Social Issues (SPSSI) as a revolt within the American Psychological Association (APA).[51]

SPSSI members in 1936 looked upon their organization as a "body for the promotion and protection of research on 'controversial' topics, the administration of timely referenda, the authoritative interpretation of the attitudes of the socially-minded psychologists respecting important group conflicts, and the support of all progressive action that promises to aid in the preservation or creation of human values."[52]

Because the American Sociological Society (ASS) in the 1930s had come to resemble the APA in its restrictiveness and social values (or alleged "value-freeness"), many sociological social psychologists were attracted to SPSSI. I was one of them. We were happy with the challenges SPSSI and its members were willing to face. We were only sorry that SPSSI was not SSSI — a Society for the Study of Social Issues — in other words a more overtly interdisciplinary body.

By the 1940s bureaucratic-managerial control of the principal professional society in sociology had become oppressive in the view of many of the problematic-technically oriented, as well as in the eyes of the humanist existentialists. The growing number of regional societies remained somewhat open and flexible, but the American Sociological Society glorified abstractions and methodological complications.

Many of us then, as now, regard social problems as being necessarily the central concern of sociologists. We look upon what dependably accurate and relevant sociology we have as the composite product of many thorough-going social-problem studies. As my wife, Elizabeth Briant Lee, and I pointed out in 1949 in our book *Social Problems in America*, "Only through seeing and understanding actual instances of white-collar criminality, unemployment, despair, poverty, panic, and riot can the sociologist bring . . . theories into some degree of correspondence with social realities. Only by studying the accumulated generalizations of other investigators can the specific instances of crime, poverty, or panic come into some more adequate perspective."[53]

During the 1940s Elizabeth and I often discussed with other sociologists the relative lack of attention in our discipline to our pyramiding social problems. We finally started a campaign to develop a sister organization to SPSSI that in 1950–51 became the Society for the Study of Social Problems (SSSP). Its original constitution and by-laws resembled those of SPSSI, but SSSP structure differed in two marked respects from that of SPSSI. The latter had become a section of the APA (American Psychological Association), but we felt that SSSP could make a more continuing contribution by remaining separate from the ASS (from 1959 the ASA, the American Sociological Association). We also did not want membership to be limited to those labeled sociologists. SSSP's budget, organization, publications, and conferences are separate from the ASA's. We hope that they remain so.

Elizabeth and I asked E. W. Burgess of the University of Chicago and A. M. Rose of the University of Minnesota to help us in our organizing efforts. Of the elder statesmen in sociology at the time, Burgess appeared to be the most sympathetic with what we were trying to accomplish. He agreed to take on the title of acting chair for 1950–51 and then of president for 1951–53 on condition that he would not have to "do the work," as he put it. Rose spent the academic year 1951–52 in France, but prior to his departure he was of some assistance in enlisting midwestern support. As acting secretary in 1950–51, vice-president in 1951–52, president-elect in 1952–53, and president in 1953–54, I joined with Elizabeth and many others to "do the work."

Elizabeth chaired the important Editorial and Publications Committee that planned and initiated SSSP's two important projects in print: Jerome Himelhoch, S. F. Fava, and S. H. Aronson launched in June 1953 the SSSP journal, *Social Problems*. Himelhoch and Fava in 1955 edited the first of a series of sponsored books that were commercially published under the auspices and for the benefit of SSSP.[54]

The formal organizational meeting of SSSP took place on September 6, 1951 in the faculty lounge of Roosevelt College, Chicago.[55] During 1950–54, the organizing year and the first three years of SSSP's formal existence, there were many occasions when the whole enterprise veered perilously near to collapse. Some who accepted office in SSSP had little interest in its success, but there were always others who "covered" the delinquencies of such, and the "show went on." The extent of SSSP's strain in our own family budget often made Elizabeth and me discuss how far we could continue to support financially our organizational speculation! Fortunately, for example, such a volunteer as Stanley H. Chapman chaired the first membership committee; his vigorous direct-mail campaign helped quadruple our membership between our 1951 and 1952 annual meetings.

Perhaps our most difficult annual meeting was the one in 1952 in Atlantic City. Those entrusted with key arrangements for that meeting did not regard the society's existence seriously, and Elizabeth and I had to take over local details with the help of some of the three hundred in attendance. What could have been—and nearly was—a catastrophe was turned into a highly successful convention, well reported in the *New York Times*. News accounts featured contributions by Florian Znaniecki, George Simpson,[56] Erwin O. Smigel, and E. W. Burgess.[57]

Twenty-five years later, in 1975–76, several of us became aware of the need for a more value-oriented society than SSSP had become. This resulted in Charles P. C. Flynn, Elizabeth, and I forming the Association for Humanist Sociology. After preliminary meetings at our home in Short Hills, New Jersey, its first convention was held at Miami University, Oxford, Ohio, October 29–31, 1976. Elizabeth and I served as the AHS's first and second presidents in 1976–78. Flynn edited a newsletter for the AHS and then its journal, *Humanity & Society,* launched in 1977. Its newsletter, under the guidance of Richard H. Wells, evolved into *The Humanist Sociologist,* a quarterly periodical that carries a range of communications reflecting membership activities and concerns. The informal annual conferences of this society take place in the fall and have grown in popularity each year.

These organizational revolts against rigidification and dehumanization modified sociological research, theorizing, and writing and penetrated sociological teaching. Above all, the SSSP, AHS, and the Sociological Practice Association (formed in 1978 as the Clinical Sociology Association) help to broaden opportunities for expression by the younger and the more nonconforming sociologists. These three organizations do not compete. They are complementary. Among them, they are doing a great deal to keep sociology relevant and vital in today's problem-wracked society.

Fortunately for the health of sociology as a viable and useful discipline, revolts against organizational inadequacy have included a number of other efforts. Women, the young, blacks and other ethnic groups, and those with religious concerns have sought and found means to organize themselves so that they might influence sociological concerns, employment, and recognition. These initiatives make the profession more flexible and adaptable. They help create more perceptive understanding of insurgent contributions.

The ideological and social-scientific crises of our time are no longer disguisable by reformist palliatives and soothing propagandas. The disillusioned and rebellious women, blacks, Hispanics, youth, and other groups demand fundamental reconsiderations of how our society operates and of how it can come or be made to operate. They are learning to understand how a thoroughly scientific approach can yield more adequate insights and thus facilitate needed reorganizations. They are coming to support a humanist-existential approach to their problems. They see it as a tool for liberation and social adaptation. It offers no panaceas. It provides sane critiques of the manipulations by the

Swiss Guards and sound bases for social planning and for actionist strategies. Increasing literacy, social sophistication, and sense of urgency may lead people to play with many panaceas, but their experiences in doing so make a broader acceptance of a humanist-existential social science increasingly likely.

11

Helping People Confront Ideas and Change

Young rebels cry out against an "establishment" that rules through "hypocrisy." Militant blacks steel themselves to action against white racist "hypocrisy." Activist women prod their less concerned sisters of the majority gender to join in destroying the sexist "hypocrisy" with which men dominate society and exploit females.

The cry is an old one. Matthew quotes Jesus as saying, "Woe unto you, scribes and Pharisees, hypocrites! For ye make clean the outside of the cup and of the platter, but within they are full of extortion and excess."[1]

The term *hypocrite* derives from a Greek word meaning to mimic or to play a part. It has come to refer to a person who assumes a false appearance, who pretends "to be what he is not, or to feel or believe what he does not actually feel or believe; especially, a false pretender to virtue or piety."[2] Thus the clean "outside of the cup" hides such contrasting inwards as "extortion and excess." Our country's alleged democracy hides its actual plutocracy and imperialism. A white "liberal" stance serves to obscure the continuing repression and exploitation of Blacks. Male plausibility—at least for them—makes male chauvinism more tenable.

But just what is hypocrisy as a societal phenomenon? How common is it? Why are people so surprised at being called hypocrites?

What do those who revolt against hypocrisy say they are trying to accomplish? What are they likely to achieve?

Hypocrisy as a Label

Hypocrisy designates as "ugly" a characteristic all socialized human beings develop as they grow up and participate in a variety of social groups within any given society. Behind hypocrisy is multivalence, or many-valuedness, or even many-mindedness. More specifically, you may see both sincerity and hypocrisy arise from another person's multivalent speech and actions. The "sincere" reactions are those you like or have in common, and the "hypocritical" ones you may fear as threats to your emotional, intellectual, or politico-economic security.

Pointing to this relationship of terms is not to be taken as an effort to apologize for outworn or overly rigid establishment values such as racism or sexism. It is an attempt to place the idea more squarely in the context of everyone's everyday human experiences. We are all hypocrites.

Society is multivalent. Any society, even quite a simple one, has a multiplicity of conflicting moral values. In our society, class, ethnic, gender, and age define groups whose moral values contrast in significant respects. These differences among relatively exclusive and somewhat homogeneous groups do not comprise the whole story of multivalence. Each individual during maturation is assimilated in turn into family, sibling, peer, and other groups, and each of these groups has its own rather distinct and contrasting value and behavior patterns. These early groups then become prototypes of later groups succeeding them in the adult world in which the expectation that we "act maturely" means that we "act like the rest of us" in the given group. The early groups are prototypes in the sense that habit patterns for action and belief typical of the group and taken on in the earlier group are assumed by maturing people to be subsequently appropriate for use in other similar groups, groups that are taken to be approximate successors to the prototype.

Boys playing freely with their friends do things they would never do before their siblings. Their behavior would also appear even more strange or outrageous to their parents. A study of boys' play groups is helpful to achieve an understanding of a football team's spirit, an infantry squad's morale, a male poker club's verbal patter, the formal and informal talk during a meeting of a corporation's salesmen, but it does not tell much about how the same men function as husbands and fathers. Similar continuities are to be observed in female patterns. Thus people who grow up within any society and become somewhat normal participants in a range of its groups, with their contrasting value orientations, achieve unexceptional normality by becoming multivalent. Contrasts between societal moral ideals and group mores help to explain the striking inconsistencies in appeals so successfully employed by politico-economic propagandists. Multivalent society requires its members to be multivalent.

Certain clubs and communities pride themselves on their monovalence, their puritanical adherence to a single code of values, but it is not clear how compulsive such patterns become. Case histories raise serious questions about such pious claims. As much can also be said about allegedly monovalent individuals.

Family, ethnic, class, gender, neighborhood, and other identities give individuals a sense of belonging they find supportive. They help people build friendly networks of associates. To what extent can such identifying be individually and socially constructive without forming the basis for individually and socially destructive bigotry and conspiracy?[3]

Value Conflicts Are Now More Obvious

In less tense times and especially in more traditional societies, contrasts among group values — group cultures or subcultures — are not ordinarily perceived as a problem. Many times custom and "social distance" obscure such differences. Social distance refers to how people with contrasting values can live and work in relatively close physical proximity and still be only superficially aware of what each other is like. It is social unawareness, ignorance, lack of empathy, nonparticipation. It permits white investment bankers to commute between Wall Street and Greenwich or Short Hills, even to be jovial with black employees or associates, and not really be aware of the nature and significance of the worlds of Harlem or Newark through which they travel each workday. When the contrasts are apparent, they are often rendered beyond question by ready-made rationalizations long present in societal and group cultures.

Classism, racism, and sexism are parts of those traditional culture-based rationalizations. They are ancient patterns of thought and action which exhibit fossilized remains of tribalism. Such intergroup tension was once of "a primitive type based upon crude criteria, and expressed in murder and robbery of the alien" and the stealing of women. Now it extends "to many and variegated modes characteristic of civilized peoples, often based upon criteria equally crude, even if expressed, in general, in less violent ways."[4]

Questions we now confront are: How does it happen that these ancient rationalizations are now so subject to attack — if and when they are? After millennia of their employment as morale-builders and soporifics in intergroup relations and struggles, in social domination and exploitation, in conspiracies against other groups, what is now making for the reexamination and hopeful revision of classism, racism, and sexism?

Our moral idealizations have always promised a great deal more to the less privileged than many individuals and groups in preferred positions found it necessary to grant. Even today, the following dictum of that great social observer and satirist of the mighty, Niccolò Machiavelli, is often verified by current behavior: He stated that "how we live is so far removed from how we ought to live, that he who abandons what is done for what ought to be done, will rather learn to bring about his own ruin than his preservation." He did recognize, it needs to be added, that even without modern mass media prying into his affairs or being helpful with their obsequious mythmaking, a prince had to be able to disguise well his faithlessness, "to be a great feigner and dissembler."[5] Our societal morals are the clean "outside of the cup" that many times can hide the "extortion and excess" of racism, sexism, classism, or whatever else might be within. We even have institutionalized and routinized large-scale moralistic feigning and dissembling in the activities of the legal, business management, and public relations professions.

These rather harsh descriptive statements are not meant to give the impression that deception is "natural" and that it is thus difficult or impossible to change such behavior to something else. Gunnar Myrdal, the Swedish statesman and scientist, warns against such a conclusion when he criticizes many American social scientists for having what he calls a "naturalistic and, therefore, fatalistic philosophy" or for permitting functional description to "lead to a conservative teleology." Myrdal makes a plea for what can also be called "the clinical study of society."[6]

Myrdal calls for the intimate observation of spontaneous behavior. This is the study of social groups and society at times when efforts are being made to change them. It focuses upon dynamics and discards abstract preconceptions and static approaches. It assigns only slight uses to such methods as opinion or so-called attitude surveys. Instead, it is behavioral in the special sense that it stresses spontaneous reactions to efforts at reform or manipulation. From this approach one can learn a great deal about how society can be changed. This approach gets behind opinions and propaganda to what people are actually doing and are likely to do. Regardless of what the approach might be called, it is essential to a more dynamic social science.

Why a Revolt Now?

Let us turn to the question of why there is a growing rebellion against discriminatory uses of differences in both social values and identities. Haven't the arts of feigning and dissembling as practiced by those in preferred positions in our society become increasingly sophisticated? Hopefully such deceptive arts are not keeping abreast of the march of literacy and of popular education among the world's women, youth, and ethnic minorities. The masses are restive. Many are dissatisfied with the existing concentrations of social power and of social benefits. Without those in preferred positions learning the arts of democratically representative leadership, they cannot possibly benefit from the advances in popular concern and awareness.

Television, picture and news magazines, alternative and experimental periodicals, "sociological" novels and short stories, "science" and "speculative" fiction,[7] the threat of the draft, implausibly explained underclared wars, together with increased female employment and vast student enrollments, have all combined to give us more clear-eyed generations. What their professors do not, cannot, or will not teach them, they try to discover for themselves. Old rationalizations of inequality and inequity are more wasted with them than their predecessors. One need not look at our youth starry-eyed, as does Charles Reich in *The Greening of America*, and assert that our young have reached a mystical and utopian stage, "Consciousness III," the spread of which will automatically solve all human problems.[8] Let's hope that the pressures and the struggles continue.

Public relations word juggling no longer can cover so well the credibility gaps between a Presidential spokesperson's statements or bulletins in the media and what eventually "leaks out" from conference rooms and "seeps back" from battlefronts. Such rhetorical efforts can no longer sustain so well the disguising of government-supported oil or fruit or steel or automobile or chemical or military power plays abroad and at home.[9] It can no longer maintain discredited union leaders in power indefinitely.

As propagandas and manipulative maneuvers wear thinner and become more transparent, the stark need for more fundamental social reorganization becomes even more pressing. Only with a redistribution of power and privilege in our society and throughout the world, only with greater egalitarianism and with more clearly representative social controls and controllers, can the current cries of dissent be stilled for any substantial period.

The kind of society we can strive for now can help us sense our interdependence upon one another not just within a limited neighborhood, region, or country, but with all humanity. It can foster conceptions of equality that glorify human personality and thus free the exceptional and all other human beings to make their contributions to human welfare — not for exploitative purposes, but in gratitude for life and human fellowship.

Can a society based upon middle-class values be our possible goal? Middle-class rationalists typically portray *the* American life style as being that of their own class members. They claim that such folks, largely contented functionaries of the status quo, give our society its stability and that the broader practice of their life style would assure the country's future. But as Robert N. Bellah and associates make clear, that way of life is drastically changing. In their *Habits of the Heart: Individualism and Commitment in American Life,* they conclude that the "communities of memory" that gave the middle-class a sense of social commitment and identity in the nineteenth century are being replaced. Corporate employment policies for administrators and professionals encourage the formation of "life style enclaves." People who individually are more mobile among corporations also seek out on their own such urban or suburban neighborhoods of similarly styled but largely unintegrated individualists. The Bellah group sees this tendency as promoting an "individualism in which the self has become the main form of reality," and they ask to what extent a society featuring this life style "can really be sustained."[10]

Participants in traditional middle-class communities benefitted from the social networks within which they lived. They took their psychological and social problems to kin, friends, family physicians, clergypeople, and even friendly public officials. Members of the current fragile enclaves, however, now turn to secular therapists for aid with such problems arising from their tensely competitive lives. Social networks have become more fragile and opportunistic. Since all of society is constantly in transition, no old class pattern can offer a panacea. Trends and possibilities in society as a whole need to be faced and diagnosed.

The society we can now have reflects our collective recognition that a mass society needs to be a humane society of participants, even a society that will frankly be called "socialistic." Some Republican and Democratic leaders in politics and their counterparts in finance and industry have been giving this conclusion grudging recognition more and more in spite of temporary setbacks under such leaders as Ronald Reagan. The problem has become not whether or not we shall have a socialistic society, but whether it shall be a plutocratic one ruled by an economic elite (often called state or national socialism), a demagogic one ruled by a political elite on the Soviet model, or a democratically participant one. The extremely ideologized examples of national socialism in Nazi Germany and Fascist Italy included in their baggage pompously charismatic leaders, militarized political parties, and racist excesses that might not be so clearly apparent in the early stages of such a development in English or American society. Similarly, the disastrous elitist-dictatorship potentialities of demagogic socialism on the Soviet pattern are not always apparent as eventualities, even though Stalin gave them dramatic exemplification. Participatory democratic socialism might conceivably grow out of the demagogic type, and it has connotations no more belittling than those in the current Swedish experience.

The steps the United States has taken away from "free enterprise" toward either plutocratic or demagogic socialism obeyed no clearcut ideological mandate. They were steps their backers assumed in each case to be in line with social necessity, that is, economic and political expediency. Whether it was a federal government bailing out a sinking corporation, industry, region, or setting up a "War on Poverty" (under the control of existing politicians) or a Medicare or Medicaid program (on the terms of private medical practitioners and hospitals), each step did have one hallmark in common with the others: It was assumed by the current power wielders to do more to strengthen than to weaken their own existing controls in our society.

This is to say that those in crucial decision-making positions cannot many times predict the consequences or the general direction of their decisions—far from it. Perhaps in the very fallibility of their social knowledge and thus of their ability to predict—usually the case with entrenched elites—lies more of gain than of loss to society. Fortunately for the well-being of us all, the leaders of certain counterelite movements in society are more likely by reason of their peripheral position to recognize the expediency of accepting and acting in terms of daringly accurate social data than are those currently vested in positions of social control. Thus, peripheral though they be, they can have weight out of all proportion to their apparent power.

What we are seeing is the growing impact of people no longer enshrouded as were their predecessors in "social distance." Time was when a famine in China or a disastrous flood in Pakistan was a ho-hum news story of little moment in the United States. Today we can almost smell the stench of rotting human bodies, and we do hear the whimper of starving children in our own living rooms. We see police dogs turned upon dissenting Americans. We see battles between police or National Guardsmen and students on our own college campuses. We are practically at the scene of sickening spectacles of our national political party conventions with their classical mixtures of a glorification and a degradation of democracy. We see *real* bullets hit *real* people—not actors—and see them actually die. We are at press conferences that are much more believably revealing of credibility gaps than are even brilliant pieces of journalistic candor.

How far can the destruction of social distance be carried? To what extent will its destruction continue to mean a growth in social empathy and understanding among the groups in our society and world? These are things that we need to know more about. These are the topics that inquiring social scientists should now be studying so that they can help us to guide social policy more wisely.

While declines in social distance are modifying somewhat the character of societal multivalence, are they influencing personal multivalence? Our youth are questioning not only intergroup differences in values, with their consequent hostilities and exploitations, but also our internalizations of differences, with consequent hypocrisy and "mature" rationalizations of inconsistencies in belief and action. Psychiatrists, psychologists, cultural anthropologists, and sociologists, as well as biographers and novelists, poets, and short-story writers, have explored aspects of this complex situation, but there is much more for us to learn. No simple pathway to the alleged monovalence of a bigot or a saint appears to be the answer. Individual multivalence has not been inspected as fully and as objectively—as irreverently—as it now should be. This is still another matter on which social scientists can help people.

Some Additional Questions

In addition to the revolts of women, nonwhites, and youth against the classist, racist, and sexist implications of entrenched societal multivalence, what other pressing symptoms of coming social reorganizations are upon us? What are other things that people need to know about and in which social scientists have provided some aid but can dig for much more?

Here are some propositions that appear to be emerging from social inquiry and societal conflict together with current questions for social scientists related to them:

1. People are finite, fallible, adaptable, and they live in what amounts to a closed "system," spaceship Earth. Does this mean that their self-destruction is as predictable as that of yeast plants in a bottle of fermenting grape juice? People, like yeast, pollute their environment. When yeast plants have converted sufficient grape juice into wine alcohol, the yeast die. Will people's belated but still possible assimilation of science into their social patterns of thought make a difference?

2. Culture and its related social structure are durable, multivalent, useful when adapted to life conditions and needs, and destructive of their carriers when they are crystallized and thus made unadapting. Can a culture and structure be kept from a deadening crystallization? How can a crystallizing culture and structure have the breath of life — of change — again suffused into it?

3. No group or groups can provide leadership in a society without depending upon popular acceptance of appropriate myths. Do all myths, even those associated with democracy and science, wear out? How? Can they be revived? How? Do all individuals and groups in positions of control forget their dependence upon the credibility of a myth?

4. People can only thrive when they have verifiable life myths with which to organize, dramatize, and embroider their routines. How many ways of verifying those myths now appear to be acceptable? Can an existential-humanist social science furnish such a process of verifica-

tion and also of modification, a kind of perpetual basis for myth renewal? How scientifically defensible can such verification become? As this book attempts to indicate in considerable detail, that process can be carried a long way through the development of an existential-humanist social science. It may be our one chance of survival.

5. Social change rarely finds expression in changed symbols, but it often does in the redefinition of existing symbols. How tenably can our treasured symbols now be interpreted so that they can continue to serve as tokens of a viable society? Is the effort worth it? Or must we just wait and face the kind of cataclysm in which old symbols get brushed aside and replaced with a "new" set? As the historian J. H. Plumb has put it, "Knowledge and understanding should not end in negation, but in action." He adds: "The old past is dying, its force weakening, and so it should. Indeed, the historian should speed it on its way, for it was compounded of bigotry, of national vanity, of class domination."[11]

6. Social change is a tricky matter. Faith that it always takes place with sedate gradualism is misplaced. Even when things appear to remain the same, subtle or even fundamental changes may well be in the making or well on their way. For example, in speaking of the adaptation of constitutional interpretation to societal change, U. S. Justice W. O. Douglas observed that justices "like Brandeis, Cardozo, Hughes, Murphy, Stone and Rutledge . . . knew that all life is change and that law must be constantly renewed if the pressures of society are not to build up to violence and revolt."[12] When changes do come, they can thus be efforts to plug threatening holes in a dike, or they can be quite dramatic, and even revolutionary. Can we learn more about social change in its many paces and manifestations — not so that we may foolishly try to prevent it, but rather so that we may learn how more wisely to welcome it and to live with it?

Notes

Preface

1. Jean-Paul Sartre, *Existentialism,* trans. Philip Mairet (London: Methuen, 1947).

2. Karl Marx, *Capital,* trans. Samuel Moore, Edward Aveling, and Ernest Untermann, ed. Frederick Engels (4th German ed., 1890; Chicago: Charles H. Kerr and Co., 1906, 1907, 1909), 3 vols.; *The German Ideology,* ed. R. Pascal (London: Lawrence and Wishart, 1938).

3. See Nicola Abbagnano, *Critical Existentialism,* trans. and ed. with an introduction by Nino Langiulli (Garden City, N.Y.: Anchor Books, 1969); Walter Odajnyk, *Marxism and Existentialism* (Garden City, N.Y.: Doubleday, 1965); Erich Fromm, ed., *Socialist Humanism: An International Symposium* (Garden City, N.Y.: Anchor Books, 1965).

4. Dumas Malone, *Jefferson and His Time* (Boston: Little, Brown, 1948–51), 2 vols.

5. Mark Twain, *Works,* ed. Frederick Anderson (Berkeley: University of California Press, 1972 et seq.), 25 vols.; Maxwell Geismar, *Mark Twain: An American Prophet* (Boston: Houghton Mifflin Co., 1970).

6. W. G. Sumner, *War and Other Essays, Earth-Hunger and Other Essays, The Challenge of the Facts and Other Essays, The Forgotten Man and Other Essays* (New Haven: Yale University Press, 1911, 1913, 1914, 1919); H. E. Starr, *William Graham Sumner* (New York: Henry Holt & Co., 1925).

7. Franz Boas, *The Mind of Primitive Man* (1911; New York: Macmillan Co., 1938), and *Race, Language and Culture* (New York: Macmillan Co., 1948); Marvin Harris, *The Rise of Anthropological Theory* (New York: Thomas Y. Crowell Co., 1968), chap. 10, "The Boasian Milieu."

8. F. W. Matson, *The Broken Image* (New York: George Braziller, 1964), p. vii.

9. Herbert Blumer, *Symbolic Interaction* (Englewood Cliffs, N.J.: Prentice-Hall, 1969), p. 39.

10. R. P. Wolensky, "The Graduate Student's Double Bind," *Sociological Spectrum* 1 (1981), pp. 393–414, pp. 393 and 401 quoted.

11. A. McC. Lee, *Toward Humanist Sociology* (Englewood Cliffs, N.J.: Prentice-Hall, 1973).

12. Lee, "Sociology for People," *Humanity & Society* 3 (1979), pp. 81–91; "On the Dread of Innovation in Universities," *Practicing Anthropology* 2, no. 1 (October 1979), pp. 3, 18–20; "Enticing Ideas That Often Distort Social Thought," *Humanity & Society* 6 (1982), pp. 103–21; "The Long Struggle to Make Sociology Useful," *Public Relations Journal* 38, no. 7 (July 1982), pp. 8–11; "Overcoming Barriers to Clinical Sociology," *Clinical Sociology Review* 2 (1984), pp. 42–50; "Some Haunting Social Problems," *SSSP Newsletter* 16, no. 2 (Winter 1985), pp. 2–3; "What Ever Happened to 'Propaganda Analysis'?" *Humanity & Society* 10 (1986), pp. 11–24.

Introduction: On Human Concerns

1. Louis Harris, "Does the Public *Really* Hate the Press?" *Columbia Journalism Review*, March/April 1984, p. 18.

2. Karl Marx, "The Poverty of Philosophy," 1847, pp. 105–212 in Marx and Frederick Engels, *Collected Works* (New York: International Publishers, 1976) 6, p. 162.

3. R. S. Lynd, *Knowledge for What?* (Princeton: Princeton University Press, 1939), pp. 217, 227, 213.

4. R. E. Kingsley, "The Function of Controversy," *Public Relations Journal* 11 (1966), p. 7.

5. S. V. Benét, "Listen to the People," *Pocket Book,* ed. Robert van Gelder (New York: Pocket Books, 1946), p. 384.

6. M. R. Davie et al., *Refugees in America* (New York: Harper and Bros., 1947); D. P. Kent, *The Refugee Intellectual* (New York: Columbia University Press, 1953); John Kosa, ed., *The Home of the Learned Man* (New Haven: College & University Press, 1968).

7. Franco Ferrarotti, *The Myth of Inevitable Progress* (Westport, Conn.: Greenwood Press, 1985); J. B. Bury, *The Idea of Progress* (New York: Macmillan Co., 1932).

8. Herbert Blumer, *Symbolic Interactionism* (Englewood Cliffs, N.J.: Prentice-Hall, 1969), p. 7.

9. H. D. Thoreau, *Walden* (1854; New York: New American Library, 1942), p. 30.

10. *The Sociology of Georg Simmel,* trans. and ed. K. H. Wolff (Glencoe, Ill.: Free Press, 1950), p. 409.

11. See A. McC. Lee, *Sociology for Whom?* 2nd ed. (Syracuse, N.Y.: Syracuse University Press, 1986), esp. chap. 9.

1 — Sociology's Images

1. See *Quarterly Journal of Doublespeak*, published since 1975 by the National Council of Teachers of English.

2. R. A. Kent, *A History of British Empirical Sociology* (Aldershot, England: Gower, 1981), pp. 1, 8.

3. R. E. Kennedy, Jr., *Life Choices: Applying Sociology* (New York: Holt, Rinehart and Winston, 1986), p. 3. See also chaps. 3 and 9.

4. Victoria Rader, "Teaching Sociology Humanistically," *Humanity & Society* 3 (1979), pp. 92–105, p. 92 quoted.

5. John Bremner quoted by Dan Reeder, "Bremner's Gospel," *The Quill* 73, no. 8 (September 1985), pp. 22–25, p. 25 quoted.

6. A. McC. Lee, *Fraternities without Brotherhood* (Boston: Beacon Press, 1955), esp. chap. 6.

7. Lee, *Multivalent Man* (New York: George Braziller, 1966), and *How to Understand Propaganda* (New York: Rinehart and Co., 1952).

8. Barrows Dunham, *Man Against Myth* (1947; New York: Hill and Wang, 1962), p. iii.

9. R. J. Barnet and R. E. Müller, *Global Reach: The Power of the Multinational Corporations* (New York: Simon and Schuster, 1974), pp. 363, 379, 364.

10. B. H. Bagdikian, *The Media Monopoly*, 2nd ed. (Boston: Beacon Press, 1987); J. H. Altschull, *Agents of Power: The Role of the News Media in Human Affairs* (New York: Longman, 1984).

11. V. F. Weisskopf, "The Frontiers and Limits of Science," *American Scientist* 65 (1977), pp. 405–11, at p. 411.

12. Robert Nisbet, "Knowledge Dethroned," *New York Times Magazine,* September 28, 1975, pp. 34 ff., at pp. 34, 37, 41, 46. *Cf.* his *The Degradation of the Academic Dogma: The University in America, 1945–1970* (New York: Basic Books, 1971). See the discussion of his *Times* article in the symposium, "Social Science: The Public Disenchantment," *American Scholar* 45 (1976), pp. 336–59.

13. Nisbet, *Prejudices* (Cambridge: Harvard University Press, 1982), pp. 287–88.

14. Nisbet, "Knowledge Dethroned."

15. Rollo May, "Introduction to the AHP Theory Conference," pp. 40–41 in Carol Guion and Tina Kelly, eds., *Satan Is Left-Handed* (San Francisco: Association for Humanistic Psychology, 1977), p. 40 quoted.

16. Oscar Wilde, "Lady Windermere's Fan," 1892, pp. 5–75 in *Four Plays by Oscar Wilde* (London: Unicorn Press, 1944), p. 56.

17. Jerome Davis, "Introduction," pp. xix–xxiv in Davis and H. E. Barnes, eds., *An Introduction to Sociology*, rev. ed. (D. C. Heath and Co., 1931), p. xxiv.

18. Steven Rose, L. J. Kamin, and R. C. Lewontin, *Not in Our Genes: Biology, Ideology, and Human Nature* (New York: Pantheon Books, 1984).

19. Statement of purpose, Society on Anthropology and Humanism, *Anthropology and Humanism Quarterly* 2, no. 1 (March 1977), and subsequent issues, inside cover.

2—Humanist Emphases in Sociology

1. Laurence Urdang, ed., *The Random House Dictionary of the English Language,* college ed. (New York: Random House, 1968), p. 645.

2. Ibid., pp. 645, 1179.

3. Willard Waller, "Insight and Scientific Method," *American Journal of Sociology* 40 (1934–35), pp. 285–97, at p. 297.

4. Max Weber, *The Methodology of the Social Sciences,* trans. and ed. E. A. Shils and H. A. Finch (Glencoe, Ill.: Free Press, 1949), p. 112.

5. Nancie L. Gonzalez, "'Science Is Sciencing,'" *Science* 219 (1983), p. 345.

6. Edward Shils, "The Calling of Sociology," pp. 1405–48 in *Theories of Sociology,* ed. Talcott Parsons, Shils, K. D. Naegele, and J. R. Pitts (New York: Free Press, 1961), p. 1414.

7. P. L. Berger, *A Rumor of Angels* (Garden City, N.Y.: Doubleday and Co., 1969), pp. 120–21; see also his *The Sacred Canopy: Elements of a Sociological Theory of Religion* (Garden City, N.Y.: Doubleday and Co., 1967).

8. Richard Quinney, "Nature of the World: Holistic Vision for Humanist Sociology," *Humanity & Society* 6 (1982), pp. 322–39, at p. 324, and *Social Existence: Metaphysics, Marxism, and the Social Sciences* (Beverly Hills, Calif.: Sage Publications, 1982), p. 18.

9. George Savile, *The Life and Letters of Sir George Savile,* ed. H. C. Foxcroft (New York: Longmans, Green and Co., 1898) 2, p. 520.

10. Edna Bonacich, "The Future of Sociology and the University: A Reply," *ASA Footnotes* 10, no. 9 (December 1982), pp. 2–3, at p. 2.

11. Cynthia B. Flynn, "An Alternative Approach to Discipline's Funding Problems," *ASA Footnotes* 10, no. 9 (December 1982), p. 2.

12. Bonacich, "The Future of Sociology", pp. 2–3.

13. Gonzalez, "'Science is Sciencing.'"

14. A. W. Gouldner, "Anti-Minotaur: The Myth of a Value-Free Sociology," *Social Problems* 9 (1962), pp. 199–213, at p. 199.

15. Joseph Gusfield, "Theories and Hobgoblins," *SSSP Newsletter* 17, no. 1 (Fall 1985), pp. 16–18, at p. 16.

16. Gonzalez, "'Science is Sciencing.'"

17. R. L. Numbers, "Medicine in the United States," *Science* 219 (1983), pp. 837–38. A review of Paul Starr, *The Social Transformation of American Medicine* (New York: Basic Books, 1983).

18. Constance Holden, "Sociology Stir at Harvard," *Science* 228 (1985), pp. 692–93.

19. "Harvard Professor Back After a Tenure Dispute," *New York Times,* Dec. 6, 1985, p. A16.

20. Derek Bok quoted by Barbara J. Culliton, "Bok Puts Computers in Their Place," *Science* 228 (1985), p. 697.

21. K. C. Kinloch, "Academic Elites as Raiders of the 'Lost' Department," *Humanist Sociologist* 7, no. 4 (December 1982), pp. 7–9.

22. Percy Black, "Science as a Way of Life," *Scientific Monthly* 71 (1950), pp. 67–68, at p. 67.

23. Herbert Spencer, *The Principles of Sociology* (New York: D. Appleton and Co., 1898), 2 vols.

24. Marvin Harris, *The Rise of Anthropological Theory* (New York: Thomas Y. Crowell, 1968), p. 128.

25. Lester F. Ward, *Dynamic Sociology* (New York: D. Appleton and Co., 1883), 2 vols.; *Pure Sociology* (New York: Macmillan Co., 1903); and *Applied Sociology* (Boston: Ginn and Co., 1906).

26. B. J. Stern, "Giddings, Franklin Henry," *Encyclopaedia of the Social Sciences* 6 (1931), pp. 654–55, at p. 654.

27. F. H. Giddings, *Democracy and Empire* (New York: Macmillan Co., 1900), and *The Western Hemisphere in the World of Tomorrow* (New York: Revell, 1915).

28. Giddings, *Americanism in War and Peace* (Worcester, Mass.: Clark University Press, 1917), and *The Responsible State* (Boston: Houghton Mifflin Co., 1918).

29. Giddings, *Principles of Sociology* (New York: Macmillan Co., 1920), and *The Scientific Study of Society* (Chapel Hill, N.C.: University of North Carolina Press, 1924).

30. W.G. Sumner, *Folkways* (Boston: Ginn and Co., 1906).

31. A. G. Keller, *Societal Evolution,* rev. ed. (New York: Macmillan Co., 1931); Marvin Harris, *Anthropological Theory,* pp. 607–11; R. C. Hinkle, *Founding Theory of American Sociology: 1881–1915* (Boston: Routledge and Kegan Paul, 1980), pp. 226–27.

32. A. McC. Lee, *Toward Humanist Sociology* (Englewood Cliffs, N.J.: Prentice-Hall, 1973), chap. 7, and *Sociology for Whom?* rev. ed. (Syracuse, N.Y.: Syracuse University Press, 1986), chap. 10.

33. R. A. Kent, *A History of British Empirical Sociology* (Brookfield, Vt.: Renouf USA, 1981), p. 1.

34. Friedrich Engels, *The Condition of the Working Class in England in 1844,* trans. Florence Wischnewetzky and others (St. Albans, England, 1976), p. 323.

35. Kent, *British Empirical Sociology,* p. 53.

36. Charles Booth, *Life and Labour of the People of London,* 3rd ed. (London: MacMillan and Co., 1902-3), 17 vols.

37. Kent, *British Empirical Sociology,* pp. 59, 61–62; T. S. and M. B. Simey, *Charles Booth: Social Scientist* (New York: Oxford University Press, 1960).

38. P. U. Kellogg, ed., *The Pittsburgh Survey* (New York: Russell Sage Foundation, 1909–14), 6 vols.

39. Philip Klein, "Preface," pp. xi–xvi in Klein and others, *A Social Study of Pittsburgh* (New York: Columbia University Press, 1938), p. xi.

40. R. S. and H. M. Lynd, *Middletown* (New York: Harcourt, Brace, 1929) and *Middletown in Transition* (New York: Harcourt, Brace, 1937).

41. R. E. Park, *Collected Papers,* ed. E. C. Hughes, C. S. Johnson, Jitsuichi Masuoka, Robert Redfield, and Louis Wirth (Glencoe, Ill.: Free Press, 1950–55), 3 vols., *On Social Control and Collective Behavior* (Chicago: University of Chicago Press, 1967), and (with E. W. Burgess) *Introduction to the Science of Sociology* (Chicago: University of Chicago Press, 2nd ed., 1924).

42. Vernon Boggs, Gerald Handel, and Sylvia F. Fava, eds., *The Apple Sliced: Sociological Studies of New York City* (New York: Praeger, 1984).

43. Lyn H. Lofland, "New York City and the Heritage of Chicago Sociology," *Contemporary Sociology* 14 (1985), pp. 15–17, pp. 16–17 quoted.

44. W. G. Sumner, *Essays,* ed. A. G. Keller (New Haven: Yale University Press, 1913–19); A. McC. Lee, "Introduction to the Transaction Edition," Sumner's *Earth-Hunger and Other Essays* (New Brunswick, N.J.: Transaction Books, 1980), pp. v–xxvii.

45. C. H. Cooley, *Human Nature and the Social Order* (1902; New York: Scribners, 1922), *Social Organization* (New York: Scribners, 1909); E. C. Jandy, *Charles Horton Cooley: His Life and His Social Theory* (New York: Dryden Press, 1942).

46. W. I. Thomas and Florian Znaniecki, *The Polish Peasant in Europe and America* (Boston: Badger, 1918–20), 5 vols.

47. W. E. B. DuBois, *The Emerging Thought of W. E. B. DuBois,* ed. H. L. Moon (New York: Simon and Schuster, 1972).

48. O. C. Cox, *Caste, Class and Race* (Garden City, N.Y.: Doubleday, 1948), and *Race Relations* (Detroit: Wayne State University Press, 1976); E. E. Harris, "Oliver C. Cox," and R. L. Goldstein, "Another Memory of Oliver C. Cox," *ASA Footnotes* 3, no. 8 (November 1975), p. 3.

49. C. W. Mills, *Power, Politics and People,* ed. I. L. Horowitz (New York: Oxford University Press, 1963).

50. Willard Waller, *On the Family, Education and War,* ed. W. J. Goode, F. F. Furstenberg, Jr., and L. R. Mitchell (Chicago: University of Chicago Press, 1970).

51. Arlene K. Daniels, "A Tribute to Erving Goffman," *ASA Footnotes* 11, no. 1 (January 1983), p. 2.

52. Abd-ar-Rahman ibn Khaldûn, *The Muqaddimah: An Introduction to History,* trans. Franz Rosenthal (1377; New York: Pantheon Books, 1958).

53. Niccolò Machiavelli, "The Prince," pp. 3–98 in his *The Prince and the Discourses,* trans. Luigi Ricci and E. R. P. Vincent (1513; New York: Modern Library, 1940).

54. Baltasar Gracián y Morales, *The Art of Worldly Wisdom,* trans. Otto Eisensch (1647; New York: Essential Books, 1947).

55. Francis Bacon, "Novum Organum," pp. 266–348 in his *Essays, Advancement of Learning, New Atlantis, and Other Pieces,* ed. R. F. Jones (1620; New York: Odyssey Press, 1937).

56. Ibid., p. 279.

57. Ibid., pp. 279–80.

58. Ibid., p. 280.

59. Ibid., p. 303.

60. N. Elias, "Professions," p. 542 in Julius Gould and W. L. Kolb, eds., *A Dictionary of the Social Sciences* (New York: Free Press, 1964).

61. C. W. Mills, *The Sociological Imagination* (New York: Oxford University Press, 1959), p. 103.

62. Lee, chair, "Report of the Committee on the Problems of the Individual Researcher," *American Sociological Review* 16 (1951), pp. 853–64.

63. Lee, chair, "Report of the Committee on Standards and Ethics in Research Practice," *American Sociological Review* 18 (1953), pp. 683–84.

64. Lee, *Sociology for Whom?* chap. 8.

65. Lee, "How Can the American Sociological Association Become More Useful?" *American Sociologist* 16, no. 2 (May 1981), pp. 93–99.

66. Walda K. Fishman and Robert Newby, "Inequality, Right-Wing Reaction, and the Humanist Imperative," chap. 8 in Fishman and C. G. Benello, eds., *Readings in Humanist Sociology* (Bayside, N.Y.: General Hall, 1986), p. 187.

67. J. M. Starr, "Cultural Politics and the Prospects for Radical Change," chap. 9 in Starr, ed., *Cultural Politics* (New York: Praeger, 1985), p. 325.

3 —To Magnify the Individual

1. See Lincoln Steffens' discussion of such experiences in *The Autobiography of Lincoln Steffens* (New York: Harcourt, Brace, 1931), p. 47.

2. C. J. Friedrich, *The New Image of the Common Man* (Boston: Beacon Press, 1950), p. 247.

3. Searches of sociological literature can readily be made through the printed indexes or the electronic services of *Sociological Abstracts*. The latter in the United States are provided through Dialog or BRS and in Europe, through Data-Star. Sociological Abstracts, Inc., is a nonprofit organization started in 1953.

4. R. E. Kennedy, Jr., *Life Choices: Applying Sociology* (New York: Holt, Rinehart and Winston, 1986), p. 5.

5. C. W. Mills, *The Sociological Imagination* (New York: Oxford University Press, 1959), pp. 5–6.

6. W. G. Sumner and A. G. Keller, *The Science of Society*, I–III, and with M. R. Davie, IV (New York: Alfred A. Knopf, 1927).

7. R. C. Hinkle, *Founding Theory of American Sociology: 1881–1915* (London: Routledge and Kegan Paul, 1980), pp. 225, 206, 335.

8. C. H. Cooley, *Life and the Student* (New York: Alfred A. Knopf, 1927).

9. E. C. Jandy, *Charles Horton Cooley: His Life and His Social Theory* (New York: Dryden Press, 1942), p. 76.

10. E. A. Ross, *Seventy Years of It: An Autobiography* (New York: Appleton-Century-Crofts, 1936).

11. P. A. Sorokin, *A Long Journey* (New Haven: College and University Press, 1963).

12. R. M. MacIver, *As a Tale That Is Told* (Chicago: University of Chicago Press, 1968).

13. W. F. Whyte, *Street Corner Society,* 2nd ed. (Chicago: University of Chicago Press, 1955), pp. 279–358.

14. John Kosa, ed., *The Home of the Learned Man* (New Haven: College and University Press, 1968).

15. C. H. Page, *Fifty Years in the Sociological Enterprise: A Lucky Journey* (Amherst, Mass.: University of Massachusetts Press, 1982).

16. H. E. Starr, *William Graham Sumner* (New York: Henry Holt and Co., 1925).

17. R. E. L. Faris, *Chicago Sociology: 1920–32* (San Francisco: Chandler Publishing Co., 1967).

18. Joseph Gusfield, "'I Gotta Be Me,'" *Contemporary Sociology* 15 (1986), pp. 7–9, at pp. 8–9.

19. Page, *Fifty Years in the Sociological Enterprise,* footnote p. 75.

20. Jerome Davis, *Peace, War and You* (New York: Henry Schuman, 1952), p. 15.

21. P. K. Bock, "Foreword: On 'Culture Shock,'" pp. ix–xii in Bock, ed., *Culture Shock* (New York: Alfred A. Knopf, 1970), pp. ix–xi.

22. Paul Von Blum, *The Critical Vision* (Boston: South End Press, 1982), p. 3.

23. Von Blum, *The Art of Social Conscience* (New York: Universe Books, 1976), p. 5.

24. Discussed at length in A. McC. Lee, *Multivalent Man* (New York: George Braziller, 1966), chaps. 18 and 19.

25. G. W. Allport, *The Nature of Prejudice* (Cambridge, Mass.: Addison-Wesley, 1954), p. 281.

26. "The Effects of Segregation: A Social Science Statement to the United States Supreme Court," pp. 371–75 in E. B. and A. McC. Lee, eds., *Social Problems in America,* rev. ed. (New York: Henry Holt and Co., 1955).

27. Lee and N. D. Humphrey, *Race Riot,* rev. ed. (New York: Octagon Books, 1968), p. 130.

28. W. G. Stephan and J. C. Brigham, eds., "Intergroup Contact," *Journal of Social Issues* 41, no. 3 (1985).

29. Danilo Dolci, "Tools for a New World," pp. 12–16 in *Saturday Review,* July 29, 1967, p. 13.

30. See also Dolci's *Outlaws* (New York: Orion Press, 1961), *Waste* (New York: Monthly Review Press, 1963), *A New World in the Making* (New York: Monthly Review Press, 1965), and *The Man Who Plays Alone* (New York: Pantheon, 1969).

31. Aldous Huxley, "Introduction," pp. vii–xi in Dolci, *Report From Palermo* (New York: Hillman/MacFadden, 1961), p. vii.

32. "Tools for a New World," p. 15.

33. Dolci quoted by Jerre Mangione. *The World Around Danilo Dolci,* new ed. (New York: Harper and Row, 1972), p. 79.

34. "Tools for a New World," p. 15.

35. Ibid.

36. Dolci quoted by Israel Shenker, "A Pacifist Revolt Is Urged by Dolci," *New York Times,* October 11, 1970.

37. Anthony Platt, "Introduction," in Platt, ed., *The Politics of Riot Commission-*

ers: 1917–1970 (New York: Macmillan Co., 1971), pp. 45–46. See also Lee and Humphrey, *Race Riot,* chap. 10.

38. A. McC. Lee, *How to Understand Propaganda* (New York: Rinehart and Co., 1952), chap. 8, esp. pp. 217–19.

39. Stuart Chase, with Marian T. Chase, *Roads to Agreement* (New York: Harper and Brothers, 1951), chap. 6, "Quaker Meeting"; R. L. Howe, *The Miracle of Dialogue* (New York: Seabury Press, 1963).

40. H. H. Kelley and J. W. Thibaut, "Group Problem Solving," in Gardner Lindzey and Elliot Aronson, eds., *The Handbook of Social Psychology,* 2nd ed. (Reading, Mass.: Addison-Wesley Publishing Co., 1969) 4, chap. 29.

41. Rachel D. DuBois and Mew-Soong Li, *Reducing Social Tension and Conflict Through the Group Conversation Method* (New York: Association Press, 1971). R. A. Straus, "Changing the Definition of the Situation," *Clinical Sociology Review* 2 (1984), pp. 51–63.

42. Holly G. Porter, "Laboratory Confrontation: A Viable Alternative to Political Violence," mimeo. (Grand Rapids, Mich.: Community Confrontation & Communication Associates, 1971).

43. Ibid., pp. 3–4.

44. Ibid., pp. 23–24. See also Louis Kriesberg, *The Sociology of Social Conflicts* (Englewood Cliffs, N.J.: Prentice-Hall, 1973), esp. chaps. 5–7.

45. E. H. Schein and W. G. Bennis, eds., *Personal and Organizational Change* (New York: John Wiley, 1965); Harry Cohen, *Connections: Understanding Social Relationships* (Ames, Iowa: Iowa State University Press, 1981); Kevin Preister and J. A. Kent, "Clinical Sociological Perspectives on Social Impacts," *Clinical Sociology Review* 2 (1984), pp. 120–32.

46. Porter, "Laboratory Confrontation," pp. 23–24.

47. Irving Goldaber and H. G. Porter, *Notes on "Laboratory Confrontation"* (Grand Rapids, Mich.: Community Confrontation & Communication Associates, n.d.), p. 2.

48. Porter, "Laboratory Confrontation," p. 32.

49. Ibid., p. 34.

50. Fletcher Knebel, "A Cop Named Joe," *Look,* July 27, 1971, p. 15.

51. Ibid., p. 19.

52. Data compiled by Irving Goldaber. See also Norman Sinclair, "Bridges to Understanding," *Engage* (United Methodist Church), May 15, 1969, and J. F. Adams, "A Confrontation That Wasn't," *Engage,* July 15, 1969.

53. T. J. Rice, "Life on the Applied/Clinical Side," *Footnotes* 14, no. 8 (November 1986), p. 8.

54. S. T. Bruyn and P. M. Rayman, eds., *Nonviolent Action and Social Change* (New York: Irvington Publishers, 1979); Gene Sharp, *The Politics of Nonviolent Action* and *Social Power and Political Freedom* (Boston: Porter Sargent Publisher, 1973 and 1980).

55. Karl Marx, "The Eighteenth Brumaire of Louis Bonaparte" (1852), pp. 95–180 in Marx and Frederick Engels, *Selected Works* (London: Lawrence and Wishart, 1968), p. 97.

56. D. H. Hammarskjold as quoted in connection with the United Nations' 1986 International Year of Peace.

1. Daniel Bell, *The End of Ideology*, rev. ed. (New York: Collier Books, 1961), pp. 393, 400, 399. See also C. I. Waxman, ed., *The End of Ideology Debate* (New York: Simon and Schuster, 1969).

2. Julius Gould, "Ideology," in Gould and W. L. Kolb, eds., *A Dictionary of the Social Sciences* (New York: Free Press, 1964), p. 315.

3. Bell, *The End of Ideology*, pp. 394–95.

4. See Richard Hofstadter, *Anti-Intellectualism in American Life* (New York: Alfred A. Knopf, 1963), esp. chap. 1.

5. W. E. H. Lecky, *History of European Morals*, 3rd ed. rev. (New York: D. Appleton, 1908) 1, p. 98, and 2, p. 40, and *History of the Rise and Influence of the Spirit of Rationalism in Europe* (London: Watts, 1910), esp. chaps. 1 and 4; H. C. Lea, *History of the Inquisition of the Middle Ages*, 2nd ed. (New York: Harper and Brothers, 1906), 3 vols.

6. See A. McC. Lee, *How to Understand Propaganda* (New York: Rinehart, 1952), p. 2, and Umberto Benigni, "Propaganda, Sacred Congregation of," *Catholic Encyclopaedia* 12 (1913), pp. 456–61.

7. Karl Mannheim, *Ideology and Utopia*, trans. and ed. Louis Wirth and E. Shils (New York: Harcourt, Brace and World, 1936), pp. 98–99, 106.

8. P. L. Berger and Thomas Luckman, *The Social Construction of Reality* (Garden City, N.Y.: Doubleday, 1966), p. 118.

9. Mannheim, *Ideology and Utopia*, pp. 13, 32, 98.

10. Edward Gibbon, *The History of the Decline and Fall of the Roman Empire* (1782; Philadelphia: Porter and Coates, 1845), 5 vols., esp. vol. 1; A. D. White, *A History of the Warfare of Science With Theology in Christendom* (New York: D. Appleton, 1896), 2 vols.

11. Mannheim, *Ideology and Utopia*, p. 99.

12. Steven Rose, "Stalking the Criminal Chromosome," *Nation* 242 (1986), pp. 732–38 at p. 732.

13. Berger and Luckman, *Social Construction*, pp. 114–15.

14. Rose, "Stalking the Criminal Chromosome," p. 732.

15. S. H. Chapman, "The Spirit of Cultural Pluralism," pp. 103–12 in H. M. Kallen et al., *Cultural Pluralism and the American Idea* (Philadelphia: University of Pennsylvania Press, 1956).

16. S. T. Bruyn and Paula Rayman, "Introduction," pp. 1–10 in Bruyn and Rayman, eds., *Nonviolent Action and Social Change* (New York: Irvington Publishers, 1979), p. 8.

17. Conceptions mentioned here are set forth in detail in A. McC. Lee, *Multivalent Man* (New York: George Braziller, 1966), chaps. 11–13.

18. E. H. Schein, "The Passion for Unanimity," in Bernard Berelson and Morris Janowitz, eds., *Reader in Public Opinion and Communication*, 2nd ed. (New York: Free Press, 1966), p. 608.

19. M. L. King, Jr., *Strength to Love* (New York: Harper and Row, 1963), p. 26.

20. J. S. Mill, *Utilitarianism, Liberty, and Representative Government* (New York: E. P. Dutton, 1951), p. 486.

21. D. L. Horowitz, *Ethnic Groups in Conflict* (Berkeley: University of California Press, 1985), p. 684.

22. M. J. Herskovitz, "Ancestry of the American Negro," *Opportunity*, January 1939, p. 30.

23. Herbert Aptheker, *American Negro Slave Revolts*, 2nd ed. (New York: International Publishers, 1963), esp. chaps. 6–14.

24. M. R. Davie, *Negroes in American Society* (New York: McGraw-Hill Book Co., 1949), p. 45.

25. Ibid., p. 54.

26. J. E. Cutler, *Lynch-Law* (New York: Longmans, Green and Co., 1905; A. F. Raper, *The Tragedy of Lynching* (Chapel Hill: University of North Carolina Press, 1933); Gunnar Myrdal et al., *An American Dilemma* (New York: Harper and Row, 1944), chap. 27.

27. M. R. Konvitz, *A Century of Civil Rights* (Westport, Conn.: Greenwood Press, 1983).

28. Carl Sandburg, *The Chicago Race Riots: July, 1919* (New York: Harcourt, Brace and World, 1969); E. M. Rudwick, *Race Riot at East St. Louis: July 2, 1917* (Carbondale: Southern Illinois University Press, 1964); Stanley Lieberson and A. R. Silverman, "The Precipitants and Underlying Conditions of Race Riots," *American Sociological Review* 30 (1965), pp. 887–98.

29. *The Marcus Garvey and Universal Negro Improvement Association Papers* (Berkeley: University of California Press, 1983), 2 vols.

30. A. D. Grimshaw, ed., *Racial Violence in the United States* (Chicago: Aldine Publishing Co., 1969), esp. chap. 12; A. McC. Lee, "Race Riots Are Symptoms," in Lee and N. D. Humphrey, *Race Riot* (Detroit, 1943), 2nd ed. (New York: Octagon Books, 1968), pp. vii–xxviii.

31. W. J. Moses, *Black Messiahs and Uncle Toms* (University Park: Pennsylvania State University Press, 1982); W. R. Witherspoon, *Martin Luther King, Jr., to the Mountaintop* (New York: Doubleday, 1985); D. J. Garrow, *The FBI and Martin Luther King, Jr.* (New York: W. W. Norton, 1981).

32. L. A. Cole, *Blacks in Power: A Comparative Study of Black and White Elected Officials* (Princeton: Princeton University Press, 1975); Manning Marable, *Black American Politics* (London: Verso, 1985).

33. King, *Strength to Love*, p. 11.

34. Ibid., p. 8.

35. Ibid., p. 12.

36. H. E. Fosdick quoted by C. H. Ward, *Builders of Delusion* (Indianapolis: Bobbs-Merrill, 1931), p. 340. See also Ray Abrams, *Preachers Present Arms* (New York: Round Table Press, 1933), and *The Essays of A. J. Muste*, ed. Nat Hentoff (New York: Simon and Schuster, 1967).

37. P. A. Sorokin, *Contemporary Sociological Theories* (New York: Harper and Brothers, 1928), p. 324, based upon F. A. Woods and A. Baltzly, *Is War Diminishing?* (Boston: Houghton Mifflin, 1915), and G. Bodart, *Losses of Life in Modern Wars* (Ox-

ford: Oxford University Press, 1916). See also M. R. Davie, *Evolution of War* (New Haven: Yale University Press, 1929), and Quincy Wright, *A Study of War,* 2nd ed. (Chicago: University of Chicago Press, 1965).

38. Sorokin, *Society, Culture, and Personality* (New York: Harper and Brothers, 1947), pp. 498–99. See also Sorokin, *Social and Cultural Dynamics* (New York: Harper and Brothers, 1937–41), 4 vols., esp. vol. 3, chaps. 9–11. *Cf.* J. D. Singer et al., *Explaining War* (Beverly Hills, California: Sage Publications, 1979), and Melvin Small and J. D. Singer, "Patterns in International Warfare, 1816-1965," in *The War System: An Interdisciplinary Approach,* ed. R. A. Falk and S. S. Kim (Boulder, Colorado: Westview Press, 1980), pp. 551–62.

39. Wright, *A Study of War,* pp. 1542–43.

40. A. D. Morse, *While Six Million Died: A Chronicle of American Apathy* (New York: Random House, 1968); Telford Taylor, *Sword and Swastika* (Chicago: Quadrangle, 1969).

41. See esp. H. E. Barnes, "The World War of 1914–1918," pp. 39–99 in Willard Waller, ed., *War in the Twentieth Century* (New York: Dryden Press, 1940); Walter Millis, *Road to War* (Boston: Houghton Mifflin, 1935).

42. Waller, "War in the Twentieth Century," pp. 3–35 in Waller, ed., *War,* pp. 13, 32.

43. See for example C. A. Beard, *An Economic Interpretation of the Constitution of the United States* (New York: Macmillan Co., 1913), *The Navy: Defense or Portent?* (New York: Harper and Brothers, 1932), and *Giddy Minds and Foreign Quarrels* (New York: Macmillan Co., 1939).

44. See for example H. E. Barnes, *The Genesis of the World War,* 2nd ed. (New York: A. A. Knopf, 1927), *The Twilight of Christianity* (New York: Vanguard, 1929), *Society in Transition* (New York: Prentice-Hall, 1939), and *An Economic History of the Western World* (New York: Harcourt, Brace, 1938).

45. G. W. F. Hegel, *Lectures on the Philosophy of History,* trans. J. Sibree from 3rd German ed. (London: George Bell and Sons, 1858), p. 6.

46. W. G. Sumner and A. G. Keller, *The Science of Society* (New Haven: Yale University Press, 1927), 1, p. 369. See also Sumner, Keller, and M. R. Davie, ibid. 4, pp. 115–52.

47. Robert Ardrey, *The Territorial Imperative* (New York: Atheneum, 1966).

48. Konrad Lorenz, *On Aggression* (New York: Harcourt, Brace and World, 1966).

49. R. E. Holloway, Jr., "Human Aggression," pp. 29–48 in *War: The Anthropology of Armed Conflict and Aggression,* ed. Morton Fried, Marvin Harris, and Robert Murphy (Garden City, N.Y.: Natural History Press, 1968), p. 31.

50. Margaret Mead, "Alternatives to War," pp. 215–28 in ibid., p. 218. See also M. R. Davie, *Evolution of War* (New Haven: Yale University Press, 1929).

51. National Commission on the Causes and Prevention of Violence, *Progress Report* (Washington: mimeo. press release, January 9, 1969), app., p. 11.

52. Office of the Secretary, U. S. Dept. of Defense, news releases.

53. National Commission . . . on Violence, *op. cit.*

54. U. S. National Center for Health Statistics, reports for 1964–68 and 1980–84.

55. V. G. Kiernan, *The Lords of Human Kind* (Boston: Little, Brown, 1969).

56. L. J. Kamin, *The Science and Politics of I. Q.* (New York: John Wiley and Sons, 1974); Marshall Sahlins, *The Use and Abuse of Biology* (Ann Arbor: University of Michigan Press, 1976).

57. K. B. Clark, *Dark Ghetto* (New York: Harper and Row, 1965), p. 128.

58. Seymour Waldman, *Death and Profits: A Study of the War Policies Commission* (New York: Brewer, Warren and Putnam, 1932), p. v.

59. P. A. C. Koistinen, *The Military-Industrial Complex* (New York: Praeger, 1980), p. 124.

60. Les Aspin, "Foreword," pp. vi–viii in ibid., p. vi.

61. Louis Kriesberg, "Clinical Sociology and Preventing Nuclear War," *Clinical Sociology Review* 4 (1986), pp. 91–106.

62. For a perceptive description and analysis of the relations of actionists and others with social change, see Goodwin Watson, *Action for Unity* (New York: Harper, 1947), esp. pp. 87–92.

63. Herbert Marcuse, *One-Dimensional Man* (Boston: Beacon Press, 1964), p. xv.

64. R. A. Seeley, *The Handbook of Non-Violence* (Westport, Conn.: Lawrence Hill and Co., 1986), pp. 232–49; Gene Sharp, *The Politics of Nonviolent Action* (Boston: Porter Sargent, 1973); Beth E. Boyle, ed., *Words of Conscience,* 10th ed. (Washington: National Interreligious Service Board for Conscientious Objectors, 1983); S. M. Kohn, *Jailed for Peace: The History of American Draft Law Violators, 1658–1985* (Westport, Conn.: Greenwood Press, 1985).

65. From slide film, "Automated Air War" (1971), sponsored by the American Friends Service Committee.

66. *Quaker Service Bulletin,* Winter 1972, p. 1; T. D. Boettcher, *Vietnam* (Boston: Little, Brown, 1985), p. 399.

67. Ibid.

68. *Quaker Service Bulletin,* Winter 1972, p. 7.

69. M. L. King, Jr., *Strength to Love,* p. 6.

70. Quincy Wright, "The Nature of Conflict," pp. 317–33 in Falk and Kim, op. cit., p. 331.

71. Center for Defense Information, "Militarism in America," *The Defense Monitor* 15, no. 3 (1986), p. 1.

72. Frantz Fanon, *The Wretched of the Earth,* trans. Constance Farrington (New York: Grove Press, 1966), p. 29.

73. Cecelia Kirkman, "Militarism and Violence against Women: The War at Home," *The Nonviolent Activist* 3, no. 7 (November 1986), pp. 3–6, at p. 3.

5 — Defenses against Manipulation

1. R. K. Manoff, "Only in America," *Progressive* 50, no. 10 (October 1986), p. 14; "Amerika: The ABC Television Miniseries," production script, MS., 579 pp.

2. Peter Clausen, editorial in *Nucleus: A Quarterly Report from the Union of Concerned Scientists* 8, no. 2 (Summer 1986), p. 6.

3. Heywood Broun, "The New York World and Other Dailies," *The Nation* 126 (1928), p. 532. See also editorial, *New York World,* May 5, 1928; editorial, "Heywood Broun," and Broun, "'Loyalty,' a Reply to the New York World," *The Nation* 126 (1928), pp. 552, 557.

4. On this, see for example, E. L. Bernays, *Biography of an Idea* (New York: Simon and Schuster, 1965).

5. J. L. Avorn and the staff of *Columbia Spectator, Up Against the Ivy Wall* (New York: Atheneum, 1969); Noam Chomsky, *American Power and the New Mandarins* (New York: Pantheon, 1969); I. L. Horowitz, *The Rise and Fall of Project Camelot* (Cambridge, Mass.: M.I.T. Press, 1967).

6. Stephen Hess, *The Government-Press Connection* (Washington: Brookings Institution, 1984); Amitai Etzioni, *Capital Corruption: The New Attack on American Democracy* (San Diego, Calif.: Harcourt Brace Jovanovich, 1984); J. W. Fulbright, *The Pentagon Propaganda Machine* (New York: Liveright, 1970); E. H. Berman, *The Influence of the Carnegie, Ford, and Rockefeller Foundations on American Foreign Policy* (Albany: State University of New York Press, 1983).

7. Patrick S. Washburn, "J. Edgar Hoover and the Black Press in World War II," *Journalism History* 13, no. 1 (Spring 1986), pp. 26–33.

8. See especially Herbert Blumer, "Collective Behavior," part 2 in Lee, ed., *Principles of Sociology,* 3rd ed. (New York: Barnes and Noble, 1969).

9. Willard Waller, *The Sociology of Teaching* (New York: John Wiley, 1932), p. 441.

10. H. J. Gans, *Deciding What's News* (New York: Pantheon Books, 1979), p. 117.

11. Michael Parenti, *Inventing Reality: The Politics of the Mass Media* (New York: St. Martin's Press, 1986), pp. xi, 89. See also Jerome Davis, *Character Assassination* (New York: Philosophical Library, 1950), esp. chaps. 5–10.

12. Louis Adamic, "The Papers Print the Riots," *Scribner's Magazine* 91 (1932), pp. 110–11.

13. E. R. Murrow, quoted by Jonathan Alter, "The Struggle for the Soul of CBS News," *Newsweek,* September 15, 1986, pp. 52, 54, at p. 52.

14. Richard Salant, quoted in "Struggle for the Soul."

15. Jonathan Alter, "Struggle for the Soul."

16. "Monolithic Media," editorial, *The Nation* 243 (1986), pp. 195–96, at p. 196.

17. *The Gag on Teaching,* 3rd ed. (New York: American Civil Liberties Union, 1940), p. 30.

18. Paul Von Blum, *Stillborn Education: A Critique of the Research University* (Lanham, Md.: University Press of America, 1986), pp. 27–28. See also Ellen W. Schrecker, *No Ivory Tower: McCarthyism and the Universities* (New York: Oxford University Press, 1986).

19. Jan M. Fritz et al., "Symposium on the History of Clinical Sociology," *Clinical Sociology Review* 3 (1985), pp. 13–38.

20. Daniel Katz et al., eds., *Public Opinion and Propaganda* (New York: Dryden Press, 1954), chaps. 1–3, 6–7, 10–12; A. McC. Lee, *How to Understand Propaganda* (New

York: Rinehart, 1952), chap. 7; Herbert Blumer, "Public Opinion and Public Opinion Polling," *American Sociological Review* 13 (1948), pp. 542–54.

21. Bernard Berelson and G. A. Steiner, *Human Behavior* (New York: Harcourt, Brace and World, 1964), pp. 540–41.

22. M. A. Maxwell, *The Alcoholics Anonymous Experience* (New York: McGraw-Hill, 1984).

23. D. M. White, "Mass Culture in America," in Bernard Rosenberg and White, eds., *Mass Culture* (Glencoe, Ill.: Free Press, 1957), pp. 13–21.

24. Kenneth Auchincloss, "Who Else Is Guilty?" *Newsweek*, April 12, 1971, p. 30.

25. A. McC. Lee, *Terrorism in Northern Ireland* (New York: General Hall, 1983), esp. chaps. 9–10.

26. Jay Peterzell, "Can the CIA Spook the Press?" *Columbia Journalism Review*, September/October 1986, pp. 29–34.

27. John Dewey, *The Quest for Certainty* (1929; New York: Capricorn Books, 1960), esp. pp. 201–04.

28. Julius Lippert, *The Evolution of Culture,* trans. and ed. G. P. Murdock (1886–87; New York: Macmillan Co., 1931); and W. G. Sumner, *Folkways* (Boston: Ginn and Co., 1906).

29. Clyde Kluckhohn, "Cultural Relativity," pp. 160–62 in Julius Gould and W. L. Kolb, eds., *A Dictionary of the Social Sciences* (New York: Free Press, 1964), p. 161.

30. Dewey, *Quest for Certainty*, p. 204.

6 — Ideologies among Sociologists

1. Franco Ferrarotti, *An Alternative Sociology,* J. W. Frieberg, ed., and trans. P. and B. Columbaro (New York: Irvington Publishers, 1979), p. 35.

2. T. S. Kuhn, *The Structure of Scientific Revolutions* (Chicago: University of Chicago Press, 1962), p. 10.

3. Ibid., p. 24. Kuhn cites Bernard Barber, "Resistance by Scientists to Scientific Discovery," *Science* 134 (1961), pp. 596–602.

4. Ibid., p. 15.

5. Gertrud Lenzer, "Auguste Comte and Modern Positivism," pp. xvii–lxviii in Lenzer, ed., *Auguste Comte and Positivism* (New York: Harper, 1975), pp. xvii–xviii.

6. Franz Adler, "Positivism," pp. 520–22 in Julius Gould and W. L. Kolb, eds., *A Dictionary of the Social Sciences* (New York: Free Press, 1964), p. 520.

7. A. W. Gouldner, *The Coming Crisis of Western Sociology* (New York: Basic Books, 1970), p. 498.

8. Cf. E. H. Erikson, *Childhood and Society,* 2nd ed. (New York: W. W. Norton, 1963), p. 251.

9. A. McC. Lee, *Multivalent Man* (New York: George Braziller, 1966), develops these theories in greater detail. For a contrasting viewpoint, see Peggy A. Thoits, "Multiple Identities: Examining Gender and Marital Status Differences in Distress,"

American Sociological Review 51 (1986), pp. 259–72. In the interests of statistical comparability, she ignores life-history and social-historical factors that would have complicated her computations.

10. L. L. and Jessie Bernard, *Origins of American Sociology* (New York: Thomas Y. Crowell Co., 1943), p. 3.

11. C. W. Mills, *The Sociological Imagination* (New York: Oxford University Press, 1959), pp. 22, 24.

12. I. L. Horowitz, "Introduction," in Mills, *Power, Politics, and People* (New York: Oxford University Press, 1963), esp. pp. 14–20.

13. R. A. Kent, *A History of British Empirical Sociology* (Aldershot, England: Gower Publishing Co., 1981), esp. chaps. 1–2.

14. Martin Bulmer, *The Chicago School of Sociology* (Chicago: University of Chicago Press, 1984).

15. Andrew Abbott, "Professions in America," *Science* 234 (1986), p. 766. See Eliot Freidson, *Professional Powers: A Study of the Institutionalization of Formal Knowledge* (Chicago: University of Chicago Press, 1986).

16. I. L. Horowitz, "Mainliners and Marginals: The Human Shape of Sociological Theory," pp. 358–83 in Llewellyn Gross, ed., *Sociological Theory* (New York: Harper and Row, 1967), pp. 370 (footnote), 375.

17. G. R. Jackall, "Engineers in the Social Order," *Science* 232 (1986), p. 1014.

18. C. W. Mills, *White Collar: The American Middle Classes* (New York: Oxford University Press, 1951), p. 131.

19. See Talcott Parsons, *The Structure of Social Action* (New York: McGraw-Hill, 1937) and *The Social System* (Glencoe, Ill.: Free Press, 1951); Parsons and E. A. Shils, eds., *Toward a General Theory of Action* (Cambridge: Harvard University Press, 1951); R. K. Merton, *Social Theory and Social Structure*, rev. ed. (Glencoe, Ill.: Free Press, 1957); S. A. Stouffer, *Communism, Conformity, and Civil Liberties* (New York: Doubleday, 1955); George Homans, *The Human Group, Social Behavior,* and *The Nature of Social Science* (New York: Harcourt, Brace and World, 1950, 1961, 1967).

20. A. W. Gouldner, "Anti-Minotaur: The Myth of a Value-Free Sociology" and other papers in Maurice Stein and Arthur Vidich, eds., *Sociology on Trial* (Englewood Cliffs, N.J.: Prentice-Hall, 1963).

21. As an example, see Louis Narens, *Abstract Measurement Theory* (Cambridge, Mass.: MIT Press, 1985).

22. Talcott Parsons, "An Outline of the Social System," pp. 30–79 in Parsons et al., eds., *Theories of Sociology* (New York: Free Press, 1961), pp. 72–73.

23. Erving Goffman, *Interaction Ritual* (Garden City, N.Y.: Doubleday, 1967), and other books; Harold Garfinkel, *Studies in Ethnomethodology* (Englewood Cliffs, N.J.: Prentice-Hall, 1967).

24. R. K. Merton and P. F. Lazarsfeld, eds., *Continuities in Social Research: Studies in the Scope and Method of "The American Soldier"* (Glencoe, Ill.: Free Press, 1950).

25. R. W. Friedrichs, *A Sociology of Sociology* (New York: Free Press, 1970), pp. 121–22.

26. J. W. Fulbright quoted by I. L. Horowitz, "The Life and Death of Project Camelot," *Trans-Action* 3, no. 1 (November–December, 1965), pp. 3–7, 44–47, at p. 3.

27. R. S. Lynd, *Knowledge for What?* (Princeton: Princeton University Press, 1939), p. 249.

28. C. L. McGehee, "Spiritual Values and Sociology: When We Have Debunked Everything, What Then?" *American Sociologist* 17 (1982), pp. 40–46, at p. 42.

29. C. S. Green, III, "Teaching Ethics in Sociology," *SSSP Newsletter* 17, no. 3 (Summer 1986), pp. 9–10, 12, at p. 9.

30. P. A. Sorokin, *Fads and Foibles in Modern Sociology and Related Sciences* (Chicago: Henry Regnery Co., 1958), pp. 104–5, 67.

31. Albert Scardino, "The Right-Thinking Campus Press: I," pp. 35–39, and Philip Weiss, "The Right-Thinking Campus Press: II," pp. 39–41 in *Columbia Journalism Review* 25, no. 3 (September/October 1986); E. Marshall, "New Group Targets Political Bias on Campus," *Science* 229 (1985), pp. 841–42.

32. Theda Skocpol, "Governmental Structures, Social Sciences, and the Development of Economic and Social Policies" (MS. New York: Social Science Research Council, 11 June 1984), pp. 1–2.

33. Jennifer Platt, in *Network,* British Sociological Association, no. 34 (January 1986), p. 20.

34. Mills, *White Collar,* p. 102.

35. Willard Waller, *The Sociology of Teaching* (New York: John Wiley and Sons, 1932), pp. 189–90.

36. H. H. Gerth and C. W. Mills, "A Biographical View," in Gerth and Mills, eds., *From Max Weber: Essays in Sociology* (New York: Oxford University Press, 1946), p. 22.

37. For candid statements by Parsons on his activities as secretary of the American Sociological Association, replies, and an assessment, see A. McC. Lee, reports as A.S.A. delegate from the Society for the Study of Social Problems, *Social Problems* 9 (1961–62), pp. 289–92, 400–401, 10 (1962–63), pp. 97–100, 293–97, 409–11, 11 (1963–64), pp. 319–21, and 12 (1964–65), pp. 356–60. See also reports by Parsons as secretary in *American Sociological Review* and his editorial column in *The American Sociologist,* 1 and 2 (1965–67).

38. Sorokin, *Fads and Foibles,* p. 300.

39. Laurence Urdang, ed., *Random House Dictionary* (New York: Random House, 1968), p. 249.

40. Sorokin, *Fads and Foibles,* p. 22.

41. Mills, *White Collar,* p. 31.

42. Talcott Parsons, *The Social System* (Glencoe, Ill.: Free Press, 1951).

43. Mills, *White Collar,* p. 72.

44. Horowitz, "Mainliners and Marginals," p. 368.

45. Note the admitted debt for ideas on "manifest" and "latent" functions to Lincoln Steffens, *Autobiography* (New York: Harcourt, Brace, 1931), esp. pp. 46–47 on the part of F. S. Chapin, *Contemporary American Institutions* (New York: Harper and Brothers, 1934), pp. 40–54. For similar debts to Steffens, see W. F. Whyte, *Street Corner Society,* 2nd ed. (Chicago: University of Chicago Press, 1955), pp. 282–83, and R. K. Merton, *Social Theory and Social Structure,* rev. ed. (Glencoe, Ill.: Free Press, 1957), pp. 75–76.

46. R. E. Park, "Introduction," in E. V. Stonequist, *The Marginal Man* (New York: Charles Scribner's Sons, 1937), pp. xiii–xviii; A. L. Kroeber, *Anthropology: Culture Patterns & Processes,* rev. ed. (New York: Harcourt, Brace and World, 1963), pp. 226–29; Lee, *Multivalent Man,* chaps. 18–19.

47. Edward Gibbon, *The History of the Decline and Fall of the Roman Empire,* ed. with notes by H. H. Milman (Philadelphia: Porter and Coates, 1845) 1, pp. 107–08. See also A. L. Kroeber, *Configurations of Culture Growth* (Berkeley: University of California Press, 1944).

48. See the penetrating analysis by Gunnar Myrdal, *Value in Social Theory,* ed. Paul Streeten (New York: Harper and Brothers, 1958), esp. pp. 44–45, 54, and by J. M. Starr, ed., *Cultural Politics: Radical Movements in Modern History* (New York: Praeger, 1985), esp. chaps. 8 and 9.

49. H. O. Mauksch, "Teaching Within Institutional Values and Structures," *Teaching Sociology* 14 (1986), pp. 40–49, at p. 40.

50. Paul Von Blum, *Stillborn Education: A Critique of the American Research University* (Lanham, Md.: University Press of America, 1986), p. 177.

51. Examples are the *Berkeley Journal of Sociology* (University of California at Berkeley), *Gender & Society* (Sociologists for Women in Society), *The Human Factor* (Columbia University, New York), *Humanity & Society* (Association for Humanist Sociology), *The Insurgent Sociologist* (University of Oregon, Eugene), and *Social Problems* (Society for the Study of Social Problems).

7 — Perplexities of Social Perception

1. C. M. Arensberg and A. H. Niehoff, *Introducing Social Change* (Chicago: Aldine, 1964), pp. 185–89. See also W. F. Whyte, *Street Corner Society,* 2nd ed. (Chicago: University of Chicago Press, 1955), esp. pp. 299–309.

2. J. F. Glass and J. R. Staude, eds., *Humanistic Society: Today's Challenge to Sociology* (Pacific Palisades, Calif.: Goodyear, 1972), part 3.

3. Karl Marx, *Early Writings,* trans. and ed. T. B. Bottomore (1844; London: C. A. Watts, 1963), pp. 122–23. Cf. G. F. W. Hegel, *The Phenomenology of Mind,* trans. J. B. Bailie, 2nd ed. (1807; New York: Macmillan, 1955).

4. Sigmund Freud, *Civilization and Its Discontents,* trans. J. Riviere (London: Hogarth Press, 1953); Herbert Marcuse, *Eros and Civilization* (Boston: Beacon Press, 1955), pp. 45ff.

5. R. E. Park, *Race and Culture,* ed. E. C. Hughes et al. (Glencoe, Ill.: Free Press, 1950), pp. 345–56. Compare with Helen M. Lynd, "Alienation: Man's Fate and Man's Hope," in J. F. Glass and J. R. Staude, eds., *Humanistic Society* (Pacific Palisades, Calif.: Goodyear Publishing Co., 1972), pp. 55–61.

6. E. C. Hughes, "Social Change and Social Protest," *Phylon,* 10 (1949), pp. 59–65; D. I. Golovensky, "The Marginal Man Concept, An Analysis and Critique," *Social Forces* 30 (1951–52), pp. 333–39.

7. A. McC. Lee, *Multivalent Man* (New York: George Braziller, 1966), esp. chap. 18.

8. Erich Fromm, *The Sane Society* (New York: Rinehart, 1955), pp. 124–25. See also Melvin Seeman, "The Urban Alienations," *Journal of Personality & Social Psychology* 19 (1971), pp. 135–43.

9. R. A. Nisbet, *The Sociological Tradition* (New York: Basic Books, 1966), p. 266.

10. J. B. Bury, *The Idea of Progress* (New York: Macmillan Co., 1932); Morris Ginsberg, *The Idea of Progress* (London: Methuen, 1953).

11. For vivid examples, see Marjorie Hope and James Young, *The Faces of the Homeless* (Lexington, Mass.: Lexington Books, 1986).

12. See for example Peter Laslett, *The World We Have Lost* (New York: Charles Scribner's Sons, 1965), esp. chaps. 1 and 5.

13. P. K. Bock, "Foreword: On 'Culture Shock,'" in Bock, ed. *Culture Shock: A Reader* (New York: A. A. Knopf, 1970), pp. ix–xii, at pp. x–xi.

14. Jay Franklin, *LaGuardia: A Biography* (New York: Modern Age Books, 1937), p. 16.

15. R. L. Gordon, *Interviewing* (Homewood, Ill.: Dorsey Press, 1969), chap. 3; Frances Henry and Satish Saberwal, eds., *Stress and Response in Fieldwork* (New York: Holt, Rinehart and Winston, 1969), esp. chaps. 3 and 5; G. D. Spindler, *Being an Anthropologist* (New York: Holt, Rinehart and Winston, 1970).

16. Hope and Young, *The Faces of the Homeless,* p. 293.

17. M. B. Clinard, *Sociology and Deviant Behavior,* 3rd ed. (New York: Holt, Rinehart and Winston, 1968), p. 446; T. S. Szasz, *Myth of Mental Illness* (New York: Dell, 1967), and *Ideology and Insanity* (Garden City, N.Y.: Doubleday, 1970); D. E. J. MacNamara and Andrew Karmen, eds., *Deviants: Victims or Victimizers* (Beverly Hills, Calif.: Sage Publications, 1983).

18. J. M. Opler, *Culture and Social Psychiatry* (New York: Atherton Press, 1967); E. D. Driver, *Sociology and Anthropology of Mental Illness* (Amherst: University of Massachusetts Press, 1970).

19. Phil Brown, *The Transfer Care: Psychiatric Deinstitutionalization and Its Aftermath* (Boston: Routledge and Kegan Paul, 1985).

20. Marc Fried, "Social Differences in Mental Health," in John Kosa, ed., *Poverty and Health: A Sociological Analysis* (Cambridge, Mass.: Harvard University Press, 1969), p. 113.

21. J. W. Coleman, *The Criminal Elite* (New York: St. Martin's Press, 1985).

22. D. R. Cressey, *Theft of the Nation: The Structure and Operations of Organized Crime in America* (New York: Harper and Row, 1969); note sharp and effective criticisms of Cressey in J. L. Albini, *The American Mafia: Genesis of a Legend* (New York: Appleton-Century-Crofts, 1971).

23. Daniel Bell, *The End of Ideology,* rev. ed. (New York: Collier, 1961), esp. pp. 138–46, discusses the "myth of the Mafia." See also Norval Morris and Gordon Hawkins, *The Honest Politician's Guide to Crime Control* (Chicago: University of Chicago Press, 1970).

24. Kenneth Mann, *Defending White-Collar Crime* (New Haven: Yale University Press, 1985).

25. D. C. Gibbons, *Society, Crime, and Criminal Behavior,* 4th ed. (Englewood Cliffs, N.J.: Prentice-Hall, 1982), p. 85.

26. Sue T. Reid, *Crime and Criminology,* 3rd ed. (New York: Holt, Rinehart and Winston, 1982), p. 48.

27. H. D. Barlow, *Introduction to Criminology,* 3rd ed. (Boston: Little, Brown and Co., 1984), p. 98. See chap. 4 on "the production and use of data."

28. H. J. Vetter and I. J. Silverman, *Criminology and Crime* (Cambridge, Mass.: Harper and Row, 1986), p. 58.

29. Lincoln Steffens, *The Autobiography of Lincoln Steffens* (New York: Harcourt, Brace, 1931), p. 47.

30. Ibid., pp. 862–64.

31. V. L. Parrington, *Main Currents in American Thought* (New York: Harcourt, Brace, 1930) 3, pp. 409–10; C. A. Beard, *An Economic Interpretation of the Constitution* (New York: Macmillan Co., 1913).

32. W. G. Sumner, *Earth Hunger and Other Essays,* ed. A. G. Keller (New Haven: Yale University Press, 1913), p. 298; see also pp. 283–300, 310–11, 316–17, 328–30, and *War and Other Essays,* ed. Keller (New Haven: Yale University Press, 1911), pp. 160, 204–7, 261–62, 325–26.

33. C. A. and M. R. Beard, *America in Midpassage* (New York: Macmillan Co., 1939) 2, p. 555.

34. Ibid., p. 949.

35. C. W. Mills, *The Power Elite* (New York: Oxford University Press, 1956), p. 9.

36. Parrington, *American Thought,* p. 409.

37. Max Weber, *From Max Weber: Essays in Sociology,* trans. and ed. H. H. Gerth and C. W. Mills (New York: Oxford University Press, 1946), pp. 78–79.

38. J. M. Starr, "Humanist Issues in Participant Observation Research," chap. 9 in Walda K. Fishman and C. G. Benello, eds., *Readings in Humanist Sociology* (Bayside, N.Y.: General Hall, 1986), p. 194.

39. Herbert Blumer, *Symbolic Interactionism: Perspective and Method* (Englewood Cliffs, N.J.: Prentice-Hall, 1969), p. 41.

40. Ibid., p. 40.

41. For a notion of the pressures brought to bear upon a great innovating social scientist because of his critical stance, see K. H. Wolff, "Introduction," to *The Sociology of Georg Simmel,* trans. and ed. Wolff (Glencoe, Ill.: Free Press, 1950), esp. letter to Max Weber quoted on p. xix.

8 — Enticing Distortions

1. See Max Weber, *From Max Weber: Essays in Sociology,* trans. and ed. H. H. Gerth and C. W. Mills (London: Routledge and Kegan Paul, 1948), pp. 78–79.

2. Patricia Wilner, "The Main Drift of Sociology Between 1936 and 1982," *History of Sociology* 5, no. 2 (Spring 1985), pp. 1–20, at pp. 1, 18.

3. R. M. MacIver, *The Web of Government* (New York: Macmillan Co., 1947), p. 4.

4. George Orwell, *1984* (New York: Harcourt, Brace, 1949).

5. George Seldes, *One Thousand Americans* (New York: Boni and Gaer, 1947), p. 111.

6. B. H. Bagdikian, *The Media Monopoly*, 2nd ed. (Boston: Beacon Press, 1987), p. 4.

7. D. D. Eisenhower, radio address, January 17, *New York Times*, January 18, 1961, pp. 1, 22.

8. J. W. Fulbright, "Militarism and American Democracy" (mimeographed), Owens-Corning Lecture at Denison University, Granville, Ohio, April 18, 1969, p. 7. See also Fulbright, *The Pentagon Propaganda Machine* (New York: Liveright, 1970), esp. p. 127.

9. D. D. Eisenhower, *Peace with Justice* (New York: Columbia University Press, 1961), pp. 37–38.

10. Scientific Committee on Problems of the Environment, *The Environmental Consequences of Nuclear War* (New York: John A. Wiley and Sons, 1985).

11. C. V. Hamilton quoted in "Black Mood on Campus," *Newsweek*, February 10, 1969, p. 53.

12. Max Weber, *Essays in Sociology*, pp. 78–79.

13. Eric Sevareid, "American Militarism: What Is It Doing to Us?" *Look*, August 12, 1969, pp. 14, 16.

14. "Meanwhile, down at the arms factory," *Development Forum* (New York: U. N. University), 12, no. 4 (May 1984), pp. 8–9. See also Ruth L. Sivard, *World Military and Social Expenditures: 1985* (New York: World Priorities, 1985).

15. Marilyn French, "Lily Tomlin," *Ms.* 14, no. 7 (January 1986), pp. 32–34, p. 32 quoted.

16. Benjamin Ginsberg, *The Captive Public: How Mass Opinion Promotes State Power* (New York: Basic Books, 1986); W. R. Neuman, *The Paradox of Mass Politics: Knowledge and Opinion in the American Electorate* (New York: Harvard University Press, 1986).

17. Plato, *The Works of Plato*, ed. Irwin Edman (New York: Simon and Schuster, 1928), pp. 410–20.

18. W. E. H. Lecky, *Democracy and Liberty*, rev. ed. (New York: Longmans, Green, 1898) 1, pp. 25–26.

19. Nancie L. Gonzalez, editorial, "In Defense of Elitism," *Science*, 213 (1981), p. 955. See J. B. Conant, *Modern Science and Modern Man* (1952; New York: Greenwood, 1983), *Shaping Educational Policy* (New York: McGraw-Hill, 1964), and *The Comprehensive High School* (New York: McGraw-Hill, 1967).

20. J. L. Walker, "A Reply to 'Further Reflections on "The Elitist Theory of Democracy,"'" *American Political Science Review* 60 (1966), p. 392.

21. *Facts on File*, October 26, 1984, p. 795, and December 31, 1984, p. 983. See also "China's Economy," *The Economist*, July 26, 1986, pp. 65–66.

22. L. J. Kamin, *The Science and Politics of I.Q.* (New York: John Wiley and Sons, 1974), pp. 1–34; Nicholas Wade, "IQ and Heredity: Suspicion and Fraud Beclouds Class Experiment," *Science* 194 (1976), pp. 916–19.

23. E. H. Erikson, *Childhood and Society*, 2nd ed. (New York: W. W. Norton, 1963), pp. 268–74.

24. Karl Marx and Friedrich Engels, *Basic Writings on Politics and Philosophy*, ed. L. S. Feuer (Garden City, N.Y.: Doubleday and Co., 1959), pp. 28, 26.

25. Barbara Goodwin and Keith Taylor, *The Politics of Utopia* (New York: St. Martin's Press, 1982), p. 252.

26. W. A. Van Winkle, "I Was a Teenage Vandal," *In These Times* 6, no. 11 (February 3–9, 1982), pp. 15–16.

27. Dave Berkman, "Dissecting the Latest National Crisis," *The Quill* 74, no. 9 (October 1986), pp. 20–23, pp. 21–23 quoted; Patricia A. Adler, *Wheeling and Dealing: An Ethnography of an Upper-Level Drug Dealing and Smuggling Community* (New York: Columbia University Press, 1985).

28. U. S. Department of Justice, *Census of Jails and Survey of Jail Inmates 1978 Preliminary Report* (Washington: Government Printing Office, 1979), p. 3.

29. E. F. McGarrell and T. J. Flanagan, eds., *Sourcebook of Criminal Justice Statistics—1984* (Washington: U. S. Department of Justice, 1985), pp. 637, 647–48, 653–54; 1985 ed. (1986), p. 537.

30. M. B. Clinard and P. C. Yeager, *Corporate Crime* (New York: Free Press, 1980); C. W. Mills, *White Collar* (New York: Oxford University Press, 1951); J. W. Coleman, *The Criminal Elite: The Sociology of White Collar Crime* (New York: St. Martin's Press, 1985).

31. The following contrast Sumner's and Keller's viewpoints: Marvin Harris, *The Rise of Anthropological Theory* (New York: Thomas Y. Crowell Co., 1968), pp. 607–11; R. C. Hinkle, *Founding Theory of American Sociology: 1881–1915* (Boston: Routledge and Kegan Paul, 1980), chap. 9; A. McC. Lee, "New Introduction," W. G. Sumner, *Earth-Hunger and Other Essays* (New Brunswick, N.J.: Transaction Books, 1980), pp. v–xxvii.

32. From a conversation with the late Howard Henderson, a vice-president of the J. Walter Thompson Co., Inc., New York, N.Y.

33. J. N. Danziger and K. L. Kraemer, *People and Computers* (New York: Columbia University Press, 1986); K. C. Laudon, *Dossier Society* (New York: Columbia University Press, 1986).

34. Buckminster Fuller, *Operating Manual for Spaceship Earth* (Carbondale: Southern Illinois University Press, 1969), pp. 15–16.

35. Stephen Stigler, *The History of Statistics: The Measurement of Uncertainty Before 1900* (Cambridge: Mass.: Harvard University Press, 1986).

36. J. M. Banner, Jr., "Press Coverage Needed to Improve Public Understanding of the Humanities," *Humanities Report* 2, no. 10 (October 1980), pp. 2–3, p. 3 quoted.

37. E. E. Slosson, quoted in *Editor & Publisher* 53, no. 48 (April 30, 1921), p. 58.

38. L. J. Rhoades, *A History of the American Sociological Association: 1905–1980* (Washington, 1981), pp. 21–22, 40–41, 57; E. B. and A. McC. Lee, "The Mission of the Society for the Study of Social Problems," *SSSP Newsletter* 17, no. 1 (Fall, 1985), pp. 9–12.

39. Charles Tilly, "Writing Wrongs in Sociology," *Sociological Forum* 1 (1986), pp. 543–52, at p. 545.

40. H. S. Becker, *Writing for Social Scientists* (Chicago: University of Chicago Press, 1986).

41. Tilly, "Writing Wrongs in Sociology," p. 551.

42. William Strunk, Jr., and E. B. White, *The Elements of Style*, rev. ed. (New York: Macmillan Co., 1972), p. 77.

43. A. McC. Lee, "How Can the American Sociological Association Become More Useful?" *The American Sociologist* 16, no. 2 (May 1981), pp. 93–97.

9 — More Intimate Distortions

1. M. L. King, Jr., *Strength to Love* (New York: Harper and Row, 1963), p. 4.

2. A. C. Kinsey, W. B. Pomeroy, and C. E. Martin, *Sexual Behavior of the Human Male* (Philadelphia: W. B. Saunders Co., 1948), p. 639. See also Ann Fausto-Sterling, *Myths of Gender* (New York: Basic Books, 1986); C. W. Franklin II, *The Changing Definition of Masculinity* (New York: Plenum, 1984).

3. Gloria Emerson, *Some American Men* (New York: Simon and Schuster, 1985), p. 315.

4. H. E. Barnes, "Introductory Note," pp. 739–43, in Barnes, ed., *An Introduction to the History of Sociology* (Chicago: University of Chicago Press, 1948), p. 741.

5. Howard Becker, p. 624, in Becker and H. E. Barnes, *Social Thought from Lore to Science*, 2nd ed. (Washington: Harren Press, 1952) p. 1.

6. Mary E. Richmond, *Social Diagnosis* (1917; New York: Free Press, 1965).

7. Jane Addams, *Twenty Years at Hull-House* (New York: Macmillan Co., 1911), and *A Centennial Reader*, ed. Emily C. Johnson (New York: Macmillan Co., 1960); Mary Jo Deegan, *Jane Addams and the Men of the Chicago School, 1892–1918* (New Brunswick, N.J.: Transaction Books, 1987).

8. Louise C. Wade, "Mary Eliza McDowell," *Dictionary of American Biography* (New York: Charles Scribner's Sons, 1958), 11, pt. 2, pp. 407–9.

9. R. E. L. Faris, *Chicago Sociology: 1920–1932* (San Francisco: Chandler Publishing Co., 1967), pp. 12, 52.

10. Martin Bulmer, *The Chicago School of Sociology* (Chicago: University of Chicago Press, 1984); F. H. Matthews, *Quest for an American Sociology: Robert E. Park and the Chicago School* (Montreal: McGill-Queens University Press, 1977).

11. Faris, *Chicago Sociology*, p. 126.

12. Elizabeth Briant Lee, *Eminent American Women*, forthcoming. See also Committee on the Status of Women in Sociology, American Sociological Association, "Sexist Biases in Sociological Research: Problems and Issues," *ASA Footnotes*, January 1980; Athena Theodore, *The Campus Troublemakers: Academic Women in Protest* (Houston, Texas: Cap and Gown Press, 1986); Joan Huber, "Trends in Gender Stratification, 1970–1985," *Sociological Forum* 3 (1986), pp. 476–95; E. D. Kahn and Lillian Robbins, eds., "Sex Discrimination in Academe," *Journal of Social Issues* 41, no. 4 (Winter 1985).

13. "Statement and Resolutions of the Women's Caucus," *American Sociologist* 5, no. 1 (February 1970), pp. 63–65.

14. Arlene K. Daniels, "A Founding Mother's Reminiscence," *SWS Network* 14, no. 2 (November 1985), pp. 4–5, at p. 5.

15. Pauline B. Bart, "Anniversary Remarks," *SWS Network,* pp. 6–7, at p. 6.

16. Joan Huber, "Why and How I Got Involved in SWS," ibid., p. 6.

17. Alice C. Rossi, "The Formation of SWS: An Historical Account by a Founding Mother," *SWS Network,* pp. 2–4, at p. 4.

18. V. G. Kiernan, *The Lords of Human Kind* (Boston: Little, Brown, 1969), esp. chaps. 1–3; T. F. Gossett, *Race* (Dallas: Southern Methodist University Press, 1963).

19. Quoted by David Holden, "A Bad Case of the Troubles Called Londonderry," *New York Times Magazine,* August 3, 1969, pp. 10–11, 29 ff., p. 29 quoted.

20. Ibid., p. 44.

21. A. McC. Lee, *Terrorism in Northern Ireland* (Bayside, N.Y.: General Hall, 1983).

22. D. S. Connery, *The Irish,* rev. ed. (New York: Simon and Schuster, 1970), p. 280.

23. Jeremy and Joan Harbison, eds., *A Society Under Stress: Children and Young People in Northern Ireland* (Somerset, England: Open Books, 1980), chap. 1.

24. Leon Uris, *Trinity* (Garden City, N.Y.: Doubleday and Co., 1976). For a laudatory review of the book, see John Hume, "As It Was in the Beginning," *Hibernia* (Dublin), October 8, 1976, p. 20. Hume is a leading Roman Catholic politician in Northern Ireland.

25. James Madison, in *The Enduring Federalist,* ed. C. A. Beard (New York: Frederick Ungar Publishing Co., 1948), p. 70.

26. For a more detailed discussion of social class, see A. McC. Lee, *Multivalent Man* (New York: George Braziller, 1966), parts 2 and 3.

27. J. S. Mill, "The Subjection of Women," pp. 259–340 in his *Collected Works,* ed. J. M. Robson (1869; Toronto: University of Toronto Press, 1984), p. 321.

28. Aristotle, *The "Art" of Rhetoric,* trans. J. H. Freese (Cambridge, Mass.: Harvard University Press, 1926), p. 105.

29. H. L. Mencken, ed., *A New Dictionary of Quotations* (New York: A. A. Knopf, 1942), p. 597.

30. G. B. Shaw, *Man and Superman* (1903; New York: W. H. Wise and Co., 1930), p. 226.

31. R. F. Hixson, *Privacy in a Public Society: Human Rights in Conflict* (New York: Oxford University Press, 1987). See also Max Radin, "Intent, Criminal," *Encyclopaedia of the Social Sciences* (New York: Macmillan Co., 1932) 8, pp. 126–31.

32. Titus Maccius Plautus' comedy, "Trinummus," quoted in Mencken, *Dictionary of Quotations,* p. 596.

33. *Brown v. Topeka Board of Education,* 148 U.S. 483 (1954).

34. *Plessy v. Ferguson,* 163 U.S. 537 (1896).

35. *Brown v. Topeka.*

36. Raymond Wolters, *The Burden of Brown: Thirty Years of School Desegregation* (Knoxville: University of Tennessee Press, 1984), pp. 3, 7, 288–89.

37. R. A. Pride and J. D. Woodard, *The Burden of Busing: The Politics of Desegregation in Nashville, Tennessee* (Knoxville: University of Tennessee Press, 1985), p. 281.

38. C. D. MacDougall, *The Press and Its Problems* (Dubuque, Iowa: W. C. Brown,

1964), p. 98. See also media advertisements in the periodicals *Advertising Age, Editor & Publisher, Sales Management, Business Week,* etc.

39. Roy Hoopes, *Ralph Ingersoll* (New York: Atheneum, 1985); John Tebbel, *The Marshall Fields* (New York: E. P. Dutton and Co., 1947).

40. J. H. Altschull, *Agents of Power: The Role of the News Media in Human Affairs* (New York: Longman, 1984), pp. 258–59.

41. J. M. Starr, ed., *Cultural Politics: Radical Movements in Modern History* (New York: Praeger, 1985), esp. Starr's chaps. 8 and 9; Abe Peck, *Discovering the Sixties: The Life and Times of the Underground Press* (New York: Pantheon, 1985).

42. Steven Emerson, *The American House of Saud: The Secret Petrodollar Connection* (New York: Franklin Watts, 1985).

43. See periodicals issued by feminist and minority actionist organizations and such books as James Aronson, *Deadline for the Media: Today's Challenges to Press, TV and Radio* (Indianapolis: Bobbs-Merrill, 1972), and D. H. Weaver and G. C. Wilhoit, *The American Journalist* (Bloomington: Indiana University Press, 1985).

44. Lincoln Steffens, *Autobiography* (New York: Harcourt, Brace and Co., 1931); E. E. Dennis and Claude-Jean Bertrand, "Seldes at 90: They Don't Give Pulitzers for That Kind of Criticism," *Journalism History* 7 (1980), pp. 81–86, 120; I. F. Stone, *Polemics and Prophecies* and *I. F. Stone's Weekly Reader* (New York: Random House, 1970, 1973); Ann M. Sperber, *Murrow: His Life and Times* (New York: Freundlich Books, 1986); Ralph Nader, ed. with others, *Whistle Blowing* (New York: Grossman, 1972), and *The Consumer and Corporate Responsibility* (New York: Harcourt, Brace, 1973).

45. N. D. Cochran, *E. W. Scripps* (1933; Westport, Conn.: Greenwood, 1972); Gilson Gardner, *Lusty Scripps* (1932; St. Clair Shores, Mich.: Scholarly Press, Inc., 1971); F. C. Clough, *William Allen White: Maverick on Main Street* (Westport, Conn.: Greenwood, 1975); Hoopes, *Ingersoll*, Tebbel, *Marshall Fields.*

46. T. R. Sarbin and V. L. Allen, "Role Theory," *The Handbook of Social Psychology,* ed. Gardner Lindzey and Elliot Aronson (Reading, Mass.: Addison-Wesley Publishing Co., 1968), 1, pp. 488–567, p. 491 quoted.

47. William James, *Psychology* (1890; New York: Collier Books, 1962), p. 192; Willard Waller, *The Family* (New York: Cordon Company, 1938), p. 163; G. H. Mead, *Mind, Self and Society* (Chicago: University of Chicago Press, 1934); Erving Goffman, *The Presentation of Self in Everyday Life* (New York: Doubleday Anchor Books, 1959); Lee, *Multivalent Man,* pp. 77–94.

48. Lee, *Multivalent Man,* pp. 127–28. See Craig Reinarman, *American States of Mind* (New Haven: Yale University Press, 1987).

49. W. G. Sumner, "War," pp. 3–40 in Sumner, *War and Other Essays,* ed. A. G. Keller (New Haven: Yale University Press, 1911), pp. 36, 38.

50. Howard Elterman, "The Vietnam War and the Media: Notes on Personal and Political Transformations," 24 pp. MS., p. 4.

10 — How Sociologists Serve People

1. C. H. Cooley, *Life and the Student: Roadside Notes on Human Nature, Society, and Letters* (New York: Alfred A. Knopf, 1927), p. 160.

2. Glenn Jacobs, preface in Jacobs, ed., *The Participant Observer* (New York: George Braziller, 1970), p. ix.

3. Howard Becker and H. E. Barnes, *Social Thought From Lore to Science,* rev. ed. (Washington: Harren Press, 1952) 2, p. 982.

4. E. C. Hughes, *The Sociological Eye: Selected Papers* (Chicago: Aldine-Atherton, 1971), p. 457.

5. Aldous Huxley, *Brave New World* (New York: Bantam, 1953), p. 2.

6. Paul Von Blum, *Stillborn Education: A Critique of the American Research University* (Lanham, Md.: University Press of America, 1986), p. 11.

7. A. H. Maslow, "Problem-Centering vs. Means-Centering in Science," *Philosophy of Science* 13 (1946), p. 329.

8. G. A. Lundberg, *Can Science Save Us?* (New York: Longmans, Green and Co., 1947), p. 144.

9. Harry Alpert, "George Lundberg's Social Philosophy," pp. 48–62 in Alfred de Grazia et al., eds., *The Behavioral Sciences* (Great Barrington, Mass.: Behavioral Research Council, 1968), p. 61.

10. W. J. Filstead, ed., *Qualitative Methodology: Firsthand Involvement With the Social World* (Chicago: Markham, 1970), esp. chaps. 3–5 by Irwin Deutscher, Herbert Blumer, and M. B. Clinard; Blumer, *Symbolic Interactionism* (Englewood Cliffs, N.J.: Prentice-Hall, 1969), esp. chaps. 1, 9, 10; Jacobs, *Participant Observer,* esp. pp. vii–x; Leonard Schatzman and Anselm Strauss, *Field Research: Strategies for a Natural Sociology* (Englewood Cliffs, N.J.: Prentice-Hall, 1973); George McCall and J. L. Simmons, *Issues in Participant Observation* (New York: Random House, 1969); and Monica B. Morris, *An Excursion into Creative Sociology* (New York: Columbia University Press, 1977).

11. Andrew Kohut and others, "Is There a Crisis of Confidence?" *Public Opinion Quarterly* 50 (1986), pp. 1–41.

12. Examples: I. F. Stone, George Seldes, Vance Packard, Fred J. Cook, Jessica Mitford, Nicholas Von Hoffman, and Paul J. Nyden, among many.

13. Thorstein Veblen, *The Higher Learning in America: A Memorandum on the Conduct of Universities by Business Men* (1918; Stanford, Calif.: Academic Reprints, 1954); Upton Sinclair, *The Goose Step,* 2nd ed. (1923; New York: AMS Press reprint); R. M. Hutchins, *The Higher Learning in America* (1962; Westport, Conn.: Greenwood Press, 1979); R. P. Wolff, *The Ideal University* (Boston: Beacon Press, 1970); Bettina Aptheker, *The Academic Rebellion in the United States* (Secaucus, N.J.: Citadel Press, 1972); Ira Shor, *Critical Teaching and Everyday Life* (Boston: South End Press, 1980); Herbert Schiller, *The Mind Managers* (Boston: Beacon Press, 1973).

14. John Goyder, "Survey on Surveys: Limitations and Potentialities," *Public Opinion Quarterly* 50 (1986), pp. 27–41.

15. W. H. Whyte, Jr., "The Social Engineers," *Fortune,* January 1952, pp. 88–91, at p. 89. See also Whyte, *Is Anybody Listening?* (New York: Simon and Schuster, 1952), esp. chap. 10.

16. Veblen, *Higher Learning* p,. 226.

17. R. W. Friedrichs, *A Sociology of Sociology* (New York: Free Press, 1970), esp. pp. 118–23; N. K. Denzin, ed., *The Values of Social Science* (Chicago: Aldine, 1970); John Lofland, *Protest: Studies of Collective Behavior and Social Movements* (New Brunswick, N.J.: Transaction Books, 1985).

18. E. W. Engstrom and E. H. Alexander, "A Profile of the Man in Industrial Research," *Proceedings of the I. R. E.,* December 1952, esp. pp. 1637–44.

19. Institute for Social Research, University of Michigan, "Proposal for a Research Program on the Administration of Research Organizations," mimeographed, April 5, 1954, p. 2.

20. Harold Anderson, ed., *Creativity and its Cultivation* (New York: Harper, 1959); Bernard Barber, *Science and the Social Order,* rev. ed. (New York: Collier, 1962).

21. Daniel Bell, "Adjusting Men to Machines," *Commentary* 3 (1947), pp. 79–88, at pp. 87–88.

22. Whyte, "Social Engineers," p. 89.

23. Hughes, *Sociological Eye,* p. 525.

24. Ann Withorn, *Serving the People: Social Services and Social Change* (New York: Columbia University Press, 1984); J. F. Handler and Michael Sosin, *Last Resorts: Emergency Assistance and Special Needs Programs in Public Welfare* (New York: Academic Press, 1983); American Friends Service Committee, *Struggle for Justice* (New York: Hill and Wang, 1971).

25. Aldon Morris, *The Origins of the Civil Rights Movement* (New York: Free Press, 1984); Robert Fisher, *Let the People Decide: Neighborhood Organizing in America* (Boston: Twayne, 1984).

26. Jan M. Fritz, *The Clinical Sociology Handbook* (New York: Garland Publishing, 1985).

27. J. W. Coleman, *The Criminal Elite: The Sociology of White-Collar Crime* (New York: St. Martin's Press, 1985).

28. Walda K. Fishman and C. G. Benello, eds., *Readings in Humanist Sociology: Social Criticism and Social Change* (Bayside, N.Y.: General Hall, 1986).

29. I. L. Horowitz, *Professing Sociology* (Chicago: Aldine, 1968), pp. 262–63.

30. James Aronson, *Deadline for the Media: Today's Challenges to Press, TV and Radio* (Indianapolis: Bobbs-Merrill Co., 1972); Michael Parenti, *Inventing Reality: The Politics of the Mass Media* (New York: St. Martin's Press, 1986).

31. K. B. Clark et al., "The Effects of Segregation and the Consequences of Desegregation: A Social Science Statement," *Appendix to Appellants' Briefs,* U.S. Supreme Court (October 1952), *Brown et al. v. Board of Education of Topeka, Kansas,* and other cases. For a summary and interpretation of testimony by expert witnesses in these cases, see Clark, "The Social Scientist as an Expert Witness in Civil Rights Litigation," *Social Problems* 1 (1953), pp. 5–10.

32. *Brown v. Board of Education, Topeka,* 347 U.S. 483 (1954).

33. *Brown v. Board of Education, Topeka,* 349 U.S. 294 (1955).

34. James Reston, "A Sociological Decision," *New York Times,* May 18, 1954, p. 14.

35. *Plessy v. Ferguson,* 163 U.S. 537 (1896).

36. Mel Ravitz, "The Crisis in Our Cities: An Action Perspective," in Leonard Gordon, ed., *A City in Racial Crisis* (Dubuque, Iowa: W. C. Brown, 1971), p. 159.

37. T. F. Hoult, "'Race and Residence' Reviewed After the Riot," in Gordon, *A City in Racial Crisis,* pp. 14–15. See also A. J. Mayer and Hoult, *Race and Residence in Detroit* (Detroit: Wayne University Institute of Urban Studies, 1962).

38. Alphonso Pinkney, *The Myth of Black Progress* (New York: Cambridge University Press, 1984); Reynolds Farley, *Blacks and Whites: Narrowing the Gap?* (Cambridge, Mass.: Harvard University Press, 1984); Jennifer L. Hochschild, *The New American Dilemma: Liberal Democracy and School Desegregation* (New Haven: Yale University Press, 1984).

39. K. B. Clark, *Dark Ghetto* (New York: Harper and Row, 1965), p. 240. See also Alice Walker, "In the Closet of the South: A Letter to an African-American Friend," *Ms.* 15, no. 5 (November 1986), pp. 32–33.

40. C. H. Page, "Sociology as a Teaching Enterprise," in R. K. Merton, Leonard Broom, and L. S. Cottrell, Jr., *Sociology Today* (New York: Basic Books, 1959), p. 587.

41. P. L. Berger, *Invitation to Sociology* (Garden City, N.Y.: Doubleday, 1963), p. 164.

42. Public Affairs Committee, 381 Park Avenue South, New York, N.Y. 10016, has published more than 600 pamphlets on a wide range of social and personal concerns since 1936, each with an average circulation of 100,000. Each pamphlet is carefully checked by a group of specialists prior to publication.

43. Called a mixture of journalism and social-scientific analysis, published by New Society Publications, 128 Long Acre, London WC2E 9QH, England.

44. Popular articles on research results written chiefly by social scientists, published since 1963, now located at Rutgers University, New Brunswick, N.J. 08901.

45. L. J. Rhoades, *A History of the American Sociological Association: 1905–1980* (Washington: American Sociological Association, 1981), pp. 21–22, 40–41. See also reports on media relations in *American Sociological Review* 4 (1939), pp. 264–66, 5 (1940), pp. 104–5, 413–14, *et seq.*

46. Published since 1952, P.O. Box 22206, San Diego, Calif. 92122.

47. Bernard Rosenberg, "Mass Culture in America," in Rosenberg and D. M. White, eds., *Mass Culture: The Popular Arts in America* (Glencoe, Ill.: Free Press, 1959), pp. 5, 9.

48. L. A. Coser, *Men of Ideas* (New York: Free Press, 1965); J. C. Gowan, G. D. Demos, and E. P. Torrance, *Creativity* (New York: John Wiley, 1967); R. N. Bellah, Richard Madsen, Anne Swidler, W. M. Sullivan, and S. M. Tipton, *Habits of the Heart* (Berkeley: University of California Press, 1985).

49. W. F. Ogburn, *Social Change,* 2nd ed. (New York: Viking Press, 1950), p. 83.

50. A. G. Keller, *Societal Evolution,* rev. ed. (New York: Macmillan, 1931), p. 92.

51. Ross Stagner, "Reminiscences About the Founding of SPSSI," *Journal of Social Issues* 42 (1986), pp. 35–42.

52. L. J. Finison, "The Early History of the Society for the Psychological Study of Social Issues: Psychologists and Labor," *Journal of the History of the Behavioral Sciences* 15, (1979), pp. 29–37, at p. 30. See also Finison, "The Psychological Insurgency: 1936–1954," *Journal of Social Issues* 42 (1986), pp. 21–33.

53. A. McC. and E. B. Lee, *Social Problems in America* (New York: Henry Holt, 1949), p. vi; rev. ed., 1955, p. v.

54. Early volumes: Jerome Himelhoch and S. F. Fava, eds., *Sexual Behavior in American Society: An Appraisal of the First Two Kinsey Reports* (New York: W. W. Norton, 1955), and A. M. Rose et al., eds., *Mental Health and Mental Disorder* (New York: W. W. Norton, 1955).

55. A. McC. Lee, "To the Editor," *Social Problems* 9 (1961–62), pp. 386–89 (some basic documents on the organization of SSSP).

56. "Loyalty Oath Held Threat to Sociology," *New York Times,* September 4, 1952.

57. "Big Business Is Found Chiselers' Favorite," *New York Times,* September 5, 1952.

11—Helping People Confront Ideas and Change

1. Matthew 23:25.

2. *Century Dictionary* (New York: Century, 1914), 3, p. 2954.

3. A. McC. Lee, *Multivalent Man* (New York: George Braziller, 1966), esp. chaps. 1–7. See also P. A. Sorokin, *Society, Culture, and Personality* (New York: Harper, 1947), esp. chap. 19.

4. W. G. Sumner and A. G. Keller, *The Science of Society* (New Haven: Yale University Press, 1927), 1, pp. 360–61.

5. Niccolò Machiavelli, "The Prince," trans. Luigi Ricci, rev. E. R. P. Vincent, in *The Prince and the Discourses,* ed. Max Lerner (New York: Modern Library, 1940), pp. 56, 64.

6. Gunnar Myrdal, *Value in Social Theory,* ed. Paul Streeten (New York: Harper, 1958), pp. 143, 151.

7. Benjamin Appel, *Fantastic Mirror: Science Fiction Across the Ages* (New York: Pantheon, 1969); Bernard Rosenberg and D. M. White, eds., *Mass Culture* (Glencoe, Ill.: Free Press, 1959); C. N. Manlove, *Science Fiction: Ten Explorations* (Kent, Ohio: Kent State University Press, 1986).

8. Charles Reich, *The Greening of America* (New York: Random House, 1970).

9. Morton Mintz and J. S. Cohen, *America, Inc.* (New York: Dial, 1971); R. L. Heilbroner et al., *In the Name of Profit* (New York: Doubleday, 1972); Noam Chomsky and E. S. Herman, *The Washington Connection and Third World Fascism* (Boston: South End Press, 1979); E. S. Herman, *The Real Terror Network* (Boston: South End Press, 1982).

10. R. N. Bellah, Richard Madsen, Anne Swidler, W. M. Sullivan, and S. M. Tipton, *Habits of the Heart* (Berkeley: University of California Press, 1985), pp. 77, 143.

11. J. H. Plumb, *The Death of the Past* (Boston: Houghton Mifflin, 1969), pp. 106, 145.

12. W. O. Douglas, *An Almanac of Liberty* (Garden City, N.Y.: Doubleday, 1964), p. 104.

Index

Darwin, Charles, 22, 23, 24, 40, 63, 148, 159
Daughters of the American Revolution, 34
Davie, M. R., xi, 216, 221, 225–26
Davis, Ann E., xi
Davis, Jerome, 13, 43, 217, 222, 228
Deegan, Mary J., 119, 237
De Grazia, Alfred, 240
Democracy, xiv–xvi, 7, 42–43, 66–67, 74, 102, 134, 152–53
Demos, G. D., 242
Deng Xiaoping, 153
Dennis, E. E., 239
Denzin, N. K., 240
Desegregation, 175, 193
Deutscher, Irwin, 240
Dewey, John, xv, 103, 120, 229
Dickens, Charles, 27
Disinformation, 83, 101
Distortions: enticing, 143–65; intimate, 166–81
Dolci, Danilo, 46–50, 56, 222
Domination: types of, 148–49
Dostoevski, Feodor, 27
Douglas, W. O., 213, 243
Dramaturgy, 112
Driver, E. D., 233
Drugs, 95, 139, 157
Du Bois, Rachel D., 223
Du Bois, W. E. B., 26, 220
Dunham, Barrows, 8, 217
Dynamic relationism, 60–61

Edman, Irwin, 235
Education, 42–43, 65, 71, 97, 103, 121, 142, 147–48, 152
Egocentrism, 171
Einstein, Albert, 20, 22, 148
Eisenhower, D. D., 90, 138, 147–48, 235
Elias, N., 220
Elitism, xv, xviii, 22, 35, 98, 122, 135, 144, 151–53, 210
Elterman, Howard, xi, 181, 239
Emerson, Gloria, 168, 237
Emerson, Steven, 239

Empathy, 38–39; intergroup, 51
Engels, Friedrich, 25, 155, 198, 215–16, 219, 223, 236
Engstrom, E. W., 241
Entrepreneurs, 13, 22, 79, 108, 118, 120
Equal Rights Amendment, 154, 156
Erikson, E. H., 120, 155, 229, 235
Ethics, 24, 30, 63, 115, 188
Ethnic groups, 66, 94, 99, 191, 206
Ethnocentrism, 12, 64, 152, 166, 171
Ethnomethodology, 112, 159
Etzioni, Amitai, 228
Evolutionism, 23, 40
Ewen, Lynda A., xi
Existential humanism, ix, xviii, 136, 212–13
Exposés, 9, 19, 114

Fads, 166, 176–79
Falk, R. A., 226–27
Fanon, Frantz, 75, 227
Faris, R. E. L., 41, 222, 237
Farley, Reynolds, 242
Fashions, 166, 176–79
Fausto-Sterling, Ann, 237
Fava, Sylvia F., xi, 201, 220, 242
Federal Office of War Information, 88, 93
Female careers, 167–70
Ferrarotti, Franco, xi, 104, 216, 229
Feuer, L. S., 236
Field, Marshall, III, 177–78
Fieldwork, 38, 139, 184
Filstead, W. J., 240
Finch, H. A., 218
Finison, L. J., 242
Fisher, Robert, 241
Fishman, Walda K., xi, 31, 119, 221, 234, 241
Flanagan, T. J., 236
Flynn, C. P. C., xi, 202
Flynn, Cynthia B., 19, 218
Fosdick, H. E., 67, 225
Franklin, C. W. II, 237
Franklin, Jay, 233
Freedom, 148–49

Ogburn, W. F., 197, 242
O'Kane, J. M., xi
Opler, J. M., 233
Oppenheimer, Martin, xi
Orthodoxy, 144–50, 159, 186; pall of, 102, 121
Orwell, George, 145, 149, 235

Packard, Vance, 240
Page, C. H., 40, 43, 222, 242
Paradigms, 105; problematic-technical, 119–21, 200; managerial-bureaucratic, 111–13, 199–200; functional-systemic, 113
Parenti, Michael, 88, 228, 241
Pareto, Vilfredo, 111, 190
Park, R. E., xi, 25–26, 109, 127, 162, 169, 183–84, 220, 232, 237
Parrington, V. L., 27, 134, 136, 234
Parsons, Talcott, 23, 111–12, 116–17, 218, 230–31
Participant observation, 9, 24–25, 35, 37–39, 47, 139, 183–84
Pascal, R., 215
Peck, Abe, 239
Pedantry, 144, 158–60
Peixotto, Jessica, 168
Perception, 23, 123–42
Personality types, 10, 166, 179–81
Peterzell, Jay, 229
Philosophy, xv, 11, 27–29; secular, 15, 18; religious, 17–18
Physicalism, 114–15
Pinkney, Alphonso, 242
Pitt, J. R., 218
Piven, Frances F., 120
Plato, 11, 22, 151, 235
Platt, Anthony, 222
Platt, Jennifer, 115, 231
Plautus, T. M., 175, 238
Plessy v. Ferguson, 175, 193, 238, 241
Plumb, J. H., 213, 243
Plutocracy, 7–9, 26, 92, 134–36, 146, 210
Policymakers, 157, 186, 188, 192–95, 199, 203
Pomeroy, W. B., 237

Popularization, 144, 160, 162–63, 196–98
Porter, Holly G., 46, 51–53, 55–56, 223
Preister, Kevin, 223
Pride, R. A., 175, 238
Prison, 71, 192
Professionalism, 20–21, 29–30, 73, 110, 159, 174
Progress, xvi, 127
Project Camelot, 113
Propaganda, 7, 11, 58–60, 71, 76, 133, 150, 157; analysis, 42, 77–103; defined, 60, 63, 78; special interest, 23, 117; techniques, 85–87, 98–102
Protagoras, 11, 22
Public Affairs Committee, Pamphlets, 89, 196, 242
Public opinion, 88, 94–97, 133; pollsters, 95–96, 159, 180, 187–88
Public relations, xv, 80, 84, 187, 207, 209

Quaker Service Bulletin, 227
Quantification, 13, 40
Quantophrenia, 114–15
Quarterly Journal of Doublespeak, 217
Quinney, Richard, 18, 218

Racism, xiii, xvi, 11, 19, 23, 54, 64–65, 71, 153, 158, 171, 173–74, 192, 205, 207
Rader, Victoria, xi, 4, 217
Radin, Max, 238
Raper, A. F., 225
Ravitz, Mel, 194, 241
Rayman, Paula, 65, 223–24
Reader, Jonathan, xi
Reagan, Ronald, 64, 87, 90, 138, 148, 157, 210
Redfield, Robert, 220
Red scares, 99–100, 115
Reeder, Dan, 217
Reich, Charles, 208, 243

Social roles, 180–81; female, 167; male, 167, 204
Social sciences, 11, 213; revolts within, 199–203
Social setting, 126, 138–39
Social structure, 83, 212
Social system, 41, 71–72, 111–12, 149
Social therapy, therapists, 187, 190–92
Socialism, 23, 210
Social power, 42, 80, 82–83, 104, 113, 126, 133–36, 152, 157, 208
Social Problems, 145, 201, 232
Society (formerly *Trans-Action*), 196
Society on Anthropology and Humanism, 12, 218
Society for Humanistic Anthropology, xi
Society for the Psychological Study of Social Issues (SPSSI), xi, 199–200
Society for the Study of Social Problems (SSSP), xi, 11–12, 24, 197, 200–202
Sociobiologists, 13
Sociodrama, 55
Sociological Abstracts, Inc., 37, 197, 221
Sociological Practice Association, xi, 202
Sociologists, sociology: abstract, 9, 12, 144, 183; as a profession, 109–10; as autobiography, 32–33, 40–41; as basic concerns, 4–5; as consciousness raisers, 41; as chamber of horrors, 3, 5, 9; as field of contention, 4–5; careers in, 1, 33, 126–42, 182–203; clinical, 18, 24, 42–43, 46, 49–51, 96, 187–95, 207–8; consultants, 19–20; critical, 19, 146; cults in, 22, 29, 107, 110, 114, 122, 151, 159, 190; defined, 1, 34–36, 57, 108; emancipatory, 18, 104; empirical, 3; focal points of, 107–13, 116, 118–19; humanist, x, 31, 43; humanist-existential, x, 119–22; ideologies in, 104–22; laboratory, 37; liberation, 5, 18, 31, 103, 195–98; mainliners, 107, 110,

Sociologists, sociology (*cont.*)
114; marginals, 107, 110, 114; market for, 109; "normal," 110–11, 115; organizations, 199–203; philosophical, 2; "pure," 31; radical, 21; teaching, 2, 32–44; technical, 3, 9, 107–8, 111; values in, 114–16; vocation-centered, 107, 111, 115
Sociologists for Women in Society, 169–70
Sons of the American Revolution, 34
Sophists, 22
Sorensen, Aage, 21
Sorokin, P. A., 40, 67–68, 109–10, 114–15, 117, 221, 225–26, 231, 243
Sosin, Michael, 241
Spanish-American War, 23
Spencer, Herbert, 23–24, 219
Sperber, Ann M., 239
Spindler, G. D., 233
Spokespeople, 19, 81–82
Sproule, J. M., xi
Stagner, Ross, 242
Starr, H. E., 41, 215, 222
Starr, J. M., xi, 31, 119, 140, 221, 232, 234, 239
Starr, Paul, 21, 218
Statistics, 20–21, 115, 117, 140, 162, 173, 183
Staude, J. R., 232
Steffens, Lincoln, 27, 134, 178, 221, 231, 234, 239
Stein, Maurice, 230
Stein, P. J., 120
Steinbeck, John, 27
Steiner, G. A., 229
Stephan, W. G., 46, 222
Stereotypes, 130–33, 136, 168, 176
Stern, B. J., 219
Stigler, Stephen, 236
Stone, I. F., 178, 239–40
Stonequist, E. V., 232
Stouffer, S. A., 24, 111–12, 230
Strauss, Anselm, 240
Strauss, R. A., 223
Streeten, Paul, 232
Structural-functionalism, 13, 159
Strunk, William, Jr., 237
Sullivan, W. M., 242–43

SOCIOLOGY FOR PEOPLE

was composed in 10 on 12 Baskerville on Digital Compugraphic Equipment by Metricomp;
printed by sheet-fed offset on 50-pound, acid-free Glatfelter Natural Hi-Bulk,
Smyth sewn and bound over binder's boards in Holliston Roxite C,
with dust jackets printed in one color
by Braun-Brumfield, Inc.
and published by

SYRACUSE UNIVERSITY PRESS
Syracuse, New York 13244-5160